D0074712

Mountains of Debt

Mountains of Debt

Crisis and Change in Renaissance Florence, Victorian Britain, and Postwar America

Michael Veseth

New York   Oxford
OXFORD UNIVERSITY PRESS
1990

Oxford University Press

Oxford   New York   Toronto
Delhi   Bombay   Calcutta   Madras   Karachi
Petaling Jaya   Singapore   Hong Kong   Tokyo
Nairobi   Dar es Salaam   Cape Town
Melbourne   Auckland

and associated companies in
Berlin   Ibadan

Copyright © 1990 by Oxford University Press, Inc.

Published by Oxford University Press, Inc.
200 Madison Avenue, New York, New York 10016

Oxford is a registered trademark of Oxford University Press

All rights reserved. No part of this publication may be reproduced,
stored in a retrieval system, or transmitted, in any form or by any means,
electronic, mechanical, photocopying, recording or otherwise
without the prior permission of Oxford University Press.

Library of Congress Cataloging-in-Publication Data
Veseth, Michael.
Mountains of debt : crisis and change in renaissance Florence,
Victorian Britain, and postwar America / Michael Veseth.
p. cm.   Includes bibliographical references.
ISBN 0-19-506420-8
1. Debts, Public—History—Case studies.   2. Debt—History—Case
studies.   3. Debts, External—Italy—Florence—History.   4. Debts,
External—Great Britain—History.   5. Debts, External—United
States—History.   I. Title.
HJ8003.v47   1990
336.3′4′09—dc20   89-49029

WIDENER UNIVERSITY
WOLFGRAM
LIBRARY
CHESTER, PA.

DISCARDED

2 4 6 8 9 7 5 3 1

Printed in the United States of America
on acid-free paper

Preface

This book is about economic crisis of a type that is often thought to be uniquely modern. The United States during the postwar years has become the world's richest and most dynamic economy, yet we have accumulated truly enormous levels of private and public debt, an unexpected and disturbing outcome. Our debts have now grown so large that they often dominate everyday decision making in both the public and private sectors, a condition that I call "fiscal crisis." How did this situation come about and how will it end?

The postwar United States is not the first rich and dynamic economy to experience fiscal crisis. Renaissance Florence and Victorian Britain were leading economies that fell into fiscal crisis in different ways, for different reasons, and with different ultimate results. There is something beneficial to be learned from these past experiences. Looking at the patterns of the past allows us to see recent trends with clearer vision. This book therefore tells the stories of economic change and fiscal crisis in Florence and Britain as prologue to a new analysis of the economic crisis of the postwar United States, an unusual way to approach the analysis of contemporary economic problems.

It is impossible to look at Michelangelo's great statue of David in the Academia in Florence without feeling a whole range of personal emotions, including a deep gratitude to Renaissance Italy for leaving us such an inspired bequest. So it was for me, too, when I first visited Florence in 1983. But as an economist—a "dismal scientist"—specializing in government finance, I was also bound to ask, "How did they finance it?"

Back home in Tacoma, I began to study the government and economy of Renaissance Florence and I found, to my surprise, that although the language, food, clothing, housing, sanitation, and many of the social customs in the Florence of, say, 1427 were different from what I am accustomed to, as far as basic economic organization and the institutions of business and government finance go, I would have been pretty much at home.

The Florentines were ahead of their time. Their cultural renaissance was accompanied by the birth and development of many modern economic institutions. The Florentine economy employed systems of production and trade that foreshadowed the later developments subsequently known as capitalism. These "real" economic institutions of production were built on a financial foundation that was almost completely modern. Double-entry accounting, for example, was invented in northern Italy; the Medici and other Florentine banking families perfected its use in trade and finance. Simple forms of most modern financial and commercial instruments and institutions—except the *Wall Street Journal*—were available in some form to the citizens of early Renaissance Florence.

Florentine government finance was also relatively modern at this time. Even their tax system looks familiar to twentieth-century eyes. This is especially true after 1427, when Florence created the very first income tax, complete with personal exemptions, itemized deductions, and the inevitable loopholes and tax returns. The Florentines also invented funded public debt in the fourteenth century. Over time their debt grew and grew until it dominated the economic and political life of the city. Florence was therefore the first great state to be overshadowed by its public debt. Renaissance Florence — its economy, tax system, and public debt — was the inspiration for the study that eventually resulted in this book.

Some people might find Renaissance Florence too old and too foreign a case to provide much insight about current economic problems, but the experiences of Victorian Britain have a more obviously modern color to them. Like Florence, Britain was the most dynamic economy of its time. Like Florence, Britain accumulated large public debts and fell into fiscal crisis. This coincidence perhaps makes the Florentine experience seem more relevant and the problems of the United States today less unexpected.

It is common knowledge that Victorian Britain became the dominant economic power of the nineteenth century because of its industrial revolution, but the role of government finance and public debt in Britain's rise and decline is less well known. Public debt and the income tax were critical innovative factors in the early development of Britain's industrial economy, but as the driving force of the economy evolved, these unchanging fiscal institutions became barriers to change and growth. While in Florence it was the huge size of the debt that created fiscal crisis, in Britain it was fear of debt, not debt itself, that created fiscal crisis and discouraged structural change.

Britain did not repeat the Florentine experience with debt and taxation, nor has the United States in the post-war period precisely replicated earlier patterns. Yet there are important similarities among these experiences and much to be learned, I think, from the differences. This book is my attempt to write down what I have learned from the study of these three critical periods in economic history and the history of public debt and taxation.

This study of economic history has been an enriching experience for me not just because I have filled in so many gaps in my general education but also because this historical analysis has given me an appreciation for the advantages of the long view over the short view when analyzing some economic problems. This book, then, takes the long view of the problem of fiscal crisis.

In the course of preparing this essay I have run up my own mountain of debts — mainly of the intellectual sort. I am particularly grateful to the anonymous donor whose generosity endowed the John T. Lantz Senior Research Fellowship that financed much of my work on this book. My academic mentors, James Papke of Purdue University and Ernie Combs of the University of Puget Sound, provided crucial support for this project at different times and in different ways. Herb Addison, my editor at Oxford University Press, contributed confidence, competence, interest, and enthusiasm.

Several of my colleagues at the University of Puget Sound reviewed pieces of this essay at one stage or another, including Wade Hands, Bruce Mann, and David F. Smith. Arpad Kadarkay, a political theorist and Renaissance scholar, read the entire manuscript and provided both critical analysis and unflagging support and friendship. I am also grateful to an anonymous reviewer who provided sound guidance, constructive criticism, and friendly encouragement. Finally, I am grateful to my wife Sue, and to all my friends, family, and students, for their love and patience throughout this project.

Tacoma, Washington   M. V.
May 1990

Contents

Mountains of Debt

Prologue

Modern economists concentrate on the short view when studying recent events. Our quantitative tools and the data on which they are based break down when applied over longer time spans, so we restrict our studies to areas where our tools will work. As a result we tend to look at many long-developing problems mostly in terms of their short-term causes and effects.

It is hard to be so short-sighted when analyzing an economy that lies five hundred years in the past. Even though the Florentines were demon record keepers, we can never mine from their account books the high-quality data required by the furnaces of modern econometric mills; so we have to rely on qualitative information at least as much as quantitative data. This frees us a little from the short view.

The analysis of the past promotes long-view economics in a second way. In the academic division of labor, economists develop general theories of societal behavior, while the task of historians is to find explanations for specific events. Historians are free to range over long periods of time in pursuit of causes and effects. Economic history gives economic analysis the useful freedom to be historical. It is hard for an economist to read the history of the Black Death, for example, without realizing that important economic effects must have remained even after several generations, long after econometric equations would have lost their statistical significance.

In taking this historical approach, I became increasingly interested in the long view of the pressing economic problems of today. I began to develop a long-view model of structural change and fiscal crisis that builds on what I have learned from my study of economic history. I hope that I can offer a new perspective on our current economic dilemma that may supplement the insights of the traditional analysis of these problems.

The present volume is therefore an experiment in comparative economic history, where I attempt to apply a model of structural change and fiscal crisis to two critical periods of the past, Renaissance Florence and Victorian Britain, as well as to recent events in the United States. It should be obvious that I did not choose these times and places randomly. They are periods of great economic changes and — not coincidentally, in my view — fiscal crisis and tax reform. In other words, these are times and places where I think the outlines of my model hold. My ultimate goal is to apply the insights provided by past episodes to an analysis of problems today.

Comparative historical analysis is, I think, a useful addition to the tools that economists use to understand how society and the economy work. But there are problems and risks. First, I am a public finance economist, not a

3

historian; and I bring to the study of past times the modern tools of my discipline. In a sense, the volumes of written history (including the work of many fine economic historians) are grist for my mill. Historians provide the raw materials, and I supply the analysis. There are, I hope, some advantages to this approach.

Second, in researching the economic history of Florence and Britain, I have worked from secondary sources. My study has been driven by questions of structural change and public finance. In searching the history books for answers to these questions, I suspect that I have overlooked some matters, subtle or obvious. I do not believe, however, that these unavoidable gaps are so wide or deep as to undermine the foundations of my arguments.

Historians may find my historical summaries rather simple, but should be interested in the economic uses to which they are put; economists may find my economic analysis fairly straightforward but should find the historical examples useful. All readers, especially people interested in public policy and current economic problems, should find interesting the chapters at the end of the essay, where I examine the current public debt problems of the United States and suggest a course of action.

In defending comparative economic history, Charles Kindleberger, in *A Financial History of Western Europe*, asserts that history is "a laboratory to test whether such theories are useful to the political economist, with his interest in policy" and that comparative economic history "can test for generality, to set aside the theories that fit only the single case" (p. 1). This is my aim, too, and, like Kindleberger, I will try to avoid becoming impressionistic or romantic where analysis degenerates into the yearning search for historical parallels.

This is not a history book but an essay that uses history to explore a profound contemporary problem, the problem of structural change and fiscal crisis. My goal is not to enlighten our understanding of the past but to use the past to improve our understanding of the present.

Chapter 1 presents basic ideas concerning structural change and fiscal crisis in the long view. I will discuss the causes of major structural economic change and its likely impact on social institutions, including the institutions of government. In chapters 2 and 3 I present in some detail the history of fifteenth-century Florence, where public debt was invented, with an emphasis on the interrelationship of changes in the economy and changes in fiscal balance.

Chapters 4 and 5 analyze the experiences of Victorian Britain in the period from the first industrial revolution to the second one, a span of over one hundred years. Like Florence, Britain gave birth to many of our present-day institutional and intellectual structures; so the story of how it dealt with structural change and fiscal crisis is timely and important. In both these cases, I believe that structural change transformed society, creating fiscal crisis and rising public debt. The specific causes, effects, and ultimate consequences are different, but the general processes involved have enough in common to interest us today.

Chapters 6, 7, and 8 examine the postwar economic events, trends, and problems of the United States. Here I trace in greater detail the pathways of change and the real and shadow movements that have led to our current and probable future fiscal crises.

Finally, chapters 9 and 10 use the past to inform us about probable futures. Here I develop the idea of the "saddle point," where changes in economic and social policy are critical to the future. I look back at Florence and Britain, to see why they failed when they reached the saddle point, and I examine the particular saddle point dilemma facing the United States. Although it is not my ultimate purpose to propose or advocate a particular set of economic policies, chapter 10 does conclude with a proposal that might well set the United States on a better path as it heads towards the future.

The theme of this book is a suitably dismal one for a "dismal scientist": economic decline. Florence and Britain squandered their many advantages, and were passed by other, more dynamic nations. The policies needed to steer us from the pathways of slow decline that Florence and Britain took are not really radical and seem to be politically possible. It is probably not too late to begin to make fundamental changes in fiscal policy that might allow the United States a more promising future.

1

Structural Change and Fiscal Crisis

The government of the Italian city-state of Florence created history's first funded public debt through legislation enacted in 1344 and 1345. The public debt was named the Monte Commune (city's fund). Ironically, *monte* means both "fund" and "mountain" in Italian and the "fund" soon became a "mountain." The Florentines who invented the public debt saw it grow into a mountain of debt that ultimately dominated the economic and civic life of their city.

Mountains of public debt crowd the horizon today. Those of us who live in the major industrial democracies find it easy to explain many of these mountains: the debts of the Latin American countries result from inefficient investment and changing terms of trade; Africa is dirt poor and doomed to debt; the debts of the East European countries are due to unwise communist economic policies; and so on. These foreign public debts create finance and development problems, to be sure; but we can easily dismiss the debts themselves to be the result of bad luck or folly.

Our own public debts are harder to understand and even harder to dismiss. In 1988, for example, the central governments of the seven largest industrial democracies (Canada, the United States, Japan, France, West Germany, Italy, and the United Kingdom) generated new public debt on the order of 3.5 percent of their nations' combined gross national products. Each one of these governments ran a deficit and increased its public debt for every year of the 1980s. These mountains of public debt are not just other people's problems, they are our problems.

The danger of the growing public debt is proclaimed by government leaders who seem utterly unable to do anything about it. It is easy for pundits to blame the deficits on weak-willed politicians, but this leaves too many questions unanswered. If lack of will has produced today's big deficits, why is it lacking everywhere and why suddenly now? What would give politicians the will to make the difficult choices necessary to reduce the deficits? To blame widespread and persistent public debt on politicians is to blame it on human nature, which explains nothing because it can explain everything.

Governments have borrowed for hundreds of years, but the causes and the consequences of their debts have varied. Some debt arises through rational

7

government policy choices, such as the countercyclical deficits of the Great Depression or the unavoidable defense deficits of World War II. Other debt is irrational — mad princes or presidents who borrow, borrow, borrow to spend, spend, spend to gain for themselves power or glory or a place in history.

I am interested in today's rich country deficits because they seem neither coolly rational nor clearly mad. We do not choose to have today's big debts, but we cannot seem to choose otherwise. I believe that today's widespread rich country, high-employment, peacetime deficit condition is a fundamentally different problem from the poor country, depression, and war deficits of recent history that tend to shape and color our analysis. It seems that the world economy has fallen out of fiscal balance, the delicate equilibrium of income and outgo that is necessary, in the long run, for economic stability.

Not only are governments unable to balance their financial accounts, but in recent years whole nations have fallen from fiscal balance. International Current Account deficits and surpluses are very large and have displayed a seemingly unsustainable persistence. Not only has the United States fallen out of fiscal balance, but there is no obvious indication that any automatic equilibrating force is at work to restore balance. If there is an international invisible hand, it is very transparent indeed and works slowly or in unforeseen ways (or not at all).

Persistent fiscal imbalance in peacetime with near full-employment among rich countries. This is not business as usual, and it is therefore not surprising that these problems are not easily or completely understood or analyzed using the usual tools and ordinary methods of economic analysis.

Today's deficits are, I think, symptoms of a much larger and more important social and economic condition that we must face today and will continue to face into the future. The problem is that the world we live in is undergoing rapid and fundamental structural change. We do not fully appreciate the nature of this condition because the vast changes have accumulated slowly, piling up like grains of sand during the postwar period (although the pace of change has accelerated in recent years). While the relatively rigid social and economic structures that we have built around ourselves over the years insulate us from change today, they make the ultimate costs of adjustment greater for us in the future.

I want to discuss, in general terms, the nature of structural change and the relationship between structural change and fiscal crisis. This chapter does not try to prove any theorem or expound any complex economic theory. Instead, I want to develop a relatively simple framework that I will use in later chapters to analyze past and present examples of structural change and fiscal crisis.

Once these basic ideas have been introduced, we can begin to explore the three case studies of structural change and fiscal crisis that make up the main body of this essay. By examining the specific problems and policies of Renaissance Florence and Victorian Britain, rich countries that experienced vast structural changes and eventually faced the dilemma of fiscal crisis, we can come to understand better how the forces of change affect government, society, and the economy. This historical perspective will help us cut through the fog of daily events somewhat in later chapters of this book, to see more clearly current problems and the policy alternatives before us.

The Process of Structural Change

The basic concept of structural change is the notion that as an economy develops or reacts to the development of other nations, the best uses of its scarce resources necessarily change. Workers move from one industry to another and often from one region to another. Old plants and stores shut down or scale back while new shops and factories open their doors. Change is necessary for economic progress, but change creates problems. The process of structural change and the problems associated with it are at the heart of the dilemma that faces us today.

Structural change is always taking place everywhere in the modern world. Indeed, what differentiates the modern world from the ossified medieval feudal system is change and the expectation of further change.

The history of the U.S. economy, from the times of the explorers through the colonial period, the westward expansion, and the rise of the modern industrial economy has been, essentially, a story of structural change. New resources, new technologies, changing trade patterns, changing political patterns, new tastes, new problems. The shape of the U.S. economy has constantly changed within a changing world.

David Ricardo's famous law of comparative advantage provides one of the oldest discussions of the problem of structural change. Ricardo's famous example of comparative advantage involved the opening of trade between Britain and Portugal. In autarchy (a state of closed self-sufficiency), Britain and Portugal would use their scarce resources as best they could to make wine and cloth. Once trade was allowed, Ricardo demonstrated that both Britain and Portugal could be made better off through exchange based on differences in opportunity cost. Both countries could consume more cloth and more wine, and together they could produce more of both items than they could separately in autarchy.[1]

The key to Ricardo's result — mutually advantageous exchange — was structural change in both economies: Britain shifts resources from wine to cloth and Portugal shifts resources from cloth to wine. Specialization and exchange were the critical processes; and specialization required structural transformation and shifts of resources according to the law of comparative advantage.

International trade is not the only force that creates incentives for structural change, although it was probably the most important (and perhaps the most obvious) in Ricardo's day. Ernst Engel, the nineteenth-century German statistician, showed that economic growth, even in a closed economy, also produces structural change. Engel's Law holds that as income rises, the proportion of income that is spent on basic items such as food declines relatively (although the dollar amount spent may grow absolutely); meanwhile the proportion of income spent on nonnecessities tends to grow both relatively and absolutely. In short, as the size of the income pie rises, there is a basic change in the way consumers divide the pie among different consumption goods.[2]

Engel's Law implies that structural change is necessary if economic growth is to be self-sustaining. Without structural change in production, no long-term income growth is possible. To see this suppose, for example, that people initially spend 60 percent of their per capita income on food and that they derive, in the aggregate, 60 percent of their per capita income from the production of food. This is a stable macroeconomic equilibrium.

Now suppose that an exogenous event causes income to rise for one time period. Following Engel's Law, the proportion of per capita income spent on food falls to 55 percent. If people continue to earn 60 percent of their income from the production of food, their income will decline in the next time period because of the lower relative expenditure in this area. (They will not spend enough on food to provide for their collective incomes.) Over time their income will spiral down to its previous level. If, on the other hand, the increase in income is accompanied by a structural change of workers leaving food production and entering other areas, such that only 55 percent of total income is earned from the food sector, a new equilibrium at the higher income-level can be attained. In short, the patterns of resource use must shift as consumption patterns shift if income growth is to be sustained (given Engel's Law).

A. G. B. Fisher advanced the study of structural change and economic growth in the 1930s. He divided the economy into three types of occupations: primary (agriculture), secondary (manufacturing, mining, construction) and tertiary (services of all sorts, including government, transportation, communications). As economies grow, Fisher noted, labor tends to move from one sector to another. Most labor is located in the primary sector in poor economies. As income rises, labor shifts from primary to secondary, and then finally to the tertiary sector.[3] In a sense, of course, these shifts are necessary according to Engel's Law if each increase in income is to be sustained. Colin Clark's detailed statistical analysis of the relationship between employment patterns and economic growth provides a solid factual base for Fisher's taxonomy and theory.[4]

Fisher's triptych of resources is, of course, only a crude picture of how structural change and economic transformation work, but it captures the essence of change, the dynamic pattern of resources moving from one use to another. Some complex images of change do not show up in this portrait of the economy but are important nonetheless. In twentieth-century Britain, for example, a generation of domestic servants moved to other "higher" service occupations (communications workers, government employees, etc.). This important structural shift is hidden in Fisher's third panel, an otherwise unnoticed redistribution of workers within the tertiary sector.

Small-scale or incremental structural change can take place with only a little fiscal friction. By that I mean that change disrupts individual markets, firms, and families, but that it does not create true economywide (or worldwide) distress. It is a microeconomic, not a macroeconomic, problem.[5]

Large-scale structural change and fiscal crisis is not produced by any single event or force. In the case studies that follow, this image will emerge. The dramatic examples of structural change that I am interested in are the result of several roughly coincident revolutions in the underlying elements of the economy, acted upon by an outside catalyst. The chemical reaction that it creates is intense, causing the intense fiscal imbalances that are observed.

Although each case study is different, Renaissance Florence, Victorian Britain, and the postwar United States all experienced an increase in the pace of economic growth. They experienced dramatic changes, or revolutions, in their populations, in the basic structure of their wealth-creating sectors, and in the connecting patterns of their financial systems.

These basic forces are strong enough to generate significant levels of structural change on their own. In each of these three cases, however, the scale and scope of structural change were at some point intensified by the outside catalyst of international trade. Changes in the nature of international trade magnified the structural transformations that were already taking place within these economies. Each economy had now to solve a very complex problem—to find a way to reallocate resources efficiently within its borders that would also fit the pattern of the changing world economy.

The cases I will examine here are therefore not typical cases of structural change and fiscal crisis. They are examples of atypically large economic shifts driven by big forces within the economy and magnified by international events. It is not surprising that long-term fiscal imbalance is one result of these enormous shifts in the way the economic systems must organize themselves.

A large, relatively sudden change in the way the world works is needed to create the types of fiscal crises discussed here. But these large-scale shifts may well appear smaller and less momentous on the whole to the individuals who actually experience them firsthand. To individuals surrounded by the protective shells of existing social institutions, even a very large change may appear on the day-to-day level as local anomalies (like a warm day in January or a dry September), not as symptoms of a major shift in the environment. Indeed, it is a fact that contemporary British economists apparently failed to notice the Industrial Revolution while it was springing up all around them.

Shadow and Substance

Structural change does not happen spontaneously. Resources need a reason to move. Economic institutions, like institutions of every stripe, are always and everywhere dominated by their own momentum. Structural change must be motivated. To see this, consider workers, who, when taken together, are society's most important productive resource. Workers are allocated to jobs through many social institutions ranging from inheritance of the family occupation in traditional economies to decentralized labor markets in capitalist economies to centralized planning bureaucracies ("command" economies) in some communist countries. An effective institutional structure will allocate different workers to different jobs in some way that tends to maximize the social value of what these workers produce. Absent any change in productivity, workers stay put for years, decades, or—as economic history has found—sometimes for centuries.

Now suppose that some event—the opening of trade or a technological development, for example—changes the pattern of labor productivity among the sectors of the economy. When relative productivity changes, labor resources are drawn as if by a magnet from low-productivity jobs to those where their work has higher social value. There is a good deal of resistance to this movement, however, and not just because people are reluctant to change where they work and what they do. Shifts in how labor resources are used must necessarily be accompanied by changes in the allocation of other scarce resources (just as changes in how technology or capital are used require changes in the labor allocation). Major shifts in how labor resources are used can only be realized if these other associated resources are also very mobile. This mobility, fundamentally, is the problem of finance.

That some types of capital can move directly from sector to sector is clear and even obvious (which is unusual for economics). A truck, for example, is mobile both in the everyday sense and also in the sense employed here. Trucks are useful on the farm, in industry, in the service sector, and as personal transportation and recreational vehicles.

Most items of capital are not so flexible as a pickup truck; capital tends to be industry-specific, site-specific, process-specific, or even firm-specific. This means that capital is often specialized and has only a narrow range of realistic potential uses. Such capital cannot easily be moved from sector to sector during the process of structural change. To the extent that capital is specific in this sense, it represents another barrier to economic change.

The fact that individual lumps of capital are inflexible does not, however, mean that capital is inflexible; immobile capital can be made to flow smoothly through efficient financial markets. Financial markets allow ownership to change freely, permitting people to transfer capital among industries and across geographic borders.

Finance is usually perceived as a sterile enterprise. Plato condemned financial manipulations (and their "unjust" profits) because they did not produce anything real but just shuffled paper. This view of finance, which is widely held today at an intuitive level, is conditioned by our everyday lives, where we shuffle checks, bankbooks, bond certificates, and stock shares back and forth, exchanging one document for another and back again in progressive transactions. To see finance this way is to look only at shadows and miss the real action.

Financial transactions involve both shadow and substance. The substance is that purchasing power—command over real assets—is exchanged for some period of time through financial exchanges. When a corporation issues a bond, for example, command over real resources is transferred from the bond's buyer (a family, for example) to the firm. This alters how resources are allocated, since the firm is unlikely to use these resources in the same way as the family. The firm is likely to have in mind a more valuable use of the resources, otherwise it would not have been able to bid them away from the family by offering an attractive return. The paper trail that these resources leave behind as they move from one use to another—the checks, forms, certificates, and receipts—are the shadows of resources on the move.

Here is the paradox of finance. We tend to think that finance is sterile because we see the shadow and not the real resources involved. But in this case real substance depends on the existence of its shadows (not the other way around). Real resources are not easily moved from those who have them to those who can best use them. The development of efficient forms of finance—clever shadows—is a necessary condition for efficient resource movements. The shadows of finance permit the freer movement of capital, which is necessary if labor and other resources are to be free to move in, and adapt to, this changing world.

Financial markets therefore play an important role in the pattern of structural change that an economy adopts and, indeed, in how successfully economic transformation is implemented. Financial markets are not perfect, however; they are social institutions and, as such, are subject to hardening and, occasionally, clogging of their fiscal arteries. This will be an important problem in the case studies that follow.

The Costs of Structural Change

Structural change is always a mixed blessing. Change is both a golden opportunity and a troublesome dilemma. Opportunity comes from the higher returns that resources will earn in their new uses. The dilemma is that people, things, and institutions are not as flexible in the real world as they are in Ricardo's textbook. Even when returns are higher in another part of the economy, people and businesses are often loath to give up what they know and find familiar for an uncertain, if more profitable, alternative.

Colin Clark's study of the movement of people from primary to secondary occupations illustrates the dilemma of structural change. A developing economy generally provides a higher return to workers in the secondary sector (manufacturing) than the primary one (the farm). But so intense are the factors that make labor and other resources immobile that according to Clark's law of transformation, the return to labor in industry must be twice that on the land before workers will make the shift in significant numbers.[6]

Because resources are not perfectly and costlessly mobile, change creates substantial private and social costs in the short run as workers and businesses are left behind in the declining sectors of the economy. The private cost is borne in the form of lost income and opportunities. The social cost is felt in many ways, including slower overall levels of growth and decreased competitiveness, particularly when other countries adjust more quickly to exogenous shocks or adapt more quickly to technological change.

Structural change in the economy puts great stress on social institutions (such as government) that have been molded to fit the needs of earlier times and then allowed to harden. When this structural change is accompanied by innovations in finance, which can dramatically increase the speed with which resources move from old to new uses, these social institutions may crack and crumble. Chaos and confusion result until new institutional arrangements evolve that are better adapted to the changed social environment. The institutions of government are strained, too. Perhaps the clearest barometer of this stress is the new mountain of debt.

Structural Change and Fiscal Crisis

Throughout this essay I will talk about the problem of *fiscal crisis*, a condition in which the fact of growing public debt and the problem of managing it becomes the overwhelming concern of public policy. In fiscal crisis, the "real" functions of government become subservient to the "shadow" problem of finance.

This is a behavioral definition of fiscal crisis, not one based on economic indicators, such as debt as a fraction of GNP. In some countries, such as Victorian Britain, relatively small levels of public debt were enough to cause fiscal crisis, so sensitive was the system to the perceived problem of fiscal balance. In modern Italy, on the other hand, even enormous levels of public debt seem not to generate fiscal crisis. To the question of just how much debt is needed for fiscal crisis, I must answer that it depends on the time, place, and economic and social structure. It seems clear, however, that the United States has reached the point of fiscal crisis in the 1990s.

Today's widespread and rising public debts are a symptom of rapid and major underlying changes in the economic and social structure that underlies government's fiscal system. The structure of government no longer matches the structure of the economic and social system it was designed to service. Government and other social institutions will need to change to better match their environment. Only then will it be possible to stabilize the mountains of debt.

Social institutions, including government, develop over time to meet the needs of society, given the existing economic, technological, and social structures. Since these structures do not usually change quickly, social institutions are able to adapt themselves to their environment and grow rigid. This institutional hardening is not necessarily undesirable in the short run because it indicates that society is successful in selecting the most efficient ways to organize economic, technological, and social relationships.

Inflexible institutions are undesirable, however, when they inhibit the evolutionary or progressive changes that are associated with economic growth. Mancur Olson is one economist who has studied the relationship between institutional rigidity and economic growth.[7] Olson believes that institutions tend to become more rigid over time as interest groups gain power and use government to make rules that institutionalize benefits for the few at a high cost to the many. As time passes, existing interest groups become more powerful and rigid; and new interest groups appear and grow until finally the economy loses its ability to grow, too set in the concrete of rules, regulations, and restrictive practices to adopt the progressive innovations it needs to remain dynamic.

If rigid social institutions can cause slower growth even in an otherwise stable economy, what happens when the underlying structures of society change suddenly and the social institutions do not? The answer is that the rigid institutions must crack or crumble; crisis and chaos in some form or other will exist until social institutions change and adapt themselves to their new environment.

Government is a social institution that attempts to do for society collectively what cannot better be done by the members of society individually. Over time, governmental institutions evolve and adapt to conform to the needs and limitations of their environments. Where the principal threat to social stability is external aggression, for example, government's main role is as protector and peacekeeper. Where the main threat is instead economic instability, government becomes more involved in employment and incomes policies. In a stable society, where the communal problems remain the same, the structures of government become entrenched, specialized, and somewhat rigid. (This would probably be true even in the absence of Olson-style interest group behavior.) Government becomes better able to deal with existing problems and interests, but in the process it loses flexibility that is useful when social problems change.

Increasing government rigidity takes many forms: bureaucracies emerge and grow and laws and regulations increase in number and complexity. One important result of this decreased flexibility (and the one on which this book focuses) is that the public sector budget also becomes less flexible, less able to give under pressure of change. The sources of government tax revenue become highly specialized—taxing the economic activities that generate wealth—but subject to the inevitable influence of powerful interest groups. Budgetary outlays also become increasingly specialized and rigid. Discretionary expenditures give way to "entitlements" that are not easily modified when circumstances change.

Government's budget, like government's laws, regulations, and programs, molds itself to fit the social environment, then grows gradually more brittle over time. The budget cannot stretch when the underlying social or economic structure changes, so it cracks.

Government budgets have four parts: expenditures, transfers, taxes, and debt. Expenditures and transfers are the two general ways that government uses its resources. Expenditures are government purchases of goods and services, such as schoolbooks, military equipment, and office supplies. Transfers are payments from government to others (including perhaps other governments) for which no direct good or service is supplied. Transfer payments include some farm subsidies, unemployment benefits, Aid to Families with Dependent Children, and social security benefits. Government finances these outlays from tax revenues (and some user fees) plus whatever debt (the deficit) is needed to make ends meet. Expenditures, transfers, and taxes must all fit the underlying social and economic system precisely if government is to be successful and fiscal balance achieved. This is perhaps most true about taxes.

Tax systems are complex because taxes must perform many tasks. First, taxes need to raise revenue so that government will have resources to allocate and transfer. Taxes do not fall equally on all productive activities, however, because of political and economic differences. Politically, many interest groups are able to escape the full burden of taxation because they are able to organize to influence the legislature to grant loopholes or preferential tax treatment. Tax preferences proliferate over time, reducing the tax base and shifting the burden on to other groups.

From the economic standpoint, taxation is a delicate matter because whereas to raise revenue in the short term the tax must be aimed at those sectors of the economy that generate wealth, to raise revenue in the long run, the tax must be aimed in such a way as to avoid killing the golden goose. Therefore, different sectors of the economy may end up bearing different real tax burdens depending on how seriously the disincentives of taxation are likely to affect their growth and survival. In other words, there are generally some sectors of the economy that cannot be taxed heavily for political reasons and others that should not be taxed heavily for economic reasons. This leaves most of the tax burden to fall on whatever is left.

Major structural changes in the economy make it difficult for tax revenues to keep up with the needs of government. Existing interest groups still want protection, but so do emerging groups that will eventually play a more important role in the economy. Tax rates and structures remain frozen while the economic base of the economy changes. Tax rates on the old sources of wealth will likely stay low while tax rates will need to be reduced or modified in other areas to accommodate emerging sources of wealth. With fewer and fewer activities subject to lower and lower tax rates, tax revenues stagnate. Major institutional change — tax reform — is needed to restore the fiscal system to working order.

Similar pressures are at work on the other side of the budget ledger. The needs and interests of the past will still demand public resources, while new needs and interests must also be served. Thus, rapid structural change increases the growth of expenditures and transfers while reducing the growth of tax revenues. Deficits and a rising public debt are the consequence unless political leaders can overcome the forces just described. If they cannot, it is probably because they are themselves trapped in political structures built for the waning world of yesterday's social needs and interests. At some point, if the economic and political system fails to adjust, the problem of the public debt can come to dominate government policy.

Structural economic and social change leads to fiscal crisis. Existing government institutions become unable to provide through taxes the additional resources that are demanded. When tax revenues are inadequate, governments resort to public debt. Mountains of public debt arise until, eventually, the revenue and expenditure institutions of government evolve to suit the new economic and social environment better or are replaced by a different set of more successful institutions.

The mountains of public debt that grow out of structural economic and social change are a problem, to be sure; but they are perhaps more interesting when viewed, as here, as a symptom of more severe changes in society and crisis in social institutions.

It is probably obvious that the shape of the economy and society influences or determines the pattern of its government in the long run. But this simple relationship is complicated by the fact that government institutions also set rewards and penalties and provide incentives for actions in the private sector. In short, government both shapes the economy and is shaped by it. This creates a fascinating dynamic tension. Structural change puts stress on the public sector institutions; and the way that government reacts determines, in part, the shape and size of the structural changes that result. Structural change and fiscal crisis thus form a complex and important dynamic interrelationship.

Crisis in the Postwar Economy

Are we presently experiencing the sort of rapid structural change just described? I think that we are. One indication is the seemingly uncontrollable growth of public debt around the world, especially in strong countries such as the United States. What is the cause of this change? It would be easy to point to technological changes, such as innovations in telecommunications and computers. I suggest that they play only a supporting role and that the real structural change now under way is a movement from an economic system based on national economies and domestic markets to one based on a worldwide division of labor, where production, assembly, distribution, and marketing practices are changing rapidly. Existing economic and political institutions base themselves on traditional notions of international trade, finance, and comparative advantage. The movement to a global economy, where resource flows are much different in nature, direction, and size, strains these institutions.

This stress is magnified by recent innovations in global finance. World financial markets have been progressively deregulated over the last decade, letting a jinni out of its bottle. Now financial shadows fly nonstop around the globe through wires and via satellites, from computer to computer, passing on the way their consequent parallel real resource movements. This "big bang" (to use the name given to deregulation of London's financial markets) has shaken the world's resources loose from their roots and thereby hastened the movement to a global economy.

It will take some time for institutions—economic, political, and social—to adjust to the changes we are experiencing. Here in the United States, for example, the goods we buy are increasingly foreign; and the firms we work for are increasingly owned by foreigners. Union power, the politics of special interest groups, and our concept of national self-interest will all change as a result of the structural transformation that we are now experiencing.

Trapped in outdated institutional structures, leaders watch while public debt grows. Why do they not effect the changes needed to restore fiscal balance? Perhaps it is folly (a self-destructive choice made despite the known existence of a superior option, as Barbara Tuchman defines it). More likely, however, the reason is a misreading of the situation. We may not appreciate until much later that the turning point was passed without decisive action.

How does a nation recover from fiscal crisis and the burden of the mountains of debt? This is the bottom-line question, the most pressing precisely because it is the most difficult to answer. What will the future bring? Perhaps a better understanding of the past and present will inform our analysis.

2

Renaissance Florence: Death, Birth, and the Fifth Element

"You Florentines are the fifth element," Pope Boniface VIII proclaimed in 1300, reflecting a popular view of the unique contributions of Florentine citizens.[1] Earth, air, water, and fire could be combined by all men to produce the simple goods of everyday life. But when the Florentine "fifth element" was added, a new and more creative alchemy was possible.

Most readers of this essay will probably assume that this fifth element, the creative spark, was that of Florentine art and culture. Surely the great works of Michelangelo, Giotto, Botticelli, and Leonardo are evidence of an artistic element not common in nature but that, when mixed with base metals, yielded up objects of timeless and special beauty and grace.

In fact, Pope Boniface's famous remark was made to a gathering of merchants of Florence, not artists or philosophers; but the essence of the fifth element — the creative spark — was probably the same for Bardi the banker as for the sculptor of David. The contributions of the people of Florence to commerce and finance are perhaps as timeless and special (in their own way) as those of Michelangelo.

Pope Boniface recognized that something made the citizens of Florence special, but he probably could not define the nature of their unique difference. Alfred Marshall, the nineteenth-century British economist, knew the elements of economics and described them this way:

> In a sense there are only two agents of production, nature and man. . . . If the character and powers of nature and of man be given, the growth of wealth and knowledge and organization follow from them as effect from cause. But on the other hand man is himself largely formed by his surroundings, in which nature plays a great part: and thus from every point of view man is the centre of the problem of production as well as that of consumption; and also of that further problem of the relations between the two, which goes by the twofold name of Distribution and Exchange.[2]

The economy of Florence was both cause and effect of the nature of the Florentine people. Nature supplied the four elements of the physical world; but the people of Florence provided the spark, the special fifth element, that caused the growth of wealth and knowledge that we call the Renaissance. The renaissance of humanism was built on the foundation of the Florentine economy, a balance of production and consumption, distribution and exchange. Motivated by individual self-interest, the people of Renaissance Florence were able to achieve prosperity that was well out of proportion to the physical resources at their command.[3] This made their prosperity uncommon for its time and place and therefore an appropriate object for an amazed pope's commentary.[4]

Consider what nature had granted Florence circa 1300. The city was situated on the Arno, an alternately meager or too-generous river of only limited commercial use. The famous Roman roads, active avenues for commerce through the centuries, neatly bypassed Florence in favor of nearby hilltop Fiesole. The rolling hills and Tuscan countryside were moderately fertile but failed even to provide adequate food for the city's population. Food, minerals, raw materials, and even workers were all necessarily imported to some degree. Nature was not generous in its physical gifts. Based on a survey of the economic geography of the area, a modern economist might predict for Florence the sort of simple and hard agrarian existence that did in fact (and to some extent still does) prevail in many Tuscan villages. It is small wonder that at least one frustrated scholar has complained that "The fact that the Florentines played the chief part in the history of the Renaissance has never been satisfactorily explained."[5]

The real wealth of Florence flowed from the energy, creativity, and vision of its people, not its rivers, roads, and soil. In commerce and finance the Florentines constantly sought opportunities to buy and sell and borrow and lend, creating wealth for themselves and ultimately for their society.

The Florentines were not unique in the Western world in their highly developed propensity to truck and trade even in the face of natural obstacles to these activities; other individuals in other places displayed equal and sometimes greater business skills. But the spark of self-interest was more concentrated in Florence, so the flame burned brighter. Why?

One important factor in the growth of the Florentine economy was the unusual degree of economic freedom and social mobility available to many Florentine citizens and, consequently, the unusual ability of, and incentive for, Florentines to undertake activities in their own self-interest. The degree of economic freedom that existed in Florence (especially compared to other states) can be seen by viewing briefly the Florentine guilds.

Medieval trade guilds have a bad name; they are generally characterized as monopolistic associations that restricted the entry into, and the output of, important occupations, crafts, and industries. The medieval English guilds, for example, are generally seen as restrictive, limiting production, opportunity, and economic growth, all in order to preserve high incomes for the guild members. An English weavers guild might control production of fabric in a geographical area, limit membership, and discourage the introduction of new technology that would threaten the status quo. Walter Bagehot wrote of English guilds, "For a long period of industrial history . . . guilds . . . kept trade apart, and prevented capital from going from one [trade] to another. They even kept the trade of city A quite apart from the same trade in city B; they would not let capital or labor flow from one to the other. . . . We now know this to be a great error; such guilds did far more harm than good."[6]

Mancur Olson has argued that these restrictive guilds must have had the cooperation of similarly restrictive governments (or made use of their coercive power) to achieve these results.[7] These guilds restricted the economic freedom of members and nonmembers alike, erecting *structural rigidities* (to use Olson's terminology) that contributed to the absence of sustained economic growth during the Middle Ages.

The guilds of Florence were different. Guild membership seems to have been relatively open, with production limits rarely imposed (although quality controls and binding contracts were typically enforced by the guilds). The noneconomic activities of these guilds, such as social activities and charitable works, were sometimes as important as the commercial factors that tied the membership together.[8]

Scholars agree that the Florentine guilds were much less restrictive than their counterparts in other countries, thus increasing the range and scope of individual economic activity in Florence, giving Adam Smith's "invisible hand" of self-interest plenty of room to maneuver. This is not to say that all Florentines had a great deal of freedom of economic choice. As the incident of the Ciompi Revolt will show us, many workers and merchants felt themselves under the thumbs of the ruling class. But this is not a uniquely Florentine problem (nor is it confined to the past). The point is that economic freedom was more widely available to the Florentines than to other European societies, providing Florence with the powerful incentive of individual self-interest to fuel its engine of economic growth. Combined with the social mobility that derived from the lack of a traditional hereditary aristocracy in Florence, economic freedom was an extremely potent force, and Florence prospered so long as it lasted.

Peter Burke has aptly described Renaissance Florence as an "unusually favourable micro-climate" for the cultivation of entrepreneurs.[9] Burke finds that Florence and the other Italian city-states possessed a "relatively favourable cultural climate for entrepreneurs by virtue of their traditional stresses on such values as achievement, competition, toleration, industry, thrift, and calculation. They were pro-enterprise cultures, where the value-system had been shaped by entrepreneurs but in turn shaped others."[10]

Burke's talk of microclimates and an entrepreneurial culture makes Florence sound more like bustling Silicon Valley than Michelangelo's quaint hometown. But Burke is right, outward appearances notwithstanding; the entrepreneurial culture that flowers in these modern microclimates is the same fifth element that Pope Boniface recognized so long ago.

The economic history of Florence during the Renaissance is a complex and intertwined story of growth, decline, and stagnation. Part of this complicated economic pattern is explained by the random cycles of nature, with its floods, famines, and plagues. Much of the fate of the Florentine economy will be found in the people themselves, how they sought to resolve nature's contradictions and how they succeeded or failed.

To a significant degree, however, the economic history of Florence during its Renaissance period (roughly 1330–1530) is the story of structural change and fiscal crisis. The Florentine economy adapted with particular success to the economic environment of the thirteenth century. It struggled to maintain this success in years that followed one of history's most complete structural changes, the black death. Finally, Florence fell into long-term decline when the already-changing economic climate was rocked in the second half of the fifteenth century by events that forced the Florentines to deal with a new world economic order.[11]

Basic Industries of the Florentine Economy

Many types of firms did business in Florence and in the *contado*, or territorial possessions outside the city walls.[12] Agriculture, of course, was an important sector that employed a large share of the total population. Provision of the many necessities of consumption also created employment for a variety of tradesmen, artisans, and merchants. During the Middle Ages these were the main and sometimes only occupations in many regions. Florence was different because it developed so far beyond the norm.

Florence was an important international economic center long before the Renaissance. Northern Italy in general (but not Florence in particular), was the home of what Raymond de Roover has called the "commercial revolution" of the thirteenth century.[13] De Roover's terminology is well-chosen, for this was not a scientific revolution or an industrial revolution but rather an important improvement in the practical techniques of organization, exchange, and finance. According to de Roover, there were five keys to the commercial revolution, which the Italians gained and mastered while others did not. The keys were

1. the ability to form larger business organizations through efficient partnerships
2. the development of sophisticated means of payment, notably the bill of exchange, which facilitated long-distance finance and exchange
3. relatively safe and secure roads
4. the development of maritime insurance, to compensate for the risks inherent in sea-borne trade
5. development of relatively modern accounting practices[14]

With these five keys in hand, the merchants of Florence built a strong economy in the Middle Ages.

The dominant theme in economic history of Renaissance Florence, however, really is the story of just two industries: cloth and finance. These were the sectors that made Florence different from other cities of this period, the two trades where the keys of the commercial revolution could be used to greatest effect.

The Cloth Industry

Cloth was the most important manufactured good in the world during this period (and remained so until late in the nineteenth century). Cloth could be a rough and rugged necessity or a fine and festive luxury. The market for wool, cotton, and silk cloth was large enough to support the degree of investment and specialization that produces an industry.[15]

Nature did not endow Florence with the resources that would give it a comparative advantage in cloth production. Italian wool was not of the highest quality, for example, and the local market was limited. Florentine workers possessed no special skills, nor did they have access to any secret process. But this did not stop the entrepreneurs of Florence.

The cloth industry grew from the roots established by the guild of the Calimala merchants (so named for the street where their shops were located). The Calimala did not so much produce cloth as market the cloth that others made. They purchased rough cloth from northern countries, dyed and refined it, and resold it. They thus took cloth produced for one market and tailored it to the tastes of a different market.[16]

Some seem to think that the Calimala Guild had access to a secret chemical or manufacturing process that allowed them to turn rough cloth into a finer article, but this seems unlikely. The greater "secret" of the Calimala merchants was their ability to coordinate a complex international trade network and to market their cloth to foreign buyers successfully in the face of established local competitors. It is clear that they worked in several different markets simultaneously and took the entrepreneur's risks. They purchased the foreign cloth, arranged for transport to Florence, paid for local refinements, arranged for transport to other foreign markets, and eventually sold their "cloth of Florence" abroad. Such complex, risky, and costly lines of distribution and exchange were rare in the medieval world. Florentine entrepreneurs were the most ready and willing to undertake these risks, so they, most of all, claimed the resulting returns.

The Calimala trade was the paramount Florentine industry early in the fourteenth century, but the Calimala Guild was soon overshadowed by the wool cloth entrepreneurs of the Arte della Lana. (The designation *Arte* refers to the guild institution, so the Arte della Lana was the "Guild of Wool.") Because local wool was of low quality, members of the Lana Guild followed the pattern set by Calimala merchants, engaging in complex, long-distance international transactions. High-quality raw wool was imported in quantity from England, Spain, and other countries. Cloth of high (but probably not the highest) quality was produced in Florence from the imported wool and sold in southern Europe and the Levant by skillful Florentine merchants.

The role of the members of the Lana Guild in all this was to bear risks and coordinate the activities of others rather than to own capital and directly manage the production process. This differentiates the Florentine entrepreneurs from, say, the eighteenth- and nineteenth-century British textile manufacturers and makes them more like the Dutch textile manufacturers of Leiden a century earlier. Agents of the Lana Guild would purchase wool abroad and ship it to Florence, where they would engage independent local craftsmen of the lesser guilds to undertake the successive steps of production.

At the top of the organization chart were the *lanaiuoli*, the Lana Guild members who coordinated the complex and intricate production process. Here is how Brucker describes their activities:

> Upon arrival in the lanaiuolo's shop, the wool was first prepared for spinning. Most of this work was performed in the shop itself, by workers whose activities were supervised by foremen. Spinning was done by women of the contado. Thus the rural areas surrounding Florence were drawn into the industry's vortex. Serving as intermediaries between the lanaiuoli and the spinners were brokers who delivered the wool, collected the yarn, and paid the women on a piece-rate basis. The yarn was given to weavers who operated looms in their shops or private dwellings. The finished cloth was then sent to another category of subcontractors, the fullers, who operated their mills along streams in outlying areas. Most of the final stages of the production process — dyeing, shearing, mending — were also carried out in small shops by independent masters. Each of these petty entrepreneurs constituted a nucleus of economic activity for they frequently hired apprentices or laborers to work in their shop. Each, too, nourished subsidiary industries, crafts, and markets.[17]

What strikes the modern reader is the complexity of cloth manufacture, how many specialized steps were involved. But there is a more important point here: the distinct separation of management from the ownership of production capital. The entrepreneurs of the Lana Guild financed and coordinated the cloth-making process; but most of the productive investments (in looms, stretching sheds, and the like) were made by the owners of small businesses, who performed specialized work on a piece-rate basis. In other words, the *lanaiuoli* supplied the raw materials and circulating capital and coordinated this process, but the fixed capital was owned by the individual independent entrepreneurs. There were no huge cloth factories in Florence (as would appear late in the Industrial Revolution) and no distinct class of capitalists, in the strict sense, either.[18]

The nature of the Florentine cloth industry contributed to the relatively high degree of social mobility that prevailed in this period. Workers needed relatively little capital to move into the class of petty entrepreneurs, and the Florentine system of finance could provide this capital through loans or through partnerships that spanned social classes. It was still unlikely that a day laborer would ever be able to enter one of the major guilds, but it was not uncommon for an able family to rise several steps on the economic ladder in only a generation or two. This degree of social and economic mobility is significant, especially when compared to the rigid feudal system that still prevailed in the rest of Europe.

Production of wool cloth became the principal industry of Florence in the fourteenth and fifteenth centuries, but by the sixteenth century silk had eclipsed wool in its economic importance. The growth of the upscale silk market (at a time when wool was in decline) added an additional complication to the production process in that highly skilled workers were needed, to master certain difficult aspects of silk production. (On the other hand many silk-processing tasks were very simple and were assigned to otherwise "underemployed" women, children, and elderly relatives, thereby expanding the effective size of the labor force.)[19] The city of Lucca was the center of the silk trades in Italy and skilled Luchese citizens were difficult to attract and hold in the competitive and combative environment of the fifteenth century.

The growth of the Florentine wool industry was built on the economic concepts of specialization and exchange. The members of the Lana Guild had the vision to see the potential for profit at the end of a complex chain of transactions and the organizational skills to coordinate the activities of perhaps hundreds of craftsmen and shop masters. Finally, they had the financial resources necessary to finance this process and the entrepreneur's willingness to take the many risks involved.

The wool trade was highly profitable for the members of the Lana Guild and for the many independent contractors who did the real work of cloth production. Cloth (plus the city's trademark gold coin, the florin) is what Florence meant to most people in Europe for most of the years covered by this study.

Florentine wool cloth may have been sturdy and durable; but, as we shall see, the Florentine cloth industry itself was surprisingly fragile. Consider the conditions necessary for the Florentine wool trade to succeed. First was needed dependable sources of imported wool and reliable markets for the finished cloth. This requires a world that is relatively stable; unexpected events in other countries could disrupt the Florentine economy. Most important, the wool trade depended on free and peaceful trade. Free trade was necessary so that Florentine merchants could have access to all necessary markets. Peace was needed because war tended to close borders, disrupt the lines of communication and transport, and disturb the flow of goods between countries and between the city and the *contado*.

Finance

Cloth was the key Florentine industry, but it would be a mistake to conclude that the wealth of Florence was built on profits from manufacturing. Florentine entrepreneurs organized the production of the cloth and took profits from these ventures, to be sure, but their largest profits came through the trade and finance activities that were associated with cloth production.[20]

Cloth required trade, and trade requires finance. The widespread activities of the Lana Guild in trade meant that they had access to many financial opportunities. Being Florentines, they did not hesitate when opportunity knocked. Thus, finance became a basic business of the city and the foundation of the wealth of Florence's great families.

Italians were dominant in financial markets throughout Europe during the period of this study. While cloth was an important industry in Florence, Florentine cloth had no monopoly in the world market and was surpassed in quantity and quality by goods produced elsewhere. But no one rivaled the Italians in general and the Florentines in particular in the field of finance. Even today, Lombard Street is the London address symbolic of international finance because that was the street where, centuries before, the Italian money changers set up shop.

There are three basic reasons for the Italians' preeminence in international finance. The first, as already noted, was their presence in every important European economic center. They were there because of their interests in the wool trade and in some cases as papal fiscal agents as well. The members of the Lana Guild specialized in coordinating the activities of many producers and sellers, and some of this coordination required finance. The wool producers in England, for example, might borrow now to cover current expenses, then repay when the wool crop came to market. Cloth merchants in France and other countries might borrow to cover the price of Florentine cloth, then repay when they resold these goods. The wheels of commerce are lubricated with the oil of quick credit, a fact that the Florentine merchants appreciated. The Calimala and Lana merchants were more successful than they would otherwise have been because their firms stood ready to arrange credit throughout the production and marketing chain. In fact, it is almost artificial to separate the cloth trade from finance, so intertwined were the activities in many cases.

The second reason Italian financiers were so successful was that the Italian people must have been frugal and saved a good deal of their incomes (a tendency that persists today), so that substantial surplus funds were available for credit transactions. This point is not widely appreciated by those who have studied Florence. Saving is required for the growth of lending; and the Florentines and their neighbors must have been unusual in their propensity to save, at least during the first part of the period we are studying.

One reason that the Italians saved so much was the existence of financial institutions that allowed them to achieve both capital growth and security. This brings us to the third reason for Italian financial success—their invention and mastery of modern accounting techniques and the institutions that go with them.

It is hard to overstate the important role that arithmetic in general and accounting in particular played in the growth of Italian finance. Early commercial arithmetic textbooks indicate clearly that the Italians knew how to use relatively complex algebraic techniques to solve business problems; their knowledge included accounting, but went well beyond it.[21]

Some aspects of accounting's importance are clear; it is obvious, for example, that systematic accounting provides a clear record of transactions and therefore grants a greater measure of certainty and security to all involved. But other factors are more subtle yet probably more important. The sophisticated use of double-entry accounting allowed the Italian entrepreneurs to see how a series of complex transactions were interrelated and how means and ends could be linked in complicated and indirect ways. Because they understood accounting principles, the Italians must have thought differently, and viewed complex economic relationships differently from others. The ability to conceive of business transactions in this abstract way was a great commercial advantage.

Accounting techniques also allowed the Italians to perceive the problem of risk and learn how to reduce it through diversification, without sacrificing return. Their modern understanding of risk and return (learned, probably, from the Venetians) was one reason the inland Tuscan bookkeepers became important providers of maritime insurance.[22] Just as they could pool the risks of cloth or loan transactions through sophisticated accounting means, so, too, they could pool the risks of otherwise chancy maritime trade. This gave them an advantage both in finance and in the international commercial exchanges it makes possible.[23]

The main firms of Florentine finance—the Bardi and Peruzzi and, later, the Medici—were members of the Arte de Cambio (Exchange Guild). The name *Cambio* (Exchange) derived from the necessity of disguising interest-bearing loans as foreign exchange transactions to avoid the church's usury prohibition. Thus the "money changers" would write loan contracts specifying repayment in a different coin at a fictional exchange rate so that the interest payment was hidden. Other loans were further disguised through the use of "dry exchange" of commodities—where fictional goods were sold and repurchased at different prices in one contract to achieve the practical effect of an interest-bearing loan.

The usury prohibition was taken seriously. Some Florentines would go to great lengths to avoid the occasion of immoral interest; priests would refuse the sacraments and last rites to usurers, demanding that they compensate society before receiving forgiveness. (Florence's beautiful churches owe at least some of their wealth to the funds thus extorted.) When credit ran dry in some Tuscan cities, local governments would aggressively seek Jews to fill the gap that church doctrine had created.[24]

A positive side effect of the usury prohibition, however, was that it drew a fair amount of capital into trade and commerce through partnerships that might otherwise have been deposited in banks.[25] In this way the usury laws provided an unintentional incentive for the development of larger and more efficient business enterprises in Italy.

Eventually church doctrines evolved to recognize the difference between loans for necessary consumption and those made for productive investment; interest was allowable on the latter but proscribed on the former. This change greatly simplified credit transactions, although it may not have affected their number in any significant way.

In fact, Bernadino of Siena and Antonio of Florence, local clerics who were later elevated to sainthood, developed innovative theories that helped absolve Florentine financiers from the sin of usury. They recognized that interest might be a payment for legitimate but subtle costs—the cost of risk and the opportunity cost of foregone present consumption or alternative investment.[26] Still later, Florentines would find absolute merit in the concept of interest. Interest payments (through the commune's dowry fund) allowed young women to marry and thus avoid the moral temptations and potential sins of unmarried life. Interest payments could also add to the accumulation of wealth, which, according to their reading of Aristotle, promoted virtue and civic responsibility.[27]

How were the Florentine banking houses organized? The large firms were partnerships, with different partners participating to different degrees in each of the many enterprises in which they might be involved. The heart of the bank was the *banco* (bench or counter) or *tavola* (table), so-called since the time of the Greeks because banking activities took place in public, with book entries made openly on the table where the banker did business.

The big finance houses established *tavolas* in many cities throughout Europe. Thus, funds received in one city could be lent elsewhere. Equally important, intercity fund transfers could be accomplished for customers by intrafirm accounting entries, making the risky physical transfer of funds unnecessary. This accounting tool, which could move gold over mountains and across seas using only paper and ink, forged a link between the Italian bankers and the Vatican. The Church of Rome was the largest fiscal institution in the world, collecting and disbursing enormous sums throughout Europe. Italian bankers soon became Rome's fiscal agents in many cities, providing financial services for the Holy See and making business connections of their own in the process.

The relationship between finance and the cloth business in Florence was somewhat complex. Surely one hand washed the other in these businesses, so close links among firms and families were desirable. Loans to the English court were used to gain access to the island kingdom's choice long-staple wool, for example, which was beneficial for Florentine wool firms. By the same measure, the wool trade opened up opportunities for gains through financial transactions. It is not unexpected, then, that many firms and families engaged themselves to finance, textile manufacture, *and* trade in order to internalize the beneficial side effects of each business.

The members of the Cambio Guild were sophisticated financiers, as capable of complex transactions as some modern Wall Street firms. The banking houses of Florence created a variety of different financial instruments for use in banking, trade, and business generally. One authority has written, perhaps overlooking the seventeenth-century innovations of the Dutch, that "What is known about the operations of the Medici bank, as well as other banks in Florence and Tuscany, justifies the conclusion that they were technically the most advanced financial institutions before the late sixteenth century and possibly the late seventeenth century and were definitely surpassed in these respects only in the nineteenth century."[28]

The success and growth of these international financial firms depended on the same necessary conditions as the wool merchants. Stable economic conditions, peace, and open markets were the ideal banking environment. Unexpected economic events, closed markets, and war all disrupted financial flows and doomed credit transactions.

One more condition was necessary for the flowering of Florentine finance—stable money. Progressive debasement of coins and the consequent inflation in prices would spell doom to a creditor economy. There is no profit in lending today at full weight to be repaid tomorrow in light coin. The Florentines themselves supplied the solution to this problem in 1252 when they began minting the gold florin. The florin was probably the most stable unit of currency in history; its real value stood solid against the forces of debasement for over two hundred years. The florin was the standard by which all other coins were judged in European trade and finance. The wide influence of Florentine merchants promoted the wide use of the florin, while the stability of the florin promoted Florence's commercial interests abroad. The Florentines clearly understood the value of their coin; the Cambio Guild imposed severe punishments on members who failed to remove altered coins from circulation.

It is hard to appreciate today how important an innovation the gold florin was in its day. In the medieval world of silver coins, the expansion of trade was generally accompanied by liquidity problems and pressure to mint more money. This pressure was normally accommodated through debasement and inflation, which caused credit to dry up and had the tendency to bring growth to a halt. The lack of a solid and stable coin was therefore a major barrier to economic growth. A reliable gold coin to supplement the traditional silver tokens was a way out of this growth trap.[29]

Economic growth took off in Italy in the thirteenth century in good measure because gold coins were introduced in Florence and Genoa. This increase in liquidity without debasement and inflation allowed international trade to be a powerful engine of commercial growth.

The economy of Florence grew and prospered between 1250 and 1320 because the environmental conditions were right for its main industries. The people were largely spared from plagues and famines. Markets were relatively, if not completely, open. Wars raged, but not enough to block the trade routes. Interest rates fell within the range that makes credit transactions mutually profitable for borrowers and lenders. Good, cheap labor was available in Florence to support cloth production.

These were good times for Florence and the firms and families involved in its commercial life. Indeed, these early years of the fourteenth century—long before the Medici came to power, well before the great works of the artistic renaissance were envisioned—this was the time of the greatest economic prosperity in Florence.

Structural Change: The Disasters of the 1340s

Florentine industry slipped into a cyclical decline in the 1330s; a famine in 1339 accelerated the trend, causing the famous chronicler of the period, Giovanni Villani to report that "every trade in Florence was in too poor a shape to make a profit."[30] But these problems pale compared to the disasters that befell the commune in the 1340s.

The economic and social environment changed radically during the 1340s; the effects were felt everywhere in the Florentine state and would continue to cause trouble for years into the future. Florence experienced structural economic changes that were as large, profound, and long-lasting as any we might imagine. To an important degree, the rest of the story of the economy of Renaissance Florence is the tale of how the Florentines sought to adjust to the world that changed suddenly in the 1340s.

The disastrous decade of the 1340s saw Florence rocked by the Great Crash of its financial sector, a serious shift in the terms of trade against Florentine interests, and finally and most devastating, famine and plague that wiped out perhaps one-third of the commune's population. Because of the complexity of the events of this period, it is best first to look at each of the major problems separately, then attempt to understand their joint impacts.

Financial Collapse

The failure of the largest Florentine banking firms, the houses of the Peruzzi (1343) and the Bardi (1346), was a severe blow to the Florentine economy that might well be compared to the stock market crash of 1929 in its effects. The collapse of these pillars of Florentine finance triggered subsequent failure of other banking firms and a general contraction of manufacturing activities because of the interdependence of finance and trade in the Italian economy. The banking collapse brought ruin to citizens of all economic and social classes and a reduction in all sorts of economic activity. The great and the small alike were bent under this burden.

How did this severe collapse happen? Why did these strong businesses fail? The great firms of Florence would not fall from any single blow, but they could not withstand the compounded battering they suffered now.

The first blow came from the Florentine communal government itself. The commune had borrowed heavily for military activities and to pay for imports of food during the famine of 1339. The public debt was to be paid from duties imposed on imports at the city gates and from other excise taxes. Revenues from these sources were declining, however, and the deficit reached such a critical mass in 1342 that Walter of Brienne, the Lord of Florence, was forced to suspend debt payments. The Florentine public debt was large and widely held, so this action caused a significant liquidity crisis that continued until 1345, when the public debt was declared negotiable and shares could be freely exchanged. In the meantime, Florentine citizens sought to regain their lost liquidity by withdrawing deposits from the main banking firms. These actions effectively transferred the liquidity crisis from the government to the people and from the people to the banking houses.

Although we are here mostly concerned with how the fiscal crisis affected the Florentine banks, it is worth noting that the government's actions at this time have historical import for other reasons. The communal debts were consolidated and formally funded from excise revenues at this point, creating the Monte Commune (City Fund), shares of which were traded much as are government bonds today. The Monte was the first modern public debt, and it will figure importantly in later parts of this narrative.

The second blow to Florentine financial stability came from Naples. Roberto, the king of Naples, and his court were major depositors with the Florentine banking firms. Florentine merchants were active in the kingdom of Naples, buying food and raw materials and selling cloth and other manufactures. Trade, as noted earlier, always involves finance, and the large Florentine firms found that the business climate was much improved by their ability to provide an attractive return to Neopolitan nobles by accepting their short-term deposits and relending these funds abroad. Florence and Naples became economic and political allies, an interdependency that did no harm to Florentine business interests. It soon became a characteristic of the Florentines to use credit to lubricate otherwise sticky transactions. In later years, for example, the Medici clan would become highly skilled at the use of finance as a tool to achieve various ends in business, politics, and diplomacy.

Suddenly, however, the Neapolitans withdrew their capital from the Florentine firms. The king of Naples became concerned about a possible shift in Florence's position in the complicated balance of power between Emperor Frederick II and the Roman church. (Florence and Naples were traditionally in the Vatican camp in this conflict.) Afraid that their funds would be lost as the commune's political allegiance changed, the Neapolitans called their short-term loans with Florence, exacerbating the liquidity crisis already under way. The Neapolitan run on the banks left the big firms in Florence staggering.

The final blow came from England. Florentine merchants had a strong interest in relations with England, which was a source of high-quality wool needed for their looms. (At one point Florence even contracted for advance purchase of the entire English wool crop for several years.) This economic dependence of the rich and strong (Florence) on the produce, and therefore the political cooperation, of the poor and weak (England) had made it easy for English kings to tap Florentine bankers for credit. Thus, the Neapolitan deposits had been lent to the English kings. Tuscan firms, the Bardi and the Peruzzi prominent among them, had financed progressively more costly English military campaigns against France during the Hundred Years' War. War in this age was meant to be self-financing. The wealth of the conquered would repay the war loans of the conquerors much as modern corporate takeover strategists expect to profit from the purchase of a firm by selling its individual assets to pay off acquisition loans. The Truce of Esplechin in 1340 made clear that England would not soon prevail in the Hundred Years' War and would, therefore, be unable to repay its debts to Florence.

England's default on its "sovereign" loans (backed as they were by the personal pledge of English royalty) pushed Florence past the brink. The Peruzzi firm collapse in 1343 was followed in 1346 by the Bardi and the other principal financial houses. The days of Florence's greatest wealth were gone; the richest families of subsequent generations (the Medici among them) would not approach the wealth that had preceded the Great Crash.

We have now taken Florence on a journey equivalent to the road between 1929 and 1932. We have destroyed Florence's great banking firms and with them the critical textile-trading firms. As wealth, income, and export production fell, workers, merchants, and craftsmen at each level passed part of their burden on to those below. Credit, of course, was impossible to come by, freezing the wheels of commerce as the dynamic Florentine economy ground to a halt.

The Great Crash of 1343–1346 (as Carlo Cipolla has called it) was by itself quite enough to change Florence's fortunes for the worse.[31] This disaster was compounded, however, by a sudden and unexpected shift in the terms of trade, which further stressed the political economy of the Florentine state.

Gold and Silver Problems

The second major setback for the Florentine economy was a shift in the terms of trade against Florence through a change in the relative value of gold and silver.[32] In simple terms, the Florentine currency appreciated, making Florentine goods more expensive to foreign buyers and reducing the profits and incomes of the trading sector of the commune's economy. Because the trade sector was the historical driving force of growth in Florence, this caused a major economic crisis. As nothing is ever very simple in international finance, how and why Florence suffered this fate requires a relatively lengthy explanation.

The Florentine economy operated on a dual currency system. Both gold (the florin) and the traditional silver coins circulated in the city, with the exchange rate between gold and silver set largely by market forces; that is, the exchange rate between the florin and a silver coin such as the *quattrino* depended approximately on the relative values of the precious metals each contained. This, in turn, depended on the forces of supply and demand.

The two types of coin had different uses and circulated in different economic spheres. The florin (3.53 grams of pure gold) was used for very large transactions and was the coin of choice for trade outside the commune. Cloth transactions were generally denominated in gold, commonly using the florin in particular (other gold coins minted elsewhere also existed but were less commonly used). The gold florin was therefore the money of the wealthier classes of the Florentine economy.

Silver was the money of the lower classes. Workers were paid in silver, and the goods of daily consumption were sold for silver. The value of the silver coins counted most for the masses in Florence; gold counted most for the elite.

Thus, we have a dual economy and a dual monetary system to go with it. For the wealthy men of the Lana Guild, the exchange rate between gold and silver coins was very important. If silver fell in value relative to gold, it meant that the cost of producing cloth (paid in silver coin) fell relative to the price of the finished product (received in gold). When silver coin depreciated and the gold florin appreciated, then the profits from cloth production and other export trades increased. Silver men (who worked in the silver-based economy) might suffer, but gold men (who engaged in gold-based trade and finance) would gain.

This distribution of gains and losses was magnified through the credit markets. Small Florentine firms would borrow from the major houses in gold, but their earnings were mostly in the silver coins that more commonly circulated within the city's walls. Thus, when silver fell, the real (silver) burden of repaying a gold loan increased. This, too, benefited the members of the major guilds and worked to the detriment of the lesser guilds, merchants, and laborers.

A change in the relative value of gold and silver, then, influenced the pattern of profits from Florentine trade and created winners and losers along rather clearly drawn lines. Although the mechanisms by which gold and silver affected individuals were indirect and complex, it was in the people's self-interest to understand and appreciate them.

This discussion is leading us to the events of 1345–1347. The relative value of gold and silver shifted throughout the Western world during this time for reasons that are not entirely clear. Silver experienced a sudden and substantial increase in its value. The gold florin fell relative to silver coins. If appreciation of the gold florin was good for the big players in Florentine business and finance (but hard on the pawns in this game), this depreciation of the florin was bad luck for all.

The fall of the florin was a blow to firms of the Lana Guild and all the many smaller firms, craftsmen, and workers who profited directly or indirectly from these activities. Falling gold and rising silver strained the major firms in two ways. First, it increased their (silver) costs relative to their (gold) revenues, cutting profits at a critical moment. Second, the rise in silver reduced the purchasing power of the gold they received in loan repayments.

The unexpected depreciation of the florin in 1345–1347 further stressed those parts of the Florentine economy that were most damaged by the banking collapses discussed earlier. Anyone who held florins or whose income was linked to the florin suffered. The burden fell heaviest on the money classes, but nearly everyone was hurt in one way or another by this exchange rate change.

The Black Death

The final blow to Florentine prosperity came from nature. Relentless rains in 1345–1346 destroyed crops in Tuscany, causing a major famine in 1347. Food prices moved higher and the public debt increased as the communal government, charged with maintaining food supplies for the urban population, paid out large sums for what little grain could be found. Crop failures and famine, combined with the effects of the financial collapse and trade reversals, assured that no one would escape hard times in Florence. But the worst was yet to come.

The Black Death came to Florence in the summer of 1348. This great epidemic of the bubonic plague originated in Central Asia and spread along the silk trade routes, reaching the port city of Genoa in 1347. The "great dying" or "great pestilence" overwhelmed Europe between 1347 and 1352. Death from bubonic plague was quick and sure, fatal to 70–80 percent of those with symptoms of the disease (painful swelling of lymph nodes on armpits, neck, or groin). A painful death followed the onset of these visible symptoms, generally within about five days.

We know now that the bubonic plague was spread by rats whose fleas bore the bacterium *Yersina pestis*. These plague-bearing fleas most efficiently spread their disease in places where humans and rats are in relatively close contact. Ships were therefore a natural breeding ground for the plague, and so were urban population centers such as Florence.

The city's population fell from eighty thousand to about forty-five thousand in a matter of months. Roughly half the population of the surrounding regions perished. The total devastation of Florence and its economy was now complete.

Financial collapse and trade problems have important short-term impacts on firms, people, and economic systems. But these effects are trivial compared to those of the Black Death. The burdens of the dead and the dying and their families were as hard as they are obvious. The impact on those who ultimately survived is more complex. Barbara W. Tuchman's *A Distant Mirror* has examined some of the unexpected social consequences of a sudden demographic collapse. Carlo Cipolla describes the economic consequences in this way: "In human terms, the plague was an unmitigated disaster. In terms of the economy, its effects were far from being disastrous. The plague in essence broke the vicious spiral of deflation. Since the number of capita was suddenly and dramatically reduced . . . cash balances were unusually large, and they were not hoarded: the prevailing mood among the survivors was that of spending."[33]

It is no wonder that the sobriquet *dismal science* has stuck so firmly to the field of economics. Perhaps only a dismal scientist would look for a silver lining in the Black Death's unparalleled destruction. But once you start looking here, many interesting trends can be found.

The economic world changed dramatically as half the population suddenly disappeared. As I have said before, it is hard to imagine so large and complete a source of structural change in any economic system. The property of the many was inherited by the surviving few, increasing the wealth of people in all walks of life. The rich were richer, but the gains of the poor and middle classes were perhaps relatively larger. People were rich and they had been spared the death that took so many others. Why save for an uncertain (and possibly very short) future? The plague could return (and periodically did). Instead, the survivors spent — and spent lavishly. Silk, not rough woolens. The best. Let us live, who have not died.

Reducing the population by half does not reduce everything by half. There are fewer workers, so less is produced. But half as many workers produce more than half as many goods because of the law of diminishing marginal returns. The last workers are assigned the least productive jobs (those with the lowest marginal returns). Therefore, if only 50 percent as many workers are employed, they are assigned to the most productive jobs, minimizing the lost output.

There are fewer consumers, so less is demanded. But those consumers are wealthy, so they demand more of the best goods and fewer inferior items. The impact of these changes on prices, incomes, and production is complex.

There is general agreement that the real wages of workers increased in the years after the Black Death. The wages that scarce workers received increased by more than did the prices of the goods that they purchased. Even the peasants who did not inherit wealth through the Black Death therefore experienced an increase in their real incomes and became wealthier.

The Consequences of Structural Change

The two centuries of Florentine commercial success prior to the 1340s was built on the conditions of easy credit, favorable terms of trade (a favorable exchange rate between silver and gold coins), and relatively plentiful and cheap productive labor. All these conditions disappeared during the dreadful 1340s. Credit was scarce and costly. Cloth was still in demand, but people wanted silk more than wool. Silk was a more specialized item, requiring skilled workers at many stages of production. These and other laborers were costly, hard to find, and unwilling to engage in the same long hours and hard physical labor as before the great plague. The workers and lesser guilds gained both economic and political power as the population balance tilted in their favor.

With all the shifts that the Black Death brought about, perhaps the most interesting one is the change in basic attitudes. People became less concerned with the future and much more concerned with their immediate needs and desires. In economic terms, their rate of time preference increased, with relatively predictable results. Consumption replaced production. Savings rates fell, reducing the growth in credit availability. Luxuries became the new necessities. Speculation replaced productive investment. A short-term feeding frenzy began without regard to the potential long-run consequences.

The impact of the Black Death on the Florentine economy as a whole was different in the short run from the long run. In the short run, the Black Death offset the contractionary impacts of the collapse of finance and trade by restoring and then increasing the wealth of the commune's populace, which had been destroyed in prior years.

In the long run, however, the basic economic patterns shifted against Florence; the commune would never again be the leading economic power it once was. Greater per capita wealth made credit less of a factor in economic life. Florence was not prepared for a world where fine silks replaced basic woolens as the most important export good.

The critical factor for the people of Florence in the years after the 1340s would be their ability to meet the challenges of the newly developing world as successfully as they had mastered the problems of the Middle Ages. The Florentine economy would experience the forces of structural change caused, more than anything else, by the falling population, higher wealth, and rising real wage rates. Coping with structural change requires flexibility. As we will see, Florence held its own so long as its people were flexible and able to adjust to changing economic conditions.

1350–1369: The Days of Fat Cattle

The historian Charles de la Roncière calls this period the time of the Florentine workers' "fat cattle."[34] The city's economic situation stabilized during the period 1350–1369 in a condition that was favorable to workers, who demanded and were paid high real wages; although economic conditions were not so advantageous to the communal economy overall.

The stable economic pattern of these two decades does not mean that times were peaceful or uninteresting. While workers enjoyed their good fortune, the consequences of the "fat" times slowly accumulated, costs to be borne another day.

The Florentine public debt increased steadily during this period, a peculiar situation during relatively good times. The commune's funded public debt, the Monte, which stood at 600 thousand florins in 1343, had increased to 1.5 million florins in 1364. An analysis of the public debt during these years reveals a great deal about Florentine society.[35]

The Monte grew during the "fat" years because communal expenditures increased while tax revenues stagnated. Wars among the Italian city-states were frequent, as they had been in the past. Florence battled the Visconti of Milan in 1351–1353 and again in 1369–1370. War was waged as well against Pisa in 1362–1364, in an attempt to gain free access to the sea. Military conflict or the threat of it was part of the status quo.

Wars are always costly, but their cost increased significantly in the years after the Black Death. Workers and peasants, enjoying their "fat cattle," were no longer a ready source of cheap infantry. Costly armies of foreign mercenaries now had to be paid. The short war with Pisa is said to have cost the commune a million florins, an enormous sum.

Tax revenues failed to rise to match the increase in military costs. The Florentines nurtured a strong prejudice against taxation. They much preferred to finance government through loans (which promised to return a profit to the private sector) than taxes (which did not).

Direct taxes, such as the *estimo*, a property tax, were very unpopular and could be imposed only in times of great crisis. Indirect taxes, the *gabelles*, were common. The *gabelles* included excise taxes levied on necessities, salt, and wine and a variety of tariffs imposed at the city gate. The Black Death and recessions of the 1340s had reduced substantially the *gabelle* tax base. Even with higher rates, these indirect taxes failed to generate significant revenue increases.[36]

Faced with inadequate tax revenues, Florence resorted to increased reliance on the public debt, levied as forced loans, to finance its growing military expenditures. Forced loans (the *prestanze*) were assessed through the tax system. The tax list of the *estimo* would be used to assess loan obligations;

creditors received negotiable shares of the Monte paying a fixed interest rate, generally about 5 percent.

This system of public finance was sustainable so long as capital remained available and the public retained confidence in the value of their Monte shares. But Florentine liquidity was not growing along with the Monte. Money was being freely spent, not saved or invested. With too much capital being absorbed into rich dresses and gold jewelry, the commune found it more difficult to raise revenues through direct taxes (a last resort) or loans, forced or otherwise.

The government responded to this credit crisis in several ways. The first was to raise interest on Monte shares from the legal maximum of 5 percent to 10 percent and then to a market-dictated rate of 15 percent. Because previous legislation had set the maximum Monte rate at 5 percent, this increase in return was accomplished through the fiction of giving two or three shares in the Monte for each florin loaned (creating the Monte *a uno due* and the Monte *a uno tre*—literally, "two-for-one" and "three-for-one"). Florentines were skilled in the use of financial fictions when legal limits and market requirements differed.

Florence's terms of trade—the price of its imports in terms of its exports (roughly the ratio of gold to silver)—remained stable over this period, allowing the large firms to recover somewhat and adapt as well as they could to their new environment. Business profits in Florence were not spectacular; the "fat cattle" fed the workers, not the entrepreneurs. High Monte interest rates were needed more to bid capital away from rival consumption than from potential investments. But these high interest rates also tended to bid capital away from the business sector. Investment in productive assets in Florence declined. Money not used for conspicuous consumption purchased shares in the Monte through forced loans.

The extent to which consumption must have consumed capital is hard for us fully to appreciate today. But consider that laws were passed restricting public displays of wealth, even including the number and extent of decoration on womens' clothing. A document from the period explains the sumptuary legislation thus:

> Considering the Commune's need for revenue to pay current expenses . . . they have enacted . . . the following:
>   First, all women and girls . . . who wear—or who wear in the future—any gold, silver, pearls, precious stones, bells, ribbons of gold or silver, or cloth of silk brocade on their bodies or heads . . . will be required to pay each year . . . the sum of 50 florins. . . . Every married woman may wear on her hand or hands as many as two rings"[37]

Women were in fact fined under these statutes, although it is not clear that the net result was greater availability of credit for communal purposes. Modern credit controls are not so obviously foolish as the Florentine sumptuary laws even if they are only a little more effective.

Later generations of workers would look back of these years as times of peace, wealth, and prosperity. They would forget that the peace was made by mercenary warriors. They would forget that their wealth was inherited from the victims of the Black Death. They would forget that the prosperity took the form of consumption today with little thought of the bleaker future that predictably arrived.

The Ciompi Revolt

Stable money, stable prices, and peace were the ideal environment for the commune's great firms and their workers and artisans. Under these desirable conditions, they could adjust as well as possible to accommodate the vast structural changes that were the legacy of the 1340s. Stability, however, was not a characteristic of the decade of the 1370s, so the economy suffered. This instability climaxed in the so-called Ciompi Revolt of 1378.

The first source of instability was monetary. The value of the gold florin rose in 1373–1375.[38] This change in the key commercial exchange rate between gold and silver brought on recession by increasing the price of Florentine goods abroad relative to the local silver currencies. Recession in the export sector filtered down and multiplied through the various levels of entrepreneurs, artisans, merchants, and workers.

The largest relative effects of the florin's appreciation were felt by the "middle class" of Florentine businessmen, who stood between the richer and more powerful entrepreneurs of the Lana and Cambio Guilds on one side and the poor and powerless day workers and peasants on the other. These middle-class artisans and merchants were paid in silver but owed debts in gold. The appreciation of the gold florin (and the implicit depreciation of silver coins) caught them coming and going; their real incomes fell just as their real debt burdens increased.

A fateful nature now conspired to increase tension within the commune. The plague returned in 1374, as it did periodically, striking the generation that had grown up since the Black Death. Poor harvests in 1375 lead to a famine, raising food costs, and increasing pressure on the commune's food budget. This combination of recession, plague, and famine caused tremendous hardship for the Florentine population.

War added to this tension in 1375–1378. The War of the Eight Saints between Florence and the forces of Pope Gregory XI further disrupted trade and imposed a substantial financial burden on the commune. The papal wars cost roughly 2.5 million florins, adding to the already-high tax burden and the growing problem of the public debt. In addition, many of Florence's external assets were seized when the pope excommunicated the Florentines and placed them under interdict. This made the war doubly costly. Finally, Florence purchased peace by paying a substantial settlement to Rome, which added more still to the cost of this episode.

At this point, in 1378, with recession, plague, famine, war, high taxes, and rising debt all about, we come to the famous Ciompi Revolt.[39] The bare outline of the Ciompi Revolt is that on July 20, 1378, an unstable coalition of economically disadvantaged groups together with some members of the higher classes rallied, marched on the city hall, and succeeded in bringing down the city government. They demanded a series of reforms designed to increase their own economic and political standing. Their revolt was short-lived; in less than six weeks the old government was reestablished.

Who were the people involved in this revolt? The confrontation takes its name — *Ciompi* — from the wool carders. The revolutionaries were not all wool carders, but a great many worked in the wool trades. They were not guild members and were, in fact, forbidden by law from having guild representation; but they were subject to the rules and discipline of the Lana Guild. And given their economic status, they were all caught on the same side of the gold-silver fence. They were paid in silver, but any debts they owed were likely payable in gold. The rise in gold relative to silver was thus unambiguously detrimental to the Ciompi and their allies.

While the revolutionaries shared this hard economic lot, they differed one from the other in several important ways. Some perched on the lowest rung of Florence's economic ladder. These were day laborers employed in wool-processing shops. They owned no capital — no tools, no equipment — and had few special skills. They were both economically and politically impotent. Contrast this group (the mob) with the smaller but more potent "petty capitalists" who were united with them. Lauro Martines describes them thus: "Small-time employers of labor, they were themselves without the legal right to form guilds and were indeed subject to the wool manufacturers and merchants of the powerful Lana Guild. Their fees, production, and work standards were determined by this guild; and they had always been denied the right to any voice in government. Now, with the help and support of four or five renegades come from the rich bourgeoisie, they seized and held power for a few fleeting weeks."[40]

Some Marxist historians choose to view the Ciompi Revolt as a class struggle pure and simple, between the masses of labor and the owners of the means of production. The facts, however, do not seem to support this hypothesis. While the groups that rallied to revolt had many economic interests in common, it cannot be said that friction between "capital" and labor was the driving force of this conflict. As already noted, the group we call the Ciompi ranged from toolless day workers to the petty capitalists and employers under whose supervision much of the cloth production actually took place (these were the dyers, washers, and soapmakers, among others).

The Ciompi Revolt was not a rebellion against "capitalism" for two reasons. First, capital was not so highly concentrated in fourteenth-century Florence as would be the case years later after the Industrial Revolution. (Indeed, it is wrong even to call the Florentine system "capitalism".)[41] Second, the lower classes (the *popolo minuto*) did not so much reject their economic system as demand a greater part in it. As Brucker states,

> Perhaps it would be more accurate to say that, like every other group in Florentine society, the popolo minuto accepted a capitalist economic system. They had been nurtured in a milieu in which buying and selling, borrowing

and lending, working for wages, were as familiar as the physical landmarks of the Arno city. And despite its harsh exploitation and its inequities, this social order, by contemporary standards, was remarkably fluid and flexible, with genuine if limited opportunity for individual advancement."[42]

Brucker holds that a few self-interested individuals used the discontent of the citizens of the lower classes to try to achieve their own selfish ends. Rather than a class struggle, the revolt seems to be a struggle based on factors that were "political, personal, concrete."[43]

Why did the Ciompi regime collapse after only a few weeks? The answer seems to be that, predictably, a group with diverse political and economic interests will, once in power, fail to achieve the consensus needed to govern. At root, the unskilled workers of the mob had as little in common with their petty capitalist allies as they did with the entrepreneurs of the major guilds.

In addition, the Ciompi found that once in power, they were no more able than the old government to solve the problems of money and finance that plagued the Florentine economy. They might pass laws to devalue gold (which they did), but neither wishing nor voting would make it happen; the exchange rate between gold and silver coins was set by larger market forces that could not be legislated by any government. This important determinant of Florence's overall economic health and the resulting distribution of income within the commune was therefore out of their hands.

The Ciompi incident did produce several lasting results. While the unpropertied peasants and day workers were to remain politically impotent, a greater role in city government was found for the petty capitalists and small entrepreneurs. In this way the distribution of political influence was expanded to reflect the underlying economic importance of different groups better. Perhaps because of this, tax reform was enacted, placing a greater burden on the rich through the *estimo*, a property tax.

In economic terms, the Ciompi Revolt is most useful as an indicator of the extent of suffering that Florentines felt during this period. The collapse of the 1340s was paradoxically made less severe (for the lucky ones!) by the Black Death, which concentrated great per capita wealth among those who survived it. This concentration of riches masked the overall economic decline that had preceded the plague. The plague of the 1370s was not severe enough to offset the decline in overall wealth and income. Perversely, because more lived, more suffered.

1380–1423: Growing Problems for the Commune

The events of this period are important in themselves, but they are perhaps most important to the extent that they laid the foundation for what came later. The interlude roughly bounded by the Ciompi Revolt (1378) and the start of the fateful war with Milan (1424) established or repeated key patterns in the economic affairs of the commune. In this prologue, then, we look for traces of themes that will reappear later.

The Florentine economy prospered when peace and stability ruled. Under these conditions, their alchemist entrepreneurs could create wealth by mixing trade and finance with their secret "fifth element." Florence grew and prospered during the few brief, peaceful pauses and stagnated through the prevailing periods of violence that characterized these times.

Peace (with its lower taxes) and prosperity made a brief appearance in the late 1380s and returned for nearly a decade between 1413 and 1423. Florentine merchants and financiers took advantage of these favorable conditions and followed the four winds, plying their trades. But for well over half of this period the Florentine economy was becalmed. A variety of events accounted for this stagnation.

The crucial wool industry did not soon recover from the internal disruptions of the Ciompi Revolt of 1378. The revolt made clear the differences in interests among the many people who together made the cloth. These differences were magnified by the tension of the shrinking woolen market. Declining markets contributed to labor problems, which in turn reduced Florence's ability to compete in foreign markets, a vicious cycle that took some years gradually to work itself out.

War and threat of war again and again beat back Florence's attempts to escape from recession. Military activities closed markets, increased risk, forced taxes higher and higher, and blocked trade routes. For example, the port of Pisa was Florence's outlet to the sea; without access to Pisa, Florentine trade was reduced to a trickle. It is therefore not insignificant that Pisa was twice shut to Florence by opposing forces—when Milan captured it (1398) and again when Naples blockaded the port (1409).

Many Florentine assets were seized when the forces of Naples invaded Rome in 1413. A merchant of the period pleads, "God grant us peace soon, so that merchandise can again come and go as it should; it seems like a thousand years [that we have been at war]!"[44] Recurrent plagues compounded trade problems.

One bright sign in this otherwise dismal scene was the slow but steady return of Florentine hegemony in Italian banking circles and the rise of the Medici firm in particular. The War of the Eight Saints between Florence and the Vatican had diverted the flow of papal funds to other hands, notably the Luchese. It is hard to imagine that Florence and the papal finances could long be separated, however. Holmes concludes that "the Pope commanded the largest financial organization in the world; the Florentines were the world's bankers. They were almost indispensable to each other."[45] The Medici gained the crucial foothold with the accession of Pope John XXIII in 1410, with whom they had formerly enjoyed friendly personal and business relations.

The financial problems of the War of the Eight Saints were compounded, however, by the Great Schism of 1378, which split the church between the Roman Pope (Urban VI) and the Avignon Pope (Clement VII). Florence allied itself with Rome in this conflict, which doubtless increased its role in Roman finance; but the resources of the Roman church were strained and declining (Rome was even conquered at one point by Avignon's Neopolitan allies), so there was less business to share.

Being the pope's banker was surely a blessing, but a mixed one. The principal benefit of this position was not the potential for profit from loans to the papal state. Although such loans were made, the terms were not always advantageous to the lenders and repayment was subject to many political and military factors. These uncertain loans were the price that the Medici and others were willing to pay to gain access to the vast flow of funds that passed through the papal court in the routine, day-to-day transactions of the church. The income to be earned through efficient management of part of the church's cash flow was the prize that the Medici won when John XXIII ascended the throne of St. Peter.

The final, and perhaps the most important, trend established in this period was the growing economic importance of the communal government. The role of government in Florence expanded, changing the nature of the city's economy. In the past government had been distinctly laissez-faire; arms and food (guns and butter?) were its main concerns. Most of the commune's food had to be imported, and a government office of *abbondanza* existed to coordinate and manage this task — to try to assure an abundance of affordable table fare in a world of uncertain harvest and unreliable sources of foreign supply. Other special government offices existed to coordinate and manage the city's military affairs, which were undertaken with mercenary forces.

These were the main tasks of the Florentine government. Most other activities that we commonly associate with modern government were left to the private sector. Much of the work of the legal system was handled privately, for example. The guilds had their own rules, regulations, and enforcement mechanisms. Noble families could resort to limited legalized violence — the vendetta — to settle disputes privately. Even tax collection was a private affair. "Tax farms" were commonly used in Florence, as elsewhere in Europe. The government sold at auction the right to collect taxes from a particular source — such as the tax on wine sold at retail. The government would receive a certain cash payment from the best bid, while the bidder or "tax farmer" would attempt to profit by collecting more in taxes than he had paid for the right to collect them. In most respects, the Florentine government up to this time had deferred to the private sector. But this slowly changed.

Money was at the root of the expanded role of government in Florence. The communal funded debt, the Monte, continued to grow in peacetime, but especially in times of war. Debt finance became the dominant source of public revenues, overshadowing excise and property taxes, which were barely able to service the growing interest on the debt. Starting in 1390, *prestanze* (forced loans) were instituted at an increasing pace. Florentine citizens were repeatedly required to lend money to the commune based on their tax liability under the *estimo* property tax. A variety of sanctions were used to compel payment of these funds. In effect, these forced loans were really interest-bearing tax payments.

One effect of the expansion of forced loans was that soon every Florentine family had acquired a substantial holding of Monte shares. Investment in the public debt began to overtake investment in the private sector as a form of private wealth. The rise of the Monte produced a dynamic interdependence. The Monte's health depended on a healthy economy—one that could pay taxes and, especially, make additional loans to the public fund. The health and wealth of private sector, however, depended on the value of the Monte shares that most families carried on their books. A healthy economy required a healthy public debt, and vice versa.

We will examine this interdependence more in the next chapter. One aspect of this scene is important to the present discussion, however—how the growing Monte caused the role of government in Florence to expand. Given the relationship between the Monte and the private economy, it was perhaps inevitable for Florentine leaders to view the Monte's ability to command resources as the solution to its problems. Using Monte funds to invest in projects beneficial to the Florentine economy, the Monte could strengthen itself by reinforcing the private sector on which it depended. Thus, over time, Monte funds went to new uses, for example, to build a Florentine fleet for use in international trade or to support a Florentine university, which would attract students and investment from other cities. Monte funds supported some profitable military operations. The conquest of Arezzo in 1384, for example, provided substantial benefits to the commune by opening new markets for Florentine firms and expanding the tax base.

Perhaps the most dramatic change in Florentine economic policy was the creation of the Monte delle Doti in 1425. With this expansion of the Monte, the communal government entered the field of social, as well as economic, policy. This Monte was a fund to provide dowries for the Florentine daughters (and also business capital for sons). As Becker notes,

> This credit institution served as a type of insurance bank in which deposits were made by families so that their daughters might be guaranteed a dowry and they might be assured progeny. In an age when a girl without a dowry had virtually no opportunity to marry, this ingenious plan would appear to have been a boon to the unfortunate. . . . The republic was now responsible not only for the defence of the Florentines, but even for the proper marriage of their children. . . . [T]his . . . induced the citizenry to look towards the state for its well-being.[46]

In the dowry fund, the Monte officials had found a way to kill two birds with one stone. The dowry fund enabled them to increase communal revenues, finance high wartime expenses, and provide a useful service to society at the same time.

Confidence in the Monte Commune tended to rise and fall with collections of the tax revenues that nominally backed its shares. Tax revenues fell off with the increase in military activities in 1424. As a result it was becoming increasingly difficult to raise funds by tax, forced loans, or voluntary loans. The Monte delle Doti was conceived first as a revenue device. The dowry fund was designed to have greater appeal to Florentine families than ordinary loans because it would, in principle, enable them to solve the problem raised by the existence of female children efficiently.

There were only two respectable situations for women in this period: marriage or the convent. In either case, a capital payment (the dowry) was needed.[47] Like a zero-coupon bond, the Monte delle Doti promised to pay a specified dowry at a date in the future (provided that the covered female had married) in return for a much smaller initial investment. Like an insurance policy, Florentine fathers were now able to buy a measure of social and economic security for their female children.

The dowry fund produced needed communal revenues and provided a useful service to Florentine families; but it may have served another more practical social purpose, namely, as part of a government population policy. Florence was underpopulated during this period. The lack of skilled workers limited the commune's industry. This labor shortage had many causes—plague, war, migration patterns. But another cause was the relative infertility of the Florentine population. Florentines married late or were often unmarried and were less fertile than might be expected. The Monte delle Doti, by increasing dowries for girls, thereby making them more marriagable, and providing capital for boys, allowing them to afford marriage and family at an earlier age, could also tend to increase the incidence of marriage, reduce the age of marriage, increase average marriage tenure, and thus, through all these means, increase fertility and population growth.

Having said all this, it must be noted that the dowry fund was not an immediate success in any of the roles assigned to it. Because it was backed by the Monte Commune, which was in turn backed by tax revenues that were inadequate in 1425, there was no great rush to purchase dowry shares. Eventually, as will be discussed a little later, the dowry fund became the most important element in Florence's system of public and private finance. But this success required substantial modification of the terms, conditions, and returns offered by the dowry fund. The dowry fund did not become a really significant factor in Florentine finance until 1433, when terms were further liberalized and the return rate on some dowry shares was boosted to nearly 21 percent. Kirshner and Mohlo conclude that "these new terms markedly reduced the depositor's risk, and the nominal rate of return could not be matched by other sources of investment in Florence. . . . Investor response was extraordinary."[48]

Florence also began to use the fiscal system to encourage certain patterns of commercial development. The silk market was expanding, while wool contracted; so it was in the commune's interest to attract silk artisans to Florence. Several incentives were established to this end. Materials used in the silk trades, including silkworms and mulberry leaves, could be imported tax-free. Artisans and investors in the silk business also received special tax preferences unavailable to others in Florence, an important concern since Florentine taxes were burdensome, especially in wartime.[49]

The period 1380–1420 was one of exaggerated cycles in the performance of the Florentine economy, including a long depression from which recovery was difficult. Florence's economic health was critically dependent on a peaceful and stable economic environment, and the frequent wars and military operations of this period were devastating. Two other trends that become clear during this time are the rise of the Medici as papal bankers and the growing role of government, especially the Monte, in Florentine economic life.

This look at Florence in the early Renaissance years illustrates the problems of structural change and how they lead to fiscal crisis. Whereas the economy operated pretty much apart from government before the Black Death and the other events of the 1340s, we can see that structural change increased the role of government, as society sought to cope with changing conditions, and established government institutions as an integral and critical part of the socioeconomic system.

We also see here the early stages of fiscal crisis and how fiscal balance became an important (if not *the* important) problem for people at virtually all levels of Florentine society through the Monte Commune and the Monte delle Doti.

The obvious questions at this point are how the problem of structural change and fiscal balance resolved itself, and what the consequences were for the Florentine economy and the Florentines themselves.

3

Mountains of Debt
and the Heart of Florence

Economics and politics are two sides of the same coin. This was particularly the case in the Renaissance when the coin was a florin.[1] Economic trends and conditions in Florence determined its political structure, which in turn affected the economy. In this way, fiscal crisis slowly worked its way throughout the body of the Florentine state until it became the central organ of the city's life. This relationship, which will dominate the rest of our discussion of structural change and fiscal crisis in Florence, is clearly seen in the economic events of the 1420s.

Florence, Milan, and Venice were the dominant states in northern Italy in 1420; Naples and Rome were rivals for hegemony in the south. As Machiavelli later wrote, "These powers necessarily had two main preoccupations: the one that no armed foreign power should invade Italy; the other than no one power among themselves should enlarge its dominion."[2]

One goal of Florentine diplomacy was therefore to achieve a balance of powers that could perpetuate peace and stability. This balance was achieved, at least for a time. The ability of any two of these northern cities to beat back the advances of the third limited expansionist tendencies and was responsible, in part, for the relative peace and prosperity that prevailed in the decade prior to 1423. Florentine officials now attempted to formalize this balance by negotiating definite "spheres of influence" with Milan, which would have greatly reduced the chance of military conflict between them.

The Visconti of Milan had no real interest in these diplomatic maneuvers; and in the summer of 1423 Milanese forces advanced, triggering yet another war, which lasted until the spring of 1428. This war was particularly costly for several reasons. The high demand for foreign mercenary troops pushed their cost to extraordinary levels. Florentine military blunders prolonged the war, and Milanese forces advanced as far as the walls of Florence on several occasions. In the end, Florentine forces were unable to beat back the Visconti forces on their own; only the eventual strategic intervention of Venetian forces on Florence's side made possible a return to the previous equilibrium.

46

A study by Molho shows just how costly this war was.[3] In 1420 Florentine expenditure for *condotta* (military mercenaries) was less than 100 thousand florins, a substantial peacetime burden and an indication of how dependent Florence was on the presence of mercenary forces. In 1424, the first year of the war with Milan, *condotta* expenditures quadrupled to over 400 thousand florins and rose yet again to over 500 thousand florins the next year. Military expenditures alone during this period were about twice as much as all communal tax revenues combined.

The frugal Florentines sought ways to limit nondefense government expenditures. In 1425 a plenipotentiary committee, a sort of quattrocento Grace Commission, issued a report that made dozens of recommendations for holding down government costs, largely by reducing the salaries of officials. But it was not enough. War costs, rising mountainlike, overshadowed all lesser fiscal concerns.

Florence's tax system could not meet the growing costs of the war with Milan. The dilemma of the Florentines at this point was generalized by Adam Smith in this way:

> The ordinary expense of the greater part of modern governments in times of peace being equal or nearly equal to their ordinary revenue, when war comes they are both unwilling and unable to increase their revenue in proportion to the increase in their expense. They are unwilling for fear of offending the people, who by so great and so sudden an increase of taxes would soon be disgusted with the war; and they are unable from not knowing what taxes would be sufficient to produce the revenue wanted. The facility of borrowing delivers them from the embarrassment which this fear and inability would otherwise occasion.[4]

Florentine leaders had a strong preference for indirect taxes — excise taxes (gabelles), whose burden fell heaviest on lower- and middle-class citizens. In times of emergency — which this clearly was — the *estimo* was levied. The *estimo* was a direct tax on physical wealth, the taxpayers' "patrimony." The *estimo* was unfair and inefficient, which accounted for its unpopularity; but it was the main source of extraordinary revenues during crises.

The *estimo* allotments were used both as the basis for the tax itself and for the *prestanze* (forced loans) that were by now a major revenue source for the commune. During the five years of the war with Milan, over 114 forced loan quotas were collected, an enormous burden on the groups hardest hit by the *estimo*. In addition, the *estimo* was expanded — against very great resistance, efforts were made to collect these taxes from the residents on the *contado*, the Florentine territories beyond the commune's walls (including conquered towns and their associated countryside).

It is not unnatural to despise a tax that is unfair, burdensome, and inefficient; but in addition the *estimo* was unpredictable. This was not so much a fault of the tax itself as a consequence of the lack of a unified public budget. The *camera* (budget) of the Florentine state was an ad hoc affair; other than the gabelles, which were constantly collected, taxes were imposed whenever the public fisc hit empty. No real attempt was made to predict future expenditure needs and systematically impose taxes and forced loans to meet these needs. It was thus impossible for households fully to anticipate tax payments that might be required of them. *Chaos* is not really too strong a word for the form and effect of this fiscal system.

Can you squeeze blood from a stone? The Florentine leaders tried because they had to. Revenue, the fiscal fluid, was required in large quantities if the commune was to survive, with the Visconti of Milan literally knocking on the city's door. But the *estimo*'s tax base was too narrow, and its distribution too uneven and unfair; so even squeezing very hard (threatening punishments — even death — to those who did not pay their taxes) yielded little. Attempts were made to revise the *estimo* assessment in 1422 and again in 1425 and 1426, but the fundamental facts that made the *estimo* a narrow, unfair, and unresponsive tax could not be overcome. In 1426 a government commission formed to analyze the situation reported that it "was impossible to live and to remain subject to the impositions distributed in this fashion."[5]

Finally, in 1427, the Florentine fiscal crisis became too severe to continue. Many citizens were ruined, unable to continue under the burden of the old tax system. Others had fled the commune to avoid punishment for failure to pay taxes (particularly a problem when silk workers and skilled artisans, invaluable to local industry, were taking flight). It was both a practical and political fact that the *estimo* could not be further squeezed for revenue.

A tax revolt ensued, which resulted in the adoption of a new tax based on one already used in Venice: the *catasto*. *Catasto* can be translated as "list" or "putting down in a fixed state," and this captures what was the essence of the *catasto* to the Florentines. They would be taxed according to fixed rules, which could not easily be bent and shaped by the rich or debased by corrupt officials. Machiavelli comments that under the *catasto*, "individual contribution would thus be determined by an invariable rule, and not left to the discretion of parties."[6]

This was a real tax reform. The *catasto* broadened the tax base to include nearly all wealth; it would be very difficult for the influential money class to avoid a careful accounting of all their assets. Machiavelli provides an account of the reaction to the proposed reforms:

> As it was found that the new method would press heavily upon the powerful classes, they used their utmost endeavors to prevent it becoming law. Giovanni de'Medici alone declared himself in favor of it, and by this means it was passed. . . . The new method of rating formed a powerful check to the tyranny of the great, who could no longer oppress the lower classes, or silence them with threats . . . as they had formerly done, and it therefore gave general satisfaction, though to the wealthy classes it was in the highest degree offensive.[7]

Other authorities disagree with Machiavelli's account in at least one respect. Schevill reports that the *catasto* was supported by many members of the financial oligarchy that dominated Florentine politics, not just the Medici. Schevill holds that these wealthy families recognized the need for additional revenues and were willing to pay their share through the *catasto* — so long as the revenue was in the form of interest-earning forced loans (as was the case) and not barren tax payments.

It was also probably in the self-interest of these wealthy men to support this tax reform because their personal fortunes were directly tied to the value of the Monte stock that they owned and the Monte depended in turn on the integrity of the communal fisc. Without new loans to the Monte the old loans would be worthless, and even the mighty would fall.

The details of the *catasto* make fascinating reading for students of modern taxation and public finance. What is perhaps most striking is how very similar the *catasto* is to the income tax of today. A brief digression on the form of the *catasto* is therefore in order.

The *catasto* legislation was passed on May 24, 1427 and communal officials began the task of compiling the census of wealth that was necessary for collection of the tax. A detailed assessment of property in the commune and eventually the *contado* was begun. The goal was to arrive at an accurate record of the net worth of each household, subject to the deductions, exemptions, and other assorted gimmicks that tax laws typically contain.

Some assets were valued directly; the market value of shares in the Monte could easily be calculated, for example. Other wealth was more difficult to value directly, so a standard method of imputing value was adopted. The value of an asset was based on the income that it produced, assuming a 7-percent rate of return; in modern language we would say that the imputed value was calculated by taking the present value of the income stream at a 7-percent discount rate. (This is, today in the United States, the method and even the discount rate that many states use in valuing farm land for property taxation.) The evidence is that assets subject to market valuation, including Monte shares and the net assets of business firms, bore higher effective tax burdens than did land and other assets, where valuation was estimated indirectly. Thus, the financial assets of the commune were suddenly much more heavily taxed than before, while labor was more lightly taxed.

Exempt from the *catasto* were income-producing assets (like oxen) and (this is noteworthy) also the taxpayer's domicile and all the furnishings and decorations therein. There was, further, a two-hundred-florin allowance for each person in the household, which assured that the poorest citizens would not fall burden to this tax. (But, as already noted, there were other taxes that weighed heavily on them.)

Taxable wealth was subject to a tax rate of .5 percent per *catasto* levy. The *catasto*, like the *estimo*, might be imposed several times in each year as uncertain fiscal necessity required, so the actual annual tax burden could be much more than the nominal .5 percent.

The flavor of the *catasto* is captured in a summary of a Medici tax return of mid-fifteenth-century vintage (Table 3.1).

The *catasto* of 1427 was a notable improvement in the science of taxation (and has proved a boon to historians because of the detailed financial records

Table 3.1. Tax Due from Cosimo and Pierfrancesco De Medici, *Catasto* of 1457

Assets (*sostanze*)	
Total value of real estate	fl 59,741
Four slaves	120
Stock in Monte Commune	8,569
Business investments	54,238
Total	122,669
Deductions (*detrazioni*)	
Administrative expenses for real estate	2,985
120 pairs of oxen	1,714
14 mouths @ fl 200	2,800
Total	7,499
Taxable wealth (*sovrabbondante*)	115,170
Computation of tax	
One-half percent of *sovrabbondante*	575
Three heads	1
Tax due	fl 576

Source: Raymond de Roover, *The Rise and Decline of the Medici Bank* (Cambridge: Harvard University Press, 1963), p. 26. Columns may not sum due to rounding.

that were compiled). The tax burden was not made any lighter overall — indeed, tax reform can best be seen as the necessary prologue to a new series of tax increases — but the burden was redistributed, falling more equitably on the real sources of Florentine wealth.

The *catasto*, based as it was on written law, not corrupt judgement, stood in stark contrast to the *estimo*. Citizens of the Florentine middle class realized that they had been unfairly taxed to pay for wars instigated by leaders who themselves paid little tax. Aroused by emotions of injustice and spite, they sought to make the *catasto* retroactive. Machiavelli provides this account:

> The excitement was appeased by Giovanni de'Medici who said, "It is not well to go into things so long past unless to learn something for our present guidance; and if in former times the taxation has been unjust, we ought to be thankful, that we have now discovered a method of making it equitable, and hope that this will be a means of uniting the citizens, not of dividing them; which would certainly be the case were they to attempt the recovery of taxes for the past, and make them equal to the present; and that he who is content with a moderate victory is always more successful; for those who would more than conquer, commonly lose."[8]

Thus, Giovanni de'Medici, the richest Florentine citizen and the man on whom the *catasto* would fall most heavily, warned his fellow citizens to accept the *catasto* compromise; else, he would withdraw his support and they would get no tax reform at all. This political lesson — that half a loaf is better than none — is one that later advocates of pure tax reforms would be forced to re-learn.

Economic Conditions in Florence Circa 1427

The records of the *catasto* of 1427 provide us with rare data concerning the Florentine economy in the early Renaissance. This first *catasto* was a relatively complete and uncorrupted census of the Florentine population, and most of the tax records have survived to the present day.[9] Herlihy and Klapisch-Zuber's fascinating study of Tuscans and their families, which gives the clearest picture yet of life in this period, is based on *catasto* records.

In later years, the *catasto* lists would become corrupt and unreliable, depriving modern scholars of reliable time-series data with which to analyze long-term trends in Florence. All that we really have is this one snapshot of Tuscan economic conditions. Let us briefly examine some of the economic highlights that this photo opportunity presents.[10] Although the *catasto* records cover a large area under Florentine control, this discussion will limit itself to economic conditions in Florence itself.[11]

The *catasto* of 1427 was a tax on wealth, so *catasto* records can provide us with information concerning the amount of wealth that the Florentines possessed in this year, the types and distribution of assets they held, and the distribution of wealth within the population. From this we learn that the Florentines had high levels of total and average wealth (for their day) and that their wealth was well diversified among different types of assets but that wealth was distributed very unevenly within the population.[12]

The gross taxable wealth of Florence in 1427 was reported by the *catasto* to be fl 10.17 million (which is equivalent to over U.S. $400 million if we take the value of the florin to be approximately $40, which is probably on the low side of its value). Of this total wealth, records show that fl 2.5 million (about $100 million) of wealth was untaxed, which left a net tax base of fl 7.67 million (or over $300 million). This shows Florence to be a rich city for 1427, especially considering that family residences and their furnishings were not counted in any of these figures.

We can get a better feel for what these figures mean if we convert them to a more personal basis. If we look at wealth per household, we find that gross taxable wealth per household averaged fl 1,022 (about $41 thousand). This is a very high average, for the quattrocento especially; but we must bear in mind two factors that tend to inflate average wealth per household by this accounting. The first problem is, of course, that this is an average and so is affected by the distribution of wealth within the population. It is clearly not true that the typical Florentine household had nonresidential wealth of fl 1000; the wealth of the typical household was far below this.

A second factor to be considered is the nature of the household. Although Florentines did not have the very large nuclear families found in other cultures, it was still true that several related families might live under one roof (especially in the palaces of the rich). Thus, this measurement of wealth per household in Florentine terms tends to overstate the amount of wealth as might be measured per capita or per family, narrowly defined.

Using these *catasto* data and adjusting them appropriately, Raymond Gold-smith has compiled approximate estimates of gross national product and in-come for Florence.[13] Goldsmith estimates the gross national product of the Florentine Republic in 1427 at about fl 3 million (or about $120 million). Of this amount, he guesses that 50–60 percent would have derived from activities in the city of Florence itself. This results in annual income per household in Florence in the neighborhood of fl 140–fl 170 ($5,600–$6,800). Taking the calculations one step further, Goldsmith puts the annual income per capita in Florence at fl 38–fl 45 ($1,520–$1,800).[14] Income in the countryside and the towns under Florentine domination was much lower (per capita incomes of fl 5–fl 6, according to Goldsmith, compared to fl 38–fl 45 in Florence).

These estimates of income are as striking to us today as the actual fact of this income must have been to contemporaries of this period. These income levels made Florence a modern economy in a medieval world. The contrast between Florence and the lesser cities must have been astounding.

Given these estimates of communal and per capita income, plus the records of the city government, we can make some rough calculations about the size and burden of government and public debt in Florence in 1427.[15] The numbers that are produced by these calculations are strikingly modern in their look and feel, although, like all such numbers, they are subject to a large degree of error. Accepting this, let us forge ahead.

The direct costs of government in Florence, as they appear in *camera* docu-ments, amounts to 27 percent of the estimates of national income. Thus, judging by its size, Florence had a modern government. Government outlays' accounting for such a large percentage of income would have been unthinkable in medieval times. Much of the cost of government, however, was the expense of mercenary troops. Military outlays were equal to more than half of the cost of government.

The tax burden (exclusive of forced loans) was also relatively high for the time. We can estimate that direct taxes amounted to between 13 percent and 16 percent of per capita income, which is not far off the modern norm.

The Monte Commune had grown to a real mountain by 1427. The public debt in that year amounted to well over 100 percent of annual income. Given the wide ownership of public debt, it is now clear why the Florentines took management of the Monte so seriously. (This would be increasingly true in future years, when the Monte would grow faster than national income, making public debt an ever-bigger item in private and public life.)

The budget deficit in 1427, which was financed through forced loans, was large by modern U.S. standards (but typical of modern postwar Italian prac-tice). The deficit in 1427 was almost 18 percent of national income for Florence.

The large deficit, which fell on top of the already-towering Monte debt, imposed a very substantial interest burden on Florentine government. Budget records show that government debt servicing costs amounted to almost 12 percent of Florentine income in 1427. This figure is also far outside the realistic range for a medieval state but completely in line with modern postwar experi-ence.

These estimates of government size and cost show us that the Florentine fiscal crisis of 1427 was really very much similar to recent trends in the United States and other modern industrial countries. This suggests that the structural changes that buffet the modern world are perhaps in their relative magnitudes not totally unlike those that rocked the Renaissance.

The wealth of Florence was invested in three main areas (aside from residential property). Of the total taxable wealth listed in the *catasto*, about 40 percent was held as assets of real property. This included property, structures, equipment, and so on. Another 34 percent was listed as "movables," or circulating capital and financial instruments. Finally, about 25 percent of this wealth was made up of public debt — shares in the Monte Commune and the Monte delle Doti, in particular. The Florentines thus held a diversified portfolio of investments: land, business, and debt.

Florence was wealthy, but this wealth was highly concentrated in the hands of a few. Goldsmith reports that 27 percent of all *catasto* wealth was held by the richest 1 percent of all households.[16] Two-thirds of all the wealth was owned by only the top 10 percent of households. Meanwhile, on the other end of the scale, the poorest 50 percent of all households held only 3 percent of total wealth.

The distribution of wealth in Florence will become important later in this study when we begin to look more closely at the economic effects of Florentine public debt. The *catasto* returns show that while all sectors of the economy owned shares in the Monte (often, for poorer households, through participation in the dowry fund), it was still true that public debt ownership was concentrated in the city of Florence (as opposed to the population outside the city gates) and, within the city, among the highest-income groups. Thus, the Monte always had the potential to transfer tax revenues from low-income households (through the gabelles) to higher-income groups, further distorting the distribution of income and wealth in the commune.

War and Fiscal Crisis Return

It would be pleasing to proponents of progressive tax policy if the implementation of the *catasto* contributed in some significant way to the solution of Florence's fiscal problems. With the broader tax base, it would be possible to raise additional revenue in a fairer and more efficient way; the commune could pay its war bills and solve its debt problems without dire political or economic consequences.

It would be pleasing to present this scenario, but grossly inaccurate. Indeed, the black years following the adoption of the *catasto* were a time of political and economic crisis. The progressive *catasto*, a much better tax than the *estimo* it replaced, created more problems than it solved, leading one authority to conclude that "in a strict sense, the reform of 1427 must be reckoned a spectacular failure."[17]

As the *catasto* was being implemented, the first Peace of Ferrara (1428) brought to an end the war with Milan. But peace was fleeting, and war resumed almost immediately. The commune, still desperate for revenues, tried to impose the *catasto* on its subject city, Volterra. Revolt erupted in Volterra, forcing the Florentines again to raise an army to restore control."[18] This action led, in 1429, to an attempt to subdue the city of Lucca. The Luchese resisted; and the resulting war, which lasted until 1433, was enormously costly. Huge mercenary armies were required. Mountains of revenues were needed. The task of producing the necessary funds fell on the *catasto*.

The period of 1429–1433, during the war with Lucca, saw tax burdens (including forced loans) rise to unprecedented levels in Florence. The *catasto* was imposed more than fifty times during this period. In fact, a single collection of forced loans equaling thirty-six *catasti* was imposed all at once in 1431. (This huge lump-sum tax was meant to provide government officials with a significant pool of money—a budget!—to use in planning the commune's military operation.) Since each *catasto* levy was equal to .5 percent of taxable wealth, the sum of the taxes during this period would exhaust, in theory, the annual income of the commune.

The real tax burdens that fell on the Florentines were not, however, as heavy in fact as they were on paper for several reasons. First, much wealth was legally exempt from taxation (including the palaces and rich decorations of the Medici and their rich friends). Second, high taxes make honesty an expensive luxury and thus induce corruption. Many of the bad old habits of the corrupt *estimo* returned.

Finally, it is important to remember that *catasto* payments took the form of interest-bearing Monte shares. Thus, tax payments created additional assets for the household, at least on paper, leaving them, in a naive bookkeeping sense, no poorer. This last point applied only to households who could make their tax payments in full; those who made only partial payment (and many in the middle class fell in this category) paid actual taxes and received no Monte shares in return. Thus, the *catasto* was an interest-bearing loan for those who could pay it in full (e.g., the Medici) and a true tax on the many others who could not.

But *can* you really get blood from a stone? No matter how much superior the *catasto* was compared to the *estimo*, the revenue it could produce was still limited by the wealth of the citizens and their willingness to part with it for public purposes. Tax reform produced a better tax; but it did not, in the short run, increase the real wealth of the population, which the heavy *catasto* burden efficiently but unevenly drained.

As an emergency measure, the officials of the Monte began supplementing forced loans with special war loans (not secured by Monte shares) at high rates of interest of 30 percent (compared to the much lower—typically 5 percent— rates paid on Monte shares). It is symptomatic of the fiscal crisis the Florentine officials were experiencing that they were forced to borrow at high interest to service debt previously acquired at lower interest in order to preserve at least the myth of fiscal stability that was necessary to secure more debt in the future.

The wealthy members of the financial oligarchy who dominated Florentine politics provided the necessary funds for war finance in the form of high-interest loans. Mohlo suggests, for example, that the profits of the Medici bank offices in Rome, Venice, and elsewhere were systematically routed to its Florence office and absorbed by loans to the communal government.

The wartime fiscal crisis continued until a second Peace of Ferrara was reached in 1433. Cosimo de'Medici was forced into exile in 1433, and a year later the *catasto* was temporarily abandoned. The Florentine experiment with tax reform had come to an end. The mountains of debt that had been created in the process remained.

What should we think of the events of this period? It has been proposed that the large debts of the Monte created a spirit of civic humanism among the wealthy in Florence. With their personal fortunes tied, through ownership of Monte shares, to the financial fate of the commune, wealthy Florentines sacrificed their self-interest for the greater good of their commune. Thus, they voted to tax themselves more heavily and provided the funds needed to finance the government and its military operations in this time of crisis. Their sacrifices in fact preserved the Florentine state, and these wealthy families were rewarded with greater political power on the one hand and a measure of opposition and resentment (e.g., Cosimo's treatment) on the other.

A different view of these same events emphasizes the benefits that accrued to the wealthy families in these times of crisis. The *catasto*, aimed at taxing the rich, ended up bankrupting the middle classes. The rich accumulated Monte shares and profited from high interest rates on the war loans needed to maintain public liquidity. In this scenario, fiscal crisis becomes a means for the financial oligarchy to exploit and further dominate the middle class and lesser entrepreneurs.

In either case, some outcomes stand clear: the growth of a huge public debt; government firmly in the hands of the wealthy families (even more so on Cosimo's return from exile); and the Florentine economy in ruins due to the poverty of the artisans, workers, and petty entrepreneurs who together created the real wealth of the city.

Florence in the Years of Cosimo De'Medici

The sixty years between 1434 and 1494 can be neatly divided into two equal spans: a generation of intermittent growth and relative prosperity (1434–1464) followed by a second period when the economic arteries of the commune began to harden, setting the pattern for the century that followed (1464–1494). It is both convenient and appropriate to identify these two generations in the life of Florence with the names of Cosimo and Lorenzo, the members of the Medici clan who led the political oligarchy in Florence in these times.

It is appropriate to focus on the Medici in the fifteenth century because of their preeminent position in Florentine affairs. By this time they were the richest Florentine family by far. But their wealth was much less than that enjoyed by the elite families of the previous century, an indication of the overall trend in the fortunes of Florence. The Medici bank during this time had grown to become the largest financial enterprise in the world. The Medici expanded their commercial interests to include cloth and silk production, so that the success of their activities is a suitable summary of the broader economy. Finally, the Medici were leaders of a financial and political oligarchy that influenced the affairs and determined the policies of Florence. The Medici were not typical Florentines by any means, but the story of the Medici is in many respects the story of the Florentine economy during these years.

Cosimo returned to Florence from exile in 1434 and established a set of political and economic relationships that served as the basis for his power and influence in the years ahead. Cosimo's genius was his understanding of human nature. This made him a good judge of character in the business and political appointments he made and a skilled diplomat in the complex web of domestic and foreign interests in which the Florentine state was constantly snared.

One important aspect of human nature that Cosimo exploited is the notion of interdependency. People who depend upon one another in a mutually advantageous relationship in one sphere of life are unlikely to enter into potentially damaging relationships in another area. Finance was the tool that Cosimo used to exploit the potential that interdependent relationships held for private and public gain.

Cosimo's financial dealings, through the Medici bank, involved many of the wealthy families of the city. Their common financial interests made them political allies as well as business associates and allowed them to control and sometimes to exploit the power of government institutions. In addition, Cosimo established mutually advantageous financial relations with the small commercial interests of the city, the many merchants who bought and sold. Although not full participants in the ruling oligarchy, these numerous small business people supported Cosimo's government. Finally, the financial policies of the Medici bank made powerful allies for Florence and the Medici in Rome and Milan.

Cosimo's vision was expansionary, both broadly for Florence as a whole and more narrowly for the Medici firm. This is noteworthy, given the trends of the times, the plague of 1437–1438 in particular. This plague, though less devastating that the Black Deaths of the previous century, was still severe enough to send perhaps 20 percent of the population to their graves. Wealth became more concentrated, as before; and real wages increased. It is not obvious that most people would see this as a time of expanding horizons, but this was part of Cosimo's peculiar genius.

For the Medici bank, this vision of expansion took several forms. First, and most important, was Cosimo's practice of the reinvesting profits from his enterprises, thereby providing a firm foundation for future growth. If there is one factor that differentiates the growth years of Cosimo from Lorenzo's time of stagnation and increasing rigidity it is the emphasis on productive investment instead of sterile and conspicuous consumption. Profits that were not plowed back into the financial fields funded construction of many private and public structures in Florence and its vicinity.

The Medici firm spread and deepened its roots. Financial ties with the papal court, already an important source of profits to the Medici bank, were strengthened. Indeed, so strong were these ties that for a time, the papal court took up residence in Florence. Vast rivers of gold and silver flowed to and from the pope's coffers from throughout Christendom; and representatives of the Medici firm followed these golden tributaries, establishing further economic relationships that involved trade, finance, or both. The Medici bank soon could boast foreign branches in London, Geneva, Bruges, and Avignon in addition to those in Rome, Venice, Milan, Pisa, and Genoa. (Representatives of the firm were also active in cities where formal branches did not exist.)

The Medici expanded their business interests, taking partnerships in two wool shops and a silk firm. Profits from these interests were not on the same scale as those from the bank, but they are still important as an indicator of the close relationship between international banking and international trade for Florentine businesses.

The city of Florence, under Cosimo's strong influence, also envisioned growth and expansion. This meant territorial expansion and the expensive military conflict that necessarily accompanied it. War disrupted the principal economic activities of the commune, but it may have proved profitable to at least two segments of Florentine society: the wealthy, who made high-interest loans that often financed the war, and the small merchants, who provided the mercenary soldiers with a variety of goods and services.

War and its heavy tax burden were constant factors in Florentine life for the twenty years between 1434 and 1454. This period was characterized by constant friction among the forces of Florence, Venice, Milan, Rome, and Naples. All were driven by the same need for territorial expansion to finance an increasingly costly state, which ironically meant that all bore the heavy costs of war and defense. A shifting and fluid balance of power among these states kept military costs high for all, without any permanent economic, political, or strategic gain for any of them.

It is possible that left alone to war, war, and war again, the great Italian city-states would have slowly strangled themselves, leaving them an easy mark for an adventurous foreign force. Fate intervened, however, in the form of the Muslim Turks. The 1453 Turkish conquest of Constantinople, the seat of the Eastern Christian church, shocked and sobered the Italians. Pope Nicholas V called for an end to infighting among the Christian states so that they could mobilize their might against the Muslim threat to the East. Venice, whose economy was much dependent on Levantine trade, felt its interests most directly threatened; but all the city-states were ready to end their costly combats. The Peace of Lodi (1454) brought to a close the wars among Italian states. After twenty years of costly combat, borders were returned to their original prewar positions.

Cosimo de'Medici, respected as a diplomat in addition to his many other talents, actively promoted and negotiated the Peace of Lodi. Cosimo apparently recognized that the Italian city-states faced a military "prisoner's dilemma." Each could benefit from expanding its territorial control, but only so long as the other powers did not react. Thus, it was in each state's self-interest to expand; but if all adopted this policy at once (which they did), the result was much the worse for all of them than if all had remained at peace. Schevill notes the benefits of the mutual peace:

> Florence perhaps benefited more and for a longer time than any other state. The policy incorporated in the Lodi document was an expression of the mature view to which Cosimo had come after an experience of twenty years as foreign minister of the Arno city. That view was that Florence, a commercial republic, was not constituted so as to be able to successfully carry on a policy of aggression and that its best hope was a mutual guaranty of peace among the Italian powers on the basis of existing boundaries.[19]

The Lodi pact did not end military conflict for long, but for Florence the scope of aggression and its cost were both reduced. Florentine trade and finance again prospered in this period of lower taxes and greater general stability. Florentine interests had a relative advantage in that other Italian city-states, particularly Venice, were still often disrupted by the costs and inconveniences of war. Venetian interests in the Levant served to keep them nearly constantly in conflict with the Turks, for example.

But the existence of peace was this time a mixed blessing because Italy was not alone in ending conflict. The Hundred Years' War reached its exhausted conclusion in 1453, freeing the European countries to the north of the disruption, expense, and heavy tax burdens that they had experienced for so long. Without wartime disturbances, the economies of these countries were able to mobilize themselves into formidable commercial competition for Florentine firms.

While the Peace of Lodi created circumstances that would, all else being equal, promote the resurgence of the Florentine economy, the end of the Hundred Years' War unleashed competitive forces that ultimately overwhelmed Florence. The commune's economy bloomed quickly in the 1450s, but by Cosimo's death in 1464 it was clearly in decline and the mid-1460s saw bank failures that recall the collapses of the previous century.

The logic behind this pattern of quick rise and long decline is worth exploring briefly, because 1453–1454 was the turning point for the economy of Renaissance Florence. The Peace of Lodi, by reducing the costs and disruptions of regional conflict among the Italian states, allowed Florence and its Italian rivals a last opportunity to venture out into their traditional southern markets. The economy benefited, in the short run, from the resurgence of traditional markets for the traditional products of Florence.

But prosperity was doomed to be temporary because of the global forces unleashed by the end of the Hundred Years' War. With peace finally restored in the north, Europe was once more a "continental" economy more than a purely regional one. The products and competitors of the north were once again a force to be reckoned with. And they were an important force. Recall that in the fourteenth century, before the Hundred Years' War bottled up northern markets, Florentine cloth manufacturers had been relegated to the relatively low status of refinishers—the merchants of the Calimala trade. The northerners had the best wool in those days and made the best cloth. Florence had found it hard to compete except on the margins of the cloth industry.

The rise of the Florentine cloth industry was driven, as I have already suggested, by a special combination of incentives, knowledge, and skills that found their nexus most clearly in Florence. But luck was also an important factor in the rise of Florentine industry. The Medici and the others had been lucky that the Hundred Years' War limited competition from the north.

Now Florence would have to adjust rapidly to a world with new markets, opportunities, and competition. Florence needed to find its comparative advantage within the new trans-European market. Although it was probably not obvious at the time, this was the turning point for the Florentine economy. Should Florence remain in the patterns that had lead to regional success in the past and contributed to the short-term post-Lodi prosperity? Or should Florence look north and find its place within Europe? In the past, Florence had found success by looking south and east for the most part. In the future, however, economic growth would come from the north and the west.

Medici Public Finance

No discussion of the economy in this period would be complete without reference to the Florentine public finances, the tax system, and the Monte in particular. The constant military operations put increasing pressure on the government's purse. Mercenary costs increased because, given the broad scope of the wars being fought, soldiers for hire were in short supply and could demand premium wages. (Some mercenary forces even changed sides midwar upon receipt of a higher bid from the enemy.)

Florence was forced to lean heavily on all its revenue sources, including excise taxes, forced loans, and special high-interest war loans. Forced loans levied according to the *catasto* were, however, the most important fiscal instrument.

The *catasto* was a superior tax tool, especially compared to the alternatives; but even a sound tool can be destructive when it is misapplied, and this is what happened. The *catasto* was abused in several ways that destroyed whatever advantages this tax originally possessed.

Because the heart of the *catasto* was its record of individual income and wealth, it was a good tax only so long as the books remained accurate and current. The original *catasto* legislation called for a new assessment every three years, with the most recent list used to levy forced loans between reassessments. This assessment cycle was met for the first (1427), second (1430), and third (1433) *catasti*. But the tax base was not refigured again until the fourth *catasto* in 1442 (then again in the years 1446, 1451, 1457, 1469/70, and 1480/81). The long periods between reassessment of the *catasto* lists was important. Households who possessed great but declining taxable wealth would bear a disproportionate burden while the newly rich would continue to pay low taxes based on their smaller previous partimony. This incidence pattern apparently satisfied the desires of Cosimo's supporters, who included many of the nouveau riche. Thus the *catasto* cycle was manipulated for political gain.

Cosimo's ruling group also used the tax system to punish their political enemies. A tax that is pure in theory can always be made corrupt in practice through biased administration. This was the case in Florence. Anyone of significance who pressed opposition to the policies of the ruling oligarchy would find themselves ruined by successive levies of forced loans.

The pressing revenue requirements caused the Medici to seek revisions in the *catasto*. Progressive tax brackets, called the *scala* (staircase), were instituted for the first time and rates were increased overall. Larger exemptions were introduced in order to moderate tax increases on the poor and so avoid the possibility of a revolt of the masses. Since Cosimo and many of his partners were rich, their adoption of higher rates appears to be either foolish or unselfish; but this assumes that their own wealth was assessed accurately, which it was not. Cosimo's own *catasto* return for 1457 is an exercise in fictional accounting. This was probably not atypical; de Roover comments that "as the case of Cosimo shows, tax evasion was a game that was not frowned upon by Florentine business men. The Medici, who should have set the example of civic spirit, were the first to conceal their wealth for the purpose of diminishing the tax burden."[20]

The fact that Cosimo de'Medici fiddled his taxes does not mean that he did not bear his share of the commune's burden. *Catasto* records show the Medici to be consistently the wealthiest family and biggest taxpayer (even with cooked books), but they should have paid even more. Their biggest contribution to the commune's coffers was through sizable high-interest war loans. These war loans, as previously noted, were backed by the Monte but carried interest yields that were much, much higher than the forced loans levied through the *catasto*. Fiddling the *catasto* was thus a way for the Medici and others to reduce their holdings of low-interest regular Monte shares acquired through the *catasto*'s forced loans and increase their holdings of high-interest war loans.

As this discussion suggests, the funded public debt, the Monte, grew to an enormous size relative to the Florentine economy during this period. Between regular Monte shares subscribed through the *catasto* and the increasingly popular and necessary Monte delle Doti (the dowry fund), management of the public debt had become a factor critical to the economic status of the Florentines individually and as a whole. The importance of the Monte is illustrated by the fact that Cosimo himself was a permanent member of the public commission that oversaw the public debt. Cosimo's personal and public participation in the Monte's administration is noteworthy, for he otherwise avoided the limelight of public office so as to influence policy more efficiently through quiet backstage maneuvers and intrigues.

The dowry fund grew dramatically during this period of Florentine history; but, more significantly, its place in the economic life of the city began to change, starting with the reforms enacted in 1441. Essentially, the dowry fund was modified with the idea of using it to manage the Monte Commune debts. In other words, the dowry fund was intended to become something akin to a "sinking fund," to use the terminology that Pitt would later employ in Britain.

For several years beginning in 1441, dowry fund deposits were made in Monte shares instead of cash. The interest income from these Monte shares was used to purchase additional Monte stock on the open market. The dowry fund thus developed a third important function in the Florentine economy, that of debt management in addition to the previous roles as revenue source and guarantor of female social security.

It is likely that in linking the dowry fund with the Monte Commune, the Florentine leaders sought to improve management of public debt so as to reduce its burden and economic importance to the life of the commune. If so, the result was exactly the opposite of their expectations. As the public debt continued to grow, it in fact became more deeply woven into the fabric of Florentine society. Monte shares held by the public formed a substantial fraction of their wealth. Monte shares held by the dowry fund guaranteed the futures of Florentine women and their potential spouses. Dowries that were paid through the dowry fund soon were increasingly made up of Monte shares instead of cash, so that public debt was passed down from generation to generation.

To an increasing extent, the economic foundation of Florence was built of public debt stock. It is not surprising, therefore, that Florentine leaders should concentrate so intently on maintaining the integrity of Monte shares.

Florence in the Years of Lorenzo the Magnificent

The period 1464-1494 vividly displays the paradox that confronts an economist who studies Renaissance Florence. The economic patterns that were established in this period created a more rigid and less dynamic Florence. As these patterns hardened, Florence changed and lost its spark. The result was that the Florentine economy soon lost its preeminent place in the European economy.

If Florence did not decline absolutely (this is controversial, as we will soon see), it clearly declined relatively to other economic powers. The next great entrepreneurs were sturdy Dutch traders, not shrewd Tuscan financiers.

The beginnings of the decline of the Florentine economy coincided with the flowering of the artistic renaissance that we now most commonly associate with Florence — a profoundly troubling coincidence that was not necessarily coincidental. The Medici leader who oversaw this great decline was Cosimo's grandson, Lorenzo de'Medici — "Lorenzo the Magnificent" to those who study the humanities instead of economics.

Robert S. Lopez divides the Florentines of this period into the pessimists and the optimists.[21] The pessimists recognized that the economy had declined from its zenith of the previous century and saw the prosperity of the current period as a low plateau from which further decline was likely. The optimists did not look back so far. They saw peace and stability as far better than war and disruption. They "settled down in sufficient comfort, felt that they had definitely and finally arrived."[22]

The pessimists were the smaller group, according to Lopez, but included "significant personalities" such as Savonarola, Machiavelli, Leonardo, and Michelangelo. They saw a correlation between the worldly ways of Lorenzo's time and the economic and moral decline of the commune. They advocated a more frugal, pious existence.

The optimists were satisfied with the economic status quo and saw their challenge as "self-fulfillment." They turned inward, seeking to link their own perceived prosperity with the learning and values of ancient Greece and Rome. Their search for self-fulfillment powered a period of conspicuous consumption among the elite of Florentine economy.

The growing problems of the economy of Florence had many specific causes, which we will discuss. But the most important factor in this decline was surely the narrowing of vision that was characteristic of this age of optimism. Business and political leaders (generally the same people in Florence) no longer saw the world as full of potential for their commercial and financial endeavors. Their attention became more self-centered and parochial, and their businesses suffered accordingly. They did not respond to the challenges of foreign markets and competition; they shrank back and sought to protect their self-interests. Brucker summarizes the mood of the period this way: "In the economic sphere, as in politics, caution and conservatism prevailed; men took fewer risks and concentrated upon maintaining rather than increasing their wealth. . . . Perhaps to compensate for diminishing opportunities in trade and industry, more patricians than ever before were utilizing their training in law and the humanities to embark upon professional careers."[23]

Thus, the leading families of Florence now produced attorneys, not entrepreneurs. This is nowhere the recipe for a dynamic economy. This focus on narrow self-interest infected Florentine politics. Whatever had been left of "civic humanism"—the spirit of self-sacrifice for communal gain—was now gone.

The self-satisfied, narrow vision of this era was apparent in the shift from productive investment to conspicuous consumption. The wealth of the economy, already in decline, was reduced further as the Florentines determined to enjoy life more, much as the survivors of the Black Death had done. The Florentine economy became poor, rigid, and divided. The artistic renaissance flowered as the economic wealth that fed it was exhausted.

This is not to say that the Florentines had it completely in their power to avoid economic decline. Several long-term factors, which I have noted earlier, ran counter to their interests. The most basic of these was the long-term demographic trend that had started with the Black Death and continued still in the fifteenth century.

We might expect that the population would recover relatively quickly following the devastating plague deaths of the 1340s and 1430s, but this was not the case. Instead, we find a continued slow decline in the population in the two centuries that followed the Black Death. Birth rates were low, death rates high, marriages came later in life. Labor shortages continued from decade to decade, raising real wage rates and making the goods that Florence produced and sold relatively more expensive and the market for those goods relatively smaller. In short, even without the increased competition from the north that followed the Hundred Years' War, Florence and its wool-based economy faced the possibility of long term decline or stagnation. But the important point is that as Florentine economic life became increasingly rigid, Florence seemingly lost the ability to adjust successfully to changing conditions. Florence became the victim of its fate under Lorenzo, not the maker of its fate, as before.

The business and political leaders of the commune turned conservative and inward looking. Banking, which had grown to be a major industry, experienced a sharp downturn, from which it did not recover. Lorenzo pulled back the far-reaching arms of the Medici bank, calling in loans and generally shrinking its scale, scope, and influence. In this he reflected the times, for banking was an industry in decline in Florence. There had been seventy-two international banks on the Arno in 1422, but this number shrank to thirty-three in 1470 and finally to six or fewer in 1494. Finance and trade were coproducts in this era, so the decline of the Florentine banks is an indication of the broader decline in the economy.

Part of the decline of Florentine banking and industry can be blamed on monetary instability. The florin remained pure gold and rock solid by all accounts. But elsewhere in Europe governments succumbed to the many pressures to debase their own silver coinage, so that the exchange rate among different coins and between the gold and the silver was unstable and uncertain. Unstable monetary arrangements were poisonous to the complex contracts required for international trade and finance. So the Florentines looked inward for secure income rather than speculating on uncertain foreign markets.

Although some of these financial troubles can be blamed on the corrupt monetary practices of others, much of the responsibility must be placed on the Florentines themselves. Many of the bad loans that ultimately brought down the Florentine banking houses were just that—bad loans that would not have been made by more prudent men. These loans financed foreign wars that were unlikely to prove profitable and paid for rich silks, gaudy jewels, and lavish festivities of all sorts that left no productive residue on which to base repayment of principle and interest. The Florentines were neither the first nor the last bankers to mistake the appearance of wealth for concrete ability to pay.

The dramatic shift from investment to consumption that Florence experienced at this time is probably both cause and effect of the decline and fall of the economy. Conspicuous consumption, especially among the wealthier families, was excessive and wasteful. Lorenzo the Magnificent noted in 1469 what we may guess to be a typical social event: "To do as others had done, I held a joust in the Piazza S. Croce at great expense and with great pomp. I find we spent about 10,000 ducats."[24]

Lavish public consumption was not only wasteful, it was also divisive, accentuating the gap between rich and poor. The famous priest Savonarola preached fiery sermons to the masses against these excesses and organized "bonfires of the vanities," where worldly goods could be destroyed. A great many Florentines were moved by this message (even Lorenzo), but Savonarola himself ultimately met his own fiery destruction because of this zealous excess.

Some scholars take a different view of this period of high consumption. Richard A. Goldthwaite, for example, views the art and buildings of this period in terms of the jobs, incomes, and skills that they stimulated within the Florentine community.[25] And it is true that based on conspicuous consumption expenditures, Florence did develop a large art and construction industry. Florentine workmen became skilled artists and craftsmen in response to the growing demand for these skills. By shifting demand to these industries (and away from the broader markets of the international economy), the wealthy families of Florence preserved for a time the commune's great wealth. Florence maintained at least the appearance of prosperity and high employment.

Florence also undertook stimulatory, albeit inward-looking, fiscal policies. Taxes and trade barriers within the Florentine territories were reduced, which stimulated both Florence and towns under its control, such as Pescia.[26] In many ways Florence made the most of the pattern that it had chosen for itself.

It is important, however, not to use these facts to paint too bright a picture of the Florentine economy. While the artistic renaissance might have slowed the relative decline of the Florentine economy, it did nothing to stop it. Most of the skills developed and fancy goods produced were aimed at the home market. Silk was the only important export, and even then the number of cloths shipped (and the employment provided) was declining dramatically.

Although there is not a lot of data available about patterns of investment in Florentine industry in this period, what data we do have suggests that Florentine families did not pull a great deal of capital out of the business sector.[27] But perhaps more significant is the lack of evidence that these firms plowed profits back into their businesses, as Cosimo and his colleagues had done. Business capital was left to wither, old vines remained firmly anchored in fields planted generations ago. There was no vision of new vines or new fields.

Florentine Taxation and the Artistic Renaissance

It is a perverse fact that the *catasto*, originally heralded as a major reform, contributed to the pattern of wasteful consumption of this period. (This is, of course, a pessimistic view; an optimist would say that the income tax helped produce the artistic wonders of the Renaissance.) The progressive tax rates were pushed higher and higher by the combination of the ever-increasing revenue needs of the commune and a tax base that was shrinking due to economic stagnation and because of taxpayer dishonesty. The *catasto*, now based on income imputed from wealth — not wealth imputed from income, as before — reached a top rate of 22 percent. This is a high nominal figure, given that the tax could be imposed several times each year. Tables 3.2 and 3.3 show the *catasto* rates and a summary of Lorenzo's return. It is noteworthy that Lorenzo's wealth in 1481 was dramatically smaller than that reported half a century

Table 3.2. Tax Rates: *Catasto* of 1481

Taxable Income (florins)	Tax Rate (%)
Below 50	7.0
50–75	8.0
75–100	11.5
100–150	14.0
150–200	16.0
200–250	18.0
250–300	20.0
300–400	21.0
400 and above	22.0

Source: Raymond de Roover, *The Rise and Decline of the Medici Bank* (Cambridge: Harvard University Press, 1963), p. 28.

earlier by others of his family. Some of this decline reflects the contracting economy, but just how much is unclear, given the dishonesty with which tax returns were prepared. High tax rates encourage dishonesty, but they also encourage even honest people to put their money where it cannot legally be taken by the taxing authorities. The biggest tax loophole in the *catasto* was the provision that exempted domicile and associated decoration from taxation. Investment in buildings, art, and decoration brought immediate pleasure, stored wealth, and was legally tax-free. Investment in business, trade, or finance was uncertain, brought only speculative future pleasures, and would be fully taxed. When tax rates were low, the tax incentive to invest in art was small as well. Higher tax rates, however, made this tax shelter a desirable one.

There is evidence to support the theory that much of the conspicuous consumption of this period was, in effect, investment in a tax shelter. Robert S. Lopez has called this an "investment in culture."[28] Lopez notes that

> Some disenchanted businessmen buried their capital in real estate; others burned it up in conspicuous consumption; quite a number converted it into books and works of art. None of this was a new departure, for merchants had

Table 3.3. Tax Paid by Lorenzo de Medici ("the Magnificent") According to the *Catasto* of 1481

Total value of property	fl 57,930
Deduction: 5% for administration	2,896
Taxable value	55,033
Annual income (7% of taxable value)	3,852
Deduction: extraordinary charges	1,500
Taxable income	2,352
Tax paid (22% of taxable income)	fl 517

Source: Raymond de Roover, *The Rise and Decline of the Medici Bank* (Cambridge: Harvard University Press, 1963), p. 29.

always bought land, luxury, and culture; but the emphasis and motivation did change. Giovanni Rucellai, the second richest man in Florence, stated that he had become a patron of art because he got greater satisfaction from spending money than from gathering it. He was too proud to add that he had been losing money for many years, and that art had become a good investment, if only as the credit card of the elite.[29]

Many of the elaborate palaces that were built in Florence, for example, were far larger than necessary for any known use (except, perhaps, to use as store-houses for art investments to be purchased later).[30] They made little sense as homes (or even business offices), but they did provide an effective shelter from the tax assessor.

Art in Florence also displayed some of the properties associated with modern tax-sheltered investments. Some works of true artistic inspiration were created in Florence in these years to be sure. It would be blasphemy to dismiss Michelangelo's David or the Medici Chapel as products of a tax loophole. But the art industry in Florence, which rose up to meet domestic demand, did not grow so large by turning out these few works of great merit.

Art was a commodity product, often sold by size with little regard for subject or quality of composition or technique.[31] Art was purchased as a relatively liquid, tax-exempt store of value. If we view art as a tax-sheltered commodity that often had little artistic value, it is not so surprising that Florence's great art industry achieved no significant exports of their fine products.[32]

The optimists of this age found a rationale for their extravagance in ancient authority. Aristotle was cited as the source for the view that wealth had moral value. The public display of one's wealth "affords an opportunity for the exercise of virtue" according to popular interpretations of Aristotelian ethics.[33] Soon other classical authorities were found to buttress the view that wealth was moral and the public display of wealth a virtue.

The rise of classical ethics, which favored visible display of wealth, together with a tax system that strongly favored investment in art, conspired to create a true investment boom in art and culture in Florence. Perhaps what made Florence the heart of the artistic renaissance is that these two forces—taxes and philosophy—were brought together most strongly in Tuscany.

It is too strong to credit a flaw in the *catasto* with the artistic wonders that Florence produced. But the exemption of domicile and its decoration from the *catasto* is thought to have contributed to this trend. Herlihy and Klapisch-Zuber note that

> the exemption of the family domicile [from the *catasto*] encouraged the build-ing of elegant palaces at Florence and of sumptuous villas outside the city. The furnishing and the decoration of these palaces similarly escaped the tax collec-tor's scrutiny. . . . These exemptions had the pernicious effect of channeling capital away from commercial enterprises. But the policy certainly aided the building industry and production of art at Florence. It may thus have contrib-uted to the city's artistic efflorescence in the quattrocento.[34]

But as Lopez notes, "One might even contend that investment in culture drove the Renaissance to untimely death."[35]

How Public Debt Became the Heart of Florence

By the late decades of the fifteenth century the focal point of wealth and power in Florence was its public debt, the Monte Commune and the Monte delle Doti. Legislation from 1470 states (or even overstates) the Monte's importance: "The Monte is the heart of this body which we call city. . . . Every limb, large and small, must contribute to preserving this heart as the guardian fortress, immovable rock and enduring certainty of the salvation of the whole body and government of your State."[36]

Perhaps a more realistic view of the Monte's role in Florentine life is found elsewhere in the records of the commune. The Monte "safeguards the income of the Commune and makes men ready to make all the payments they have to make to it, because they see that all its income is transformed either into an increase in the purses of the citizens and of the whole people with regard to dowries and interests, or into a saving for them."[37]

In an uncertain world, with surprises and disasters lurking around each corner, the now-conservative Florentines found comfort in the government-guaranteed returns of the Monte Commune. Finance, trade, and production had been the basis of Florentine growth in the entrepreneurial past; but in the late fifteenth century the Florentines sought safe and stable returns to finance their humanistic pursuits.

But it is important to note that the Monte Commune was not the strong fiscal heart that its proponents might like. Monte stock traded at a relatively deep and increasing discount on the open market (trading at 20 percent of par in 1458, for example).[38] This is not surprising, given that actual payments of interest fell to as little as 1 percent in 1490, much lower than the promised rate. The weakening of the Monte was reflected in the rise of the dowry fund and the growing use of unsecured "emergency" war loans to members of the oligarchy at very high rates of interest.

The provision of dowries was absolutely crucial to the Florentine social system. Marriage was out of the question without a dowry. In the uncertain world of the late fifteenth century, dowries secured by private investments were unreliable and the human and social consequences of failed investments, therefore, was quite high. Thus, the Monte delle Doti had greater importance in the social system of the period than its economic role alone (which was significant) suggests. The existence and stability of the dowry fund were necessary conditions for the existence and stability of Florentine society.

It is hard to predict what might have happened to the Florentine economy if the Monte Commune and the Monte delle Doti had remained separate institutions. The Monte was originally the key to war finance. For many years Monte Commune shares were thought to be such a fine investment as to attract funds from abroad. But confidence in the Monte did not remain so high; shares traded at a substantial discount in the market. And special war loans (at higher interest rates) were increasingly being used to fund extraordinary government expenses.

The Monte delle Doti played a really important role in the social security of the city. As the financial reforms of Cosimo's era became set in stone, the link between the Monte Commune and the dowry fund grew stronger. (More and more of the assets of the Monte delle Doti were Monte Commune shares.) Thus, the larger problem of 150 years' worth of Monte Commune war debts, which totaled millions, was transferred to the dowry fund.

It was not easy to raise revenues by any means in the last years of the fifteenth century (or later in the sixteenth century).[39] Even the dowry fund was not an immediate success when first introduced; the interest return had to be increased to relatively high levels to draw the necessary revenues.

The high returns on dowry fund shares plus the useful social function that they played eventually worked to attract Florentine capital like a magnet of gold. Productive investment in the real economy could not compete with the perceived security of investment in government debt. The paradox of this is, of course, that the security of the Monte derived from faith, not substance. The Monte was secure because the people thought it was and were therefore willing to continue to lend money and purchase shares. Without new loans, however, the old shares could not be redeemed and interest paid. Effective management of the public debt so as to continue the illusion of substance that was necessary to the stability of economic and social systems became the essential element of public policy.

The task of managing the public debt was complex. By the late 1400s the public debt had accumulated obligations that fell into three general types: regular Monte shares, shares in the dowry fund, and the special war loans placed at higher rates of interest with members of the financial oligarchy. Over time, Monte shares were systematically converted into dowry fund obligations, making management of this fund the largest and most important public debt problem. Since dowry shares promised an eventual cash payment, it was not long before the Monte delle Doti was by far the largest class of Monte obligations. This created a continuing liquidity crisis. Payments from the dowry fund could not be financed by new purchases of dowry shares, since these purchases were being made with existing illiquid regular Monte shares.[40]

Additional sources of revenue were required at all times to finance a continuous stream of dowry redemptions. This liquidity was provided by the third type of Monte obligation — short-term "war loans" made at high rates of interest. These funds were provided by the wealthy families of Florence who made up the ranks of the Monte commission. Interest rates on these special loans ranged from 12 percent to 40 percent or more. The liquidity needs of the public debt provided a profitable opportunity for a few powerful and wealthy individuals.

Thus, the richest of the Florentines, like those of lesser means, found the government debt obligations a better investment than any found in the productive economy. Even more, the rich could profit handsomely at the expense of the many when the Monte was forced, as it almost always was, to borrow to maintain liquidity. One scholar, examining these short-term loans, remarks that "war itself could be a source of profit to the moneylenders."[41]

The high returns on public debt drew capital that might otherwise have been invested in new businesses, financing the economic growth and structural change that Florence's economy badly needed at this time. How severe this "crowding out" problem was, however, is hard to gauge, because the dominant "optimistic" view argued against investment and in favor of the public display of wealth. Thus, it might be more accurate to consider that the public debt redistributed consumption among citizens rather than diverting private investment to public debt. But this ignores the fact that private investment would have been heavily taxed, which discouraged even the pessimists from expanding their operations or entering new fields. So perhaps the best analysis is that the combination of Florentine taxes and its public debt institutions crowded out private investment.

The fact that the public debt served a social need—dowries—made the debt acceptable to the public and masked the economic damage that was being done. Essentially, the current generation of Florentine families was using debt to guarantee their children's social security at the cost of their economic security.

Although the dowry fund was nominally a sound capital "investment," it was in fact a pay-as-you-go system. Dowry fund shares were backed, through the complex debt management system, by Monte Commune stock, which paid a return that might, in theory, provide for future dowry disbursements. But Monte Commune shares were backed only by current tax revenues. The survival of the Florentine system of public debt clearly depended on a source of continually increasing liquidity; future tax revenues had to rise at least as fast as future dowry fund obligations to make the system work.

A pay-as-you-go system like this can work if the economy is growing, due to population growth or rising productivity. Indeed, the economy of Florence had sustained the Monte for 150 years. But the economy began to run dry in the 1480s. Plagues and the low fertility that was a plague legacy prevented population from rising at the necessary rate. Florentine fiscal policy had systematically siphoned off capital from the hands of entrepreneurs, investors, and producers. Ultimately a liquidity crisis was inevitable. One such crisis came in 1478, for example, when the dowry fund began to run a deficit. It became clear that the Monte della Doti could not meet its cash dowry obligations.

The Florentine money wizards found many ways to shore up the foundations of the public debt temporarily, as the fine account of Marks makes clear. The reform of 1478, for example, so boosted confidence in the dowry funds that it began to attract far too much capital and the government had to impose investment limits. But ultimately, there were not resources enough in Florence and its territories to honor the obligations of the Monte.

Florence resolved the Monte's liquidity crisis in what was probably the only possible way, given that no major new source of increased liquidity was available without debasing the sacred gold florin. Stuck with illiquid assets, they gave in to the necessity of illiquid obligations. Immediate cash payment of dowry debts was abandoned. Shares in the Monte delle Doti were assembled into a series of "lists," which earned higher interest rates but could not quickly be redeemed. Their intent was to slowly pay the principle of first one list, then the next, and so on. Marks notes that "with this measure the evolution of the Monte delle Doti was complete. . . . The original purpose of the dowry fund had been forgotten and in its place there was now a new form of investment which was profitable and more secure. . . . The Monte delle Doti continued to be the principal method by which the large body of Florentine citizens was able to exploit the revenues of the state."[42]

It is probably too harsh to say that the "original purpose" of the dowry fund was forgotten at this point. Studies of the records of the dowry fund suggest that its stated function remained a very important concern.[43] Florentine fathers continued to use the Monte delle Doti to provide their daughters with the capital they needed to become respectable wives. It is also clear, however, that the public debt became an end in itself during these years and not just a means to an end, as it had been in prior years.

The great irony of the dowry fund is that because it became a pay-as-you-go system (not unlike today's social security system in this respect), it depended on the growing economy for stability in the long run. But its obligations needed to be maintained in the short run, too, and the need for funds now meant high interest rates and high taxes. Ironically, these fiscal imperatives drained away the capital that might have helped Florence adjust to the new world economy and grow in the future. The need to keep the "heart" of Florence alive in the short run thus forced fiscal actions that weakened the body of the Tuscan city in the long run.

Florence in the Sixteenth Century

The years that followed were anything but dull. Lorenzo "the Magnificent" died in 1492, but the Medici clan remained influential. Lorenzo's son Giovanni would eventually become Pope Leo X, for example. An agent of the Medici bank, Amerigo Vespucci, would have his name given to two continents. The French invaded Italy in 1494, on their way to battle Naples, and brought down the Medici-led oligarchy in Florence. But after two decades of republican government, Medici dukes and grand dukes again ruled Florence. Savonarola, the "pessimist" dissident priest, went too far in his reformist, antimaterialist crusade, offending both the civil and church authorities, and was both hanged and burnt in the Piazza della Signoria in 1498.

Art and literature flourished in Florence. The fine arts industry boomed in terms of commodity quantity and artistic quality, as the lasting works of Michelangelo, Leonardo da Vinci, and Machiavelli attest. Lots of junk art (the Florentine equivalent of junk bonds?) was also produced, which has not survived through the years.

But by 1494 the future pattern of the Florentine economy was set and Florence's years of economic power and influence were over. The great Florentine houses of trade and finance never again possessed such wealth, wielded such power, or dominated world markets. The artistic flower of the Florentine Renaissance bloomed for a while still, but the economic roots that supported it were already in relative decline.

It is generally agreed that the European economy suffered a prolonged depression in the sixteenth century (although the data necessary to really prove this hypothesis is lacking).[44] Florence entered this period with important assets and great wealth, so reports that the Florentine economy did not suffer this depression equally with other states are not unexpected. But Florence did decline.

The Florentine cloth industry suffered a significant decline at this time, experienced an "Indian Summer" later in the sixteenth century, then collapsed completely in the seventeenth century. Not only did the countries to the north have access to fine raw materials, but they soon acquired the special skills necessary to compete with Florentine craftsmanship. As the economy of Florence declined, some skilled masters fled the region, looking for better opportunities elsewhere. They took with them their skills, which they taught to others, particularly in Flanders and England.[45]

With better materials and equal skills, northern cloth producers could dominate the high end of the market and also undercut Florentine prices at the lower levels. Soon the Italians had lost much of their export markets and were suffering from the inroads made by imports into their domestic markets as well. Not all the great Italian city-states suffered industrial decline at precisely the same time or in the same way, but decline came to them all eventually.[46]

Competition also appeared suddenly in the financial markets that Florence and the other Italians had long monopolized. Northern firms that would include the famous Fuggers appeared suddenly, and the Florentines just as suddenly disappeared. Between 1490 and 1520 Florence slipped dramatically into the second rank of finance powers.[47] The Medici bank failed in 1494, and others followed.

Bergier sees the decline of Florentine banking fortunes as the result of the "optimistic" attitudes of the time. In answer to the question of how we can explain Florence's sudden decline in its main areas of business, he cites a kind of myopia. Florence continued to look for success where they had found it in the past, not where it now was clearly visible to others. This myopia, Bergier states was "a simple lack of imagination, a habit that had grown up during more than a century of good business, easy business on a short-term basis, whereas now it was suddenly becoming necessary to plan for the long term."[48]

Falling incomes throughout Europe (combined with greater competition from northern countries) reduced the demand for Florentine wool cloth. Florence did remain competitive in the luxury silk trade, but it is not clear that this industry provided jobs and income on the same scale as did wool. The gap between the rich and poor in Florence therefore grew wider and wider. The problems of external change and internal decline were exacerbated by plagues, more wars, and a growing tax burden.

Merchants of Florence began to rely on their government to an even greater extent to compensate for problems abroad. In the 1540s, for example, rules were issued that fixed more prices and strengthened the restrictive powers of the guilds.[49] This is the type of policy that Olson would predict, a further stiffening of the institutional rigidities that would lead, in turn, to even less dynamism and even slower growth in the future. The economic status quo became even more firmly established and the broad fifteenth century vision disappeared. The new focus was to conserve, restore, and maintain.

Florentine foreign policy had always been undertaken with economics in mind. Beginning in 1495 Florence's governments established stronger and stronger links with France because of the markets and business opportunities that seemed likely in the growing French sphere of influence. In this, the Florentines were also following the pathways of the past rather than striking out onto new ground. This may have been the best strategy available, but the French connection ultimately contributed to the further decline of Florence.[50]

Florentine bankers repeated the mistakes of their ancestors the Bardi and the Peruzzi. They made large loans to the French king and his noblemen. Bank failures and depression followed when these loans could not be repaid.

Links with the French still grew stronger, and Florence began to depend more and more on access to French-controlled markets. Many Florentine families moved to France to be closer to their new economic interests (and to escape political problems in Tuscany). Even those families that remained became imbued with the French rentier attitude.[51] For nearly three hundred years it had been common for rich Florentines to maintain active participation in business (unlike rich aristocrats elsewhere). Now, under French influence, business was "out of fashion."[52] The economy became less and less able to change, to deal with the changing world economy. Rigid Florentine businesses were maintained and conserved, but they did not grow or change.

While the new aristocracy of Florence looked to government for assistance in preserving their economic situation, they were not willing to pay the taxes necessary to support these activities. Even with repeated tax reforms, direct tax collections seem to have fallen systematically, replaced by high-interest loans. Thus, Florentine aristocrats saw their government as a double source of profits; they demanded probusiness policies and also earned high interest on Monte "investments."

Florence had become a hollow economy. Cochrane points out that "Hence, the many handsome new palaces that were embellishing the face of Florence were not all signs or instruments of growing wealth. More often they were simply . . . mausoleums of once-lucrative and now liquidated international corporations. They served not to reinforce public confidence in the business ventures of the proprietors, but to drain capital out of production and into consumption."[53]

In this condition, Florence could not hope permanently to withstand the forces of structural change in the world around it. The wool market collapsed in the 1580s. The remaining Florentine businesses suffered a rash of bankruptcies. The guilds tightened their grip on the economy, trying to preserve what remained. And so Florence finally turned inward and lost its place on the international scene.

The physical wealth of Florence remained, the hollow palaces containing great works of art. The myth of Florentine financial wealth was preserved through the institutions of the Monte until the 1630s. But finally even the Monte Commune had to face reality.

Unable to pay interest on Monte stocks by any means, the Florentine government finally was forced to cut interest rates on its debt (rather than resort to the kinds of manipulations that had previously been used to disguise the true condition of the public debt).[54] The market value of Monte shares fell dramatically, and in one stroke even the myth of Florentine wealth was destroyed.

The Fifth Element

What became of the "fifth element" that made Florence and the Florentines so noteworthy in the first pages of this study? Some would say that the special spark that fired Florence was smothered by historical forces beyond human control: plague, declining population, rising real wages, the need for territorial expansion, and the constant parade of wars that expansion produced. These forces were bigger than the Florentines and account for the fact that their dismal economic fate was widely shared by others.

Others might say that Florence's fifth element was not destroyed but was transformed by some alchemy into a different form. The spark that ignited commerce and finance in the thirteenth and fourteenth centuries reappeared in the fifteenth and sixteenth centuries in the fields of art, literature, and science. It is clear that by the second half of the fifteenth century Florence's vision had shifted. It is perhaps no accident that the economic decline coincides with artistic growth.

Finally, we may suppose that the very ideas that powered the Florentine's rise were responsible for their fall. Marks holds that "it was the basic financial structure which proved decisive in the long-term development of the city. The subordination of all financial arrangements to the dictates of the credit mechanism was the major factor. It means that the state itself had come to be looked on as a source of profit, an outlook which contributed greatly to the emergence of a rentier mentality among the wealthier Florentine families."[55]

In this view, the financial innovations that contributed so much to the growth of Florence and the wealth of the Florentines ultimately evolved into a set of institutions that removed the incentives that had lead to economic growth. Dry, paper finance had replaced the real productive investment. The forces of the *catasto* and the Monte etched a conservative pattern on the economic life of the Florence, which deepened over the years until the fate of Florence was set.

Cipolla's study of the economic decline of Italy concludes that the increasing rigidity of its economic structure was the real cause of the post-Renaissance collapse. Italian cloth producers refused to adapt to changing market conditions. The cloth they made was of excellent quality and perhaps even worth its very high cost, but the buyers of the time did not think so. They wanted cheaper, if shoddier, cloth and garments. The inability of producers to change, compounded by the increasingly rigid guild system, tax system, and high wage structure, caused Florence and Italy to be overtaken by other more adaptable economies.[56]

The critical point in the economic history of Renaissance Florence appears to be 1453–1454, when peace suddenly and unexpectedly appeared. Without persistent war to stir things up, the world economy began, rather quickly, to settle into layers. Once at the top of the turbulent mixture, Florence now settled toward the lower-middle part of the world economy.

Florence had found sparkling solutions to the problems raised by the commercial revolution of the late Middle Ages. These same basic solutions were good enough to keep Florence at the top of the southern regional economy in the century after the Black Death. But Florence did not change when change was needed after the 1450s and suffered the long-term decline of its economy that we see here.

The 1450s were also a turning point in the history of Florentine public finance. Before this time it can be said that generally, the tax and debt system of Florence represented a reasonable solution to the problems of the fiscal crisis it experienced. After the 1450s, however, debt and taxes became part of the problem, not part of the solution.

In the end, the Florentines seem to have utterly lost their ability to distinguish between shadow and substance. They focused entirely on the shadow world of public debt and in the process allowed all opportunities to advance their real substance to escape.

4

Simple Patterns: Britain and the Industrial Revolution

The Exhibition of the Industry of All Nations opened in London's Hyde Park on May Day 1851 in its specially constructed home, the Crystal Palace. A glittering glass building held together by a delicate skeleton of iron and wood, the Crystal Palace was a monument to British technical superiority, a great national greenhouse enclosing

> no fewer than 772,784 square feet or about 19 acres; thus presenting an edifice about four times the size of St. Peter's, at Rome, and six times that of St. Paul's. . . .
>
> The first impression conveyed to the mind of a visitor, inexperienced in the science of architecture, on entering the building, is a sense of insecurity, arising from the apparent lightness of its supports as compared with the vastness of its dimensions. But this feeling is soon dispelled when he is informed how severely the strength of every separate part has been tested, and with what extreme care the connexion of all the supports with each other has been considered, so as to present the greatest possible combination of strength.[1]

Prince Albert challenged the nations of the world to send the finest stuff their industries and technology could produce to be displayed side by side with Britain's best. The bright light that flooded through the Crystal Palace revealed to Queen Victoria's insecure subjects the gaudy fact of Britannia's dominance. The Crystal Palace made it clear: British industry was number one.

The *Times* description of the Crystal Palace and its contents concludes boldly that "all contributed to an effect so grand and yet so natural, that it hardly seemed to be put together by design, or to be the work of human artificers."[2] Indeed, the exhibition must have seemed a miracle to many of the British people. The miracle of the Industrial Revolution was on display for all to see. And the employers did make sure that their workers saw it.

> The Exhibition has been shown to be a great Peace movement, a great moral movement, and a great industrial movement—all of which it most un-

doubtedly is. Within the last few weeks, a novel and unexpected result has been witnessed. . . .

. . . Clergymen and landed proprietors in remote rural districts have organized plans by which whole troops of agricultural laborers, with their wives and children, have been enabled to visit London . . . to see the marvels of art, skill, and industry congregated together. . . . Manufacturers in the provincial towns, and extensive employers of labour in the metropolis and its environs, have not only given their workpeople a holiday to enable them to visit the Exhibition, but have in numerous instances paid the expenses both of the trip and their admission.[3]

Perhaps no other exhibition in history has had so profound an effect on its society. The gaudy, vulgar domestic decorations defined style and good taste for a generation of middle-class households and set a standard for the aspirations of the working class. The great gleaming engines and machines were sculptures of iron and steel that told the story of man's triumph over nature. These were monuments to progress and the industrial age. The clear superiority of British products and technology over their foreign counterparts inspired the myth of the Industrial Revolution. The *Art Journal* summed up the national attitude well:

[I]t is to the honour of Great Britain that, notwithstanding the generous risk incurred by inviting competitors from all the nations of the world — prepared as they had been by long years of successful study and practical experience — the fame of British manufacturers has been augmented by this contest: and there can be no doubt that when His Royal Highness Prince Albert issues his summons to another competition, British supremacy will be manifested in every branch of Industrial Art.[4]

In fact, the confident promise of the Great Exhibition of 1851 was not fulfilled. By 1876, when the world gathered in Philadelphia to compare artistic and industrial wares, proud Britannia's torch of leadership clearly had been passed to the scientific Germans in some fields and to the ingenious Americans in others.[5] British industry and technology had been overtaken; the long-lasting consequences of this event were to influence profoundly the social, economic, and political lives of the British people for generations.

How did Britain ascend to the peak that the exhibition of 1851 defines, and why did Victorian Britain fail? — that is, why did the panoramic midcentury visions of British industrial supremacy become yellowed memories, not sterling achievements?[6] Why did Britain slip from the top rung of the industrial countries? These are big questions that have challenged historians and economists for many decades.

The rise and decline of Victorian Britain is a variation on the theme of structural change and fiscal crisis that we have just seen played out in the case of Renaissance Florence. History did not repeat itself in Victorian Britain, but certain underlying themes of human nature can be found in these two important periods. In the next two chapters I examine the British experience with structural change and fiscal crisis and prepare for the analysis of the postwar United States that will follow.

Britain adapted extremely well to one set of very large structural changes, the ones that created the Industrial Revolution. But the patterns that led to that success became rigid and prevented Britain from responding to a second set of structural changes late in the nineteenth century. The result was that Britain, like Florence, was overtaken by other nations and slipped from the top rank. The decline was most dramatic at the point where the world economy opened up and Britain had to adapt to find its place within the global market system.

Fiscal crisis also plays an important role in this saga. The British, like the crafty Tuscans who in many ways taught them their trade, created financial instruments that were remarkably successful in meeting the needs of private and public finance. In particular, the British created powerful weapons in their national debt and income tax. Their financial instruments and tax policies worked efficiently when needed early in the Industrial Revolution and account in good measure for Britain's early industrial success. (The lack of modern private and public finance is one reason France, for example, did not industrialize along with Britain.)

But British finance got stuck in a rut, which is a common problem for both money and men. As the world economy changed and expanded, the tools of public and private finance that had been so successful years before now worked against change and contributed to the rigid patterns of decline. The next chapter will focus specifically on how fiscal crisis and public finance unintentionally promoted structural rigidity and relative decline at the end of the nineteenth century.

The Myth of the Industrial Revolution

Arnold Toynbee coined the phrase *Industrial Revolution* in his Oxford lectures on this subject in 1880–1881.[7] The words Toynbee chose suggest that structural change was quick and focused on industry. Toynbee named it a revolution — not evolution, slow growth, or gradual change; a revolution to most people means a short, sharp change or reversal in direction. The adjective modifying *Revolution* is *Industrial*, suggesting that the change was not agricultural or commercial; and the image that comes to most minds is that of big machines and boiling factories. Toynbee's *Industrial Revolution*, then, suggests a rapid change from the happy, bucolic life to a world dominated by dark, sweaty Dickensian factories and workshops.[8] Given our cultural context, the story implicit in Toynbee's two little words is so clear and complete as to discourage further investigation of the matter.

Some of the misconceptions that we cannot blame on Toynbee's ability to turn a memorable phrase we can lay at the door of W. W. Rostow, an equally able wordsmith. Rostow's analysis of the British growth experience was colored by Toynbee's terms and informed by sparse and misleading historical data. Rostow saw Britain as an airplane. Before 1783 the British economy was grounded, stuck in a no-growth, subsistence, agrarian state. By the early nineteenth century Britain was in flight, the first nation to experience self-sustaining economic growth. The critical difference was the sudden takeoff into sustained growth that Rostow perceived. The massive energy needed for such a takeoff came from the engines of the "leading sector," which Rostow saw to be the cotton-woolen industry. The British takeoff of 1783–1802 was "the great watershed in the life of modern societies."[9]

Rostow's airplane metaphor is even more descriptive than Toynbee's simple phrase and has deeply conditioned our perception of British growth in particular and the process of economic development in general.[10] Rostow's language reinforces our perception of the Industrial Revolution as a sharp social transformation from the slow-paced life of pastoral meadows to today's high-flying, fast-lane, mechanized urban rat race. In viewing the Industrial Revolution this way we are guilty of a variation on an error pointed out by Walter Bagehot: "Reasoners like economists . . . turn history not into an old almanac but into a new one; they make what happens now to have happened always, according to the same course of time."[11]

The images that Arnold Toynbee and W. W. Rostow created have been woven into our cultural consciousness. Like the Crystal Palace, which itself shaped our perception of this period, the Industrial Revolution erupted suddenly, rising out of the fields and soaring brilliantly toward the sky.

The conventional wisdom regarding the Industrial Revolution may be summarized by a short list of stylized facts. Perhaps no single author has ever presented as distorted a view of British economic development as these stylized facts portray, but the impression they leave is perhaps not unlike that which casual students might absorb.[12]

- The Industrial Revolution was a relatively short period of time (1780–1800, less than one generation) during which the nature of life in Britain changed fundamentally. Workers left the land and moved to the cities, where they worked in huge impersonal factories.
- British workers had little choice in leaving the land. The Enclosure Acts forced them out of their traditional farming employments.
- The Industrial Revolution took place in Britain because the British were more innovative. The Industrial Revolution was built on technological change.
- The cotton industry was the leading sector of British economic growth. British technological innovations (the fly shuttle, Hargreave's spinning jenny, Arkwright's waterframe, Crompton's mule) caused the construction of huge capital-intensive factories that employed thousands of workers.
- The trend toward mechanization of the textile mills was complemented and reinforced by British innovations in the iron and steel industry (Cort's puddling and rolling process, Darby's coke-smelting techniques), transportation (canals and railroads), and, perhaps most important, Watt's steam engine, which powered all these industries.

- London's slickly modern financial institutions further complemented this industrial process by efficiently providing the huge capital sums that the mills and factories required.
- Britain grew, but working-class families (especially the children), who toiled long hours in the mills, factories, and mines and managed a dreary existence in urban centers like Manchester and Leeds, found their industrial lives dismal and hard compared to the memories of their country hearths.
- Influenced by Adam Smith's philosophy of "laissez-faire," British government and society tolerated the poverty, abuse, and exploitation of the Industrial Revolution.
- Britain became the "workshop of the world," trading its high technology manufactures for the raw materials of foreign lands.

One reason these stylized facts are compelling is that a grain of truth can be found in each exaggerated notion. "Facts" vaguely like these are learned in school. After the exam complexity is purged from our minds, and these simple memorable images remain. The record of the Industrial Revolution, as modern economic historians interpret it, is more complicated and less dramatic.

The Industrial *Evolution*

It might be better to call this period the Industrial *Evolution*, as some have done. *Evolution*, not *revolution*, because the pace of change was slow and the nature of change was incremental. The total effect was large to be sure, but it came about as the result of relatively small effects compounded again and again over time. This is clearly the opposite of the picture that *revolution* suggests.

McCloskey calls this a "quiet revolution." According to him, the Industrial Revolution's "immediate impact on culture or politics was slight." The population grew and moved from the country to the cities and mills. Yet McCloskey notes, "So strange were these events that before they happened they were not anticipated, and while they were happening they were not comprehended."[13] Other scholars have also commented on the degree to which the "revolution" was overlooked by the writers of the time.

Adam Smith, writing in 1776, thought he saw the future in a pin factory, where specialization of labor limited only by the size of the market increased productivity. Machines and technology had no special place in Smith's industrial vision. Writing in middle of the "revolution" (1828, twenty-five years after the critical takeoff, according to Rostow), the French economist Jean-Baptist Say proclaimed the limits of technology: "No machine will ever be able to perform what even the worst horses can."[14]

If the Industrial Revolution was slow and unexpected, went nearly unnoticed, and had little immediate effect, why does everyone now believe in it, think it obvious, and assign such ex post importance to it? To understand the paradox of the Industrial Evolution, it will help to search for parallels in nature.

In the mountains near my office, glaciers creep forward, moving constantly on a microscopic scale from snowy peaks down toward the high meadows. I have never really seen them move. But the landscape outside my window has been shaped far more by the gradual, invisible movements of glaciers than by the sudden, visible hand of man.

What is important about glaciers is not that they move slowly but that they move at all while the land all about them lies still and is transformed by them. This is what was important about the British economy during the Industrial Revolution. The economy grew and changed very slowly, but it grew and continued to grow until growth became the norm. The world around it was not growing, had no prior experience of sustained change or growth, and did not expect to grow.

When the glacier moves, the whole glacier moves, not just its "leading sector." Geologists tell us that not all the glacier moves at precisely the same rate. Some parts of a glacier can race inches ahead of the rest in a year. Glaciers are powerful, however, because their pieces work together as a whole.

It was the same with the Industrial Revolution. Growth and change took place slowly, but not just in the industrial sector. Like a glacier, all of Britain changed (at different paces, and not precisely at the same time) during the Industrial Revolution. The power of this period derives from the combined force of many different movements in many sectors over a sustained period.

Scholars have tried to capture the breadth of this pattern of change artificially, by dividing the Industrial Revolution into several component "revolutions." Phyllis Deane, for example, talks of revolutions in demography, agriculture, commerce, and transport. To Deane's list Dickson adds a "revolution" in finance (an early one: 1688–1720), and Hartwell contributes one more in the service sector. A precise taxonomy of revolutions is unimportant; what is important is that the Industrial Revolution was not so narrow a phenomenon as many imagine but rather was the result of a gathering of many forces and a sustained joint action.

A better way to describe the process at work here is to use the language of "structural change," which looks at the economy in terms of very large sectors. Structural change takes place as resources (labor, capital) are shifted from the primary sector (agriculture, natural resources) to the manufacturing sector to the services sector (including transportation, finance, and government). Structural change was clearly the combined effect of all the revolutions we see at work in Britain during the eighteenth and nineteenth centuries.

The Industrial Revolution is important not so much because change and growth were fast (the takeoff) or slow but because there was growth or change at all. Britain moved more like a glacier than like an airplane. Growth came from the combined effects of many sectors, not just one. The microchanges had the macroeffect of altering the overall structure of the British economy, not simply creating an industrial sector.[15]

It is hard for us to understand why the Industrial Revolution should go largely unnoticed while it was in process. I will argue in this section that it was the evolutionary nature of change in a world where change was unexpected that caused the revolution to be so silent. But it may also be true that the Industrial Revolution fell between two other types of events that were more memorable to individuals. On the one hand there are the personal and family events (births, deaths, marriages, even big storms) that are so important in a world that was as closed and narrow as preindustrial Britain. On the other hand—and more important to historians—we have the long and fateful military conflicts of the period, especially the Napoleonic wars. These, I think, were the events that defined this age to the people who lived it. The Industrial Revolution, existing as a slow process that overlapped several generations, provided the people no convenient single image with which to define or identify themselves.

One way to see the evolutionary rather than revolutionary nature of economic change is to consider how industrialization might have affected families of this era. Consider, for example, the life of a small-scale rural English farming family (who might have owned the land they tilled or might have worked another's land under a variety of rental or sharecropping arrangements). Production here was a family affair, with all members of the household, down to the children, putting in long hours under harsh conditions. Sunrise and sunset marked the boundaries of their workday. Given the tools and techniques of the seventeenth and eighteenth centuries, farming was a low-productivity industry, so lots of inputs were needed to generate adequate output.

Farming was the family's principal occupation, but it was not enough to support them. The long, cold, dim months between growing seasons needed to be put to productive use; and textiles were the answer. By tradition the man of the hearth would operate the loom, weaving some cotton cloth, but mostly woolen cloth. Women and children would prepare raw materials and spin the yarn that the loom demanded.

Spinning was the bottleneck in the textile business. Slow and inefficient compared to weaving, it took many small hands spinning to provide enough yarn to keep one man's loom supplied. The differences in productivity between spinning and weaving were too great to allow production to remain wholly within the family. Using the "putting-out" system, petty capitalists would supply families with raw wool, than return to collect yarn. Weavers would be given yarn and be paid when they supplied the finished cloth. The whole process was slow, uncertain, and risky for the entrepreneur, since it was difficult to monitor production. Both spinners and weavers had the opportunity to siphon off materials for their own use. Circulating capital, which the entrepreneur supplied from his own pocket, was far more important to the production process than were the small investments in fixed capital.

If we wanted to paint a picture of preindustrial Britain using oversimplified but still meaningful stylized facts, it would be this:

- *Production was centered around home and family*. All members of the family contributed to production, children included. Working conditions and the standard of living were poor by most objective standards.
- *Specialization of labor was the exception, not the rule*. Rural families typically engaged in both farming and home-based textile production.

- *Most people worked for others.* Eighty percent of agricultural land was worked by tenant farmers. Even those who owned the land they worked supplemented their farm incomes by working in the textile trade.
- *Productivity in both agriculture and manufacturing was low.* Working capital was more important than fixed capital in all these sectors.
- *There were obvious bottlenecks that limited an increase in productivity.* Inefficient spinning techniques hampered the growth of textile production. Open fields and the three-field system of crop rotation meant that much agricultural land had very low productivity at any given time.

Let me now introduce as another set of stylized facts three "revolutions"—relatively small changes that taken together, had a very large impact:

- *Population growth.* Increases in the rate of population growth due to a combination of factors, including higher birth rates and, perhaps more important, reduced mortality due to diseases (including the plague).
- *Increased productivity in agriculture.* While there is a tendency to look for one big reason for the rise in agricultural output (hence an unjustified emphasis on enclosures), it is probably more accurate to view the increases in agricultural productivity as the result of many small marginal innovations that, taken together, had a large effect. Some of the innovations were mechanical (the Rotherham plow, Jethro Tull's seed drill), while others involved changing centuries-old customs of production (wider use of the turnip as a nitrogen-fixing fodder crop, more effective field rotation systems). Good luck was also a factor; nature provided weather conditions that compounded these productivity gains.
- *Increased productivity in industry.* As in agriculture, a number of small innovations increased productivity in textiles and elsewhere in the manufacturing sector. A number of innovations accumulated in the textile industry without great effect because they improved the weaving process, while the bottleneck remained in the production of yarn in general and strong cotton yarn in particular. As improvements in spinning arrived, they therefore had a multiplier effect on output because they allowed introduction of previously unused weaving techniques.

By and large the innovations in both agriculture and manufacturing were improvements on existing practices, not completely new systems of production, and did not require large capital commitments. One reason for this was that the innovations themselves were made by working craftsmen who had little capital to use. Canals and the railways that came after them were the projects that ate large chunks of capital. Industry was relatively labor-intensive.

This last fact creates a puzzle. If the increase in textile production was not based on huge capital investments, why were the great cotton factories built? Modern observers think of factories as large lumps of integrated capital to which workers must be brought. But British factories were not as capital-heavy as those in other countries. It would, in fact, have been possible to introduce the early textile innovations within the cottage-based putting-out system. So modest were the capital requirements that the cottage workshop was viable for many years, even alongside larger factories. But the problem of monitoring production and raw material usage argued against decentralized production. The first factories were not built so much to bring workers to machines as to allow both workers and machines to be monitored efficiently. (Later, of course, steam-powered machinery would build a stronger case for capital-intensive centralized production, but British factories were still relatively labor-intensive.)

These three gentle but sustained increases—in population, in agricultural productivity, and in industrial productivity—slowly wrought large-scale structural changes in the British economic system. What made the changes difficult to perceive at the time was that at least initially, they involved changes in degree, not direction. For example, the immediate effects of the innovations in agriculture and textile production was a change in the allocation of labor within the household. The fraction of total labor within the family allocated to spinning and weaving increased. Labor became somewhat more specialized, while family production was still divided between cloth and farm goods. The specialization of labor within the family was mirrored by a specialization of labor within the community. Slowly, over the course of several generations, labor was shifted to manufacturing. Finally some families completely specialized in production of textiles or other manufactured goods. At this point, we enter the urban industrial landscape of factories, mills, and workshops.

This structural reallocation did not result in a dramatic population shift to the cities from the countryside. The growth in population meant that the size of the agricultural population could remain very large while the ranks of urban factory workers also increased. To people living at the time, the most important source of structural change was probably not industrialization but war. The long years of the European wars drew men from all over Britain, changing their lives forever. Much of the structural change from farm to factory and service sector was the result of discharged soldiers seeking work in the city rather than the now overcrowded countryside of their childhood. It is not foolish to think that these soldiers would have viewed the war as the great discontinuity, not industrialization. It is left for modern-day economists to make this mistake.

Life in the urban factory towns was not bliss. Wages were low. People worked from sunrise to sunset. Children worked from an early age. The standard of living was low. What strikes us as we look back at this situation is how dreadful the living and working conditions were. But in fact, to the people living at the time, the conditions in the city were not all that much different from life on the farm. In each particular—length of day, child labor, and so on—conditions in the city mirrored those in the countryside. In fact, the early factories and workshops apparently tended to employ family groups in production, continuing the practice of family production that had existed in the rural cottages.

What was different—and what struck reformers then and now—was how concentrated these problems were in the cities. No one paid too much attention to child labor conditions on the farm, for example, because this social problem was decentralized and took place within the confines of the family. Put dozens of children together in one place working for an unfatherly boss, however, and the same social problem is both easier to see and more shocking.

The Industrial Revolution was not so much a discrete jump as a change in ratio and proportion and, because it was so subtle (at least compared to the Napoleonic Wars), it was unappreciated. The real lesson that the industrial revolution teaches us (or should teach us) regarding structural change is that even relatively small changes in the trend lines of resource growth and technological change can have a very large impact on the structure of the economy when allowed to compound over a series of decades or generations. This is a lesson we will return to in later chapters that deal with recent changes in the postwar U.S. economy.

The Pattern of Industrial Development

> Its whole life is pervaded almost unconsciously by a few simple ideas which are interwoven in that pleasant harmony that gives their charm to Oriental carpets.   Alfred Marshall, *Principles of Economics*

Alfred Marshall intended this sentence[16] to describe the backward traditional economies of earth's equatorial belt. Unconsciously, however, Marshall provides us with an apt analogy for the British economy. Oriental carpets are produced using simple capital and large quantities of relatively unskilled labor. The beauty of a fine Persian rug comes not from its strikingly original modern design but, as Marshall noted, from a complex pattern built on the subtle repetition and transposition of a few elementary colors and shapes.

There are strong similarities between Marshall's rug and industrial development of Britain during the nineteenth century. British industrial growth was based on the use of relatively simple capital combined with a growing labor force. The workers, given the prevailing educational system, could not be described as highly skilled. Large, strikingly original modern factories were the exception rather than the rule. (But, like the medallions found at the center of some Oriental rugs, these exceptions attracted the most attention.) The primary pattern of industrial development was based on the progressive repetition of small factories and workshops linked to markets and to each other by the bold lines of canals and railways.

The early canals and the later railways were important factors in Britain's economic development. The iron industry had for many decades been small and impermanent because of its dependence on charcoal fuel. The iron works would move into a forested area and remain so long as the trees held out. When the forests were gone and no more charcoal could be produced, the factories pulled up stakes and moved on. Darby's invention of a coke-smelting technique made it possible to take advantage of Britain's abundant coal fields, but transportation problems remained. British roads were so poor that coal was often moved using pack animals—an incredibly slow and expensive system. The development of the iron industry depended on a mechanism to move coal to foundry and iron to market.

The canal was the solution to the iron industry's bottleneck. Typically for Britain, the first successful canal was a very private venture. The Bridgewater Canal, built in 1759–1761, was financed privately by the duke of Bridgewater. It linked the duke's own coal mines at Coalbrookdale in Shopshire with the nascent factory town of Manchester. The canal was entirely artificial; James Brindley, it architect, eschewed natural waterways so as to avoid the vagaries of nature. The cheap, reliable canal barges made it possible for the duke to undercut other coal suppliers in Manchester and make a fortune.

Encouraged by the Bridgewater Canal's success, canals were planned and built in other places. Private finance dominated these enterprises, at least initially. Capital came most often from mine owners and foundry operators, who could benefit directly from lower coal prices and expanding markets. Only when these sources failed did entrepreneurs venture to the City of London (Britain's Wall Street) for money. This meant that the public canal stocks offered through the City's finance houses probably represented the riskiest and most long-term of these ventures.

"Canal mania," a financial bubble, was one result of this peculiar pattern of transport finance. Not all the canals that subscribed stock were finished or made a profit. But not all were failures, either. The practice of raising capital for such large-scale projects through the city's finance houses was established.

The canal builders' financial route to the City of London did have its use. Railroad builders followed the same route for finance in the nineteenth century. The City's financial markets were conservative, at least in the sense that they preferred to follow well-traveled paths ("Capital flows in channels," says Kindleberger)[17] even if they did not always lead to guaranteed profit. The City's markets first specialized in government bonds but soon learned to love foreign bonds, domestic canal (and railway) stocks, and finally foreign canal and railway stocks. These financial channels covered a lot of ground, but there were many significant unserved sectors. Notable among these were the British manufacturers.

Iron, steel, and textiles were the most famous industries of the Industrial Revolution, although other sectors, including chemicals and instrument manufacturing, were likewise "revolutionized." As has already been noted, the scale of these factories and workshops was relatively small even after the introduction of steam power. One reason for this has to do with the peculiar British system of financial channels.

Public stock corporations were a British innovation, and many casual scholars credit Britain's early growth to the advantages of this modern capitalist institution. In fact, however, the contribution of corporate finance to industrial development was small and came rather late in the Victorian period. The City had been burnt badly by "corporate stocks" (of a different nature, to be sure) in the South Sea Bubble of 1719–1720 and did not really trust them (aside from canal and railway issues) despite their improvements.

The typical Victorian manufacturing firm was therefore a small partner-
ship, with all the capital limitations that this form of organization suggests.
Capital for the initial business came from the partners, and capital for business
expansion came from retained earnings. The growth of Victorian firms was
therefore self-financed and incremental, as each year's profits allowed marginal
improvements, repairs, or expansion in some part of the workshop or factory.
Chapman reports that in the cotton industry

> the provincial money market was evolving from very elementary beginnings,
> and the entrepreneurs in need of capital drew on very diverse sources. The
> favourite source of capital was retained earnings and during the restricted
> growth period of Arkwright's patents (1769–85) profit rates were known to be
> very high. . . . Even so, working capital requirements were so much larger
> than fixed capital, and the time-lag between decision to build and profits so
> long, that financial difficulties could be experienced. . . . Small firms that
> could not feed their own growth usually turned to their own families, and then
> to local business and social contacts for help, but of course not all had such
> connections."[18]

The sorts of manufacturing firms that resulted from this pattern of start-up
finance and expansion were large compared to Adam Smith's pin factory but
small compared to the factories that most people imagine and smaller, in fact,
than similar factories in similar trades on the continent.

British factories were small, at least until the 1870s; grew only slowly; and
made changes in technology or capacity in small steps if at all. The fact that
individual factories did not become truly huge does not mean that whole
industries did not expand. In fact. the relatively modest capital requirements of
Victorian industry encouraged the entry of new firms. Workers who could
master the technology of an industry and accumulate a little capital might
combine with partners to form new firms and build new factories that differed
only in detail from existing manufacturers.

Technological change within these factories took place, but at a modest
pace. Most progress was made by craftsmen fiddling with the existing machines
and processes, not by scientists and engineers working with a clean sheet of
paper. The scope of innovations was not wide and the use of self-finance
encouraged the preservation of the status quo.

As British industry expanded in size over time, then, it did so in a pattern
that generally, if not always, repeated itself. A little more capital, more factory
workers, and the expansion of an existing market, especially through trade, was
the pattern of British industrial growth.

The Political Economy of Structural Change

Structural change affects the people in the economy in many important ways.
Income changes. The distribution of income changes. Wealth changes. The
sources of wealth in the economy changes. The nature of the economic and
social problems facing society changes.

As the distribution of income and wealth changes, so does the distribution of political power in society. Nouveau "haves" will seek political influence to match their economic clout. A political struggle ensues because no group willingly gives up political influence.

As the distribution of political power shifts, government policies also change to reflect the interests of the newly dominant groups. Laws and regulations change, and so must the tax system. The tax system reflects a balance between the opposing forces. On one hand, interest groups will seek to limit the tax burden they bear and attempt to shift taxes onto others. However, the economic sectors that create wealth are, in the long run, the only ones that can provide for the revenue needs of government.

The political economy of structural change in the Victorian economy is a history of changing interests that clashed over public policy and the role of government. A brief survey of reform legislation will help us understand more about structural change and its effect on private interest and society.

It would be fair to say that prior to the Industrial Revolution, British economics and politics was dominated by the interests of property. Landowners—men of property—occupied the top rungs of both the economic and political ladders.

From an economic point of view, land was the critical resource of an agricultural economy. Unlike workers, land was a fixed factor, immobile and pretty much irreplaceable. Property was the principal form of real wealth and the focal point of production and consumption.

Property's primacy was reflected in the structure of British politics and laws. Politics was the exclusive domain of landed interests in the eighteenth century. Parliament, for example, was composed of men who did not directly represent the people; members of Parliament (MPs) represented property and parliamentary districts that did not reflect the population distribution.

Government policy clearly acted in the interest of property in the years before 1830. The Speenhamland poor relief system (adopted in 1795) and the Corn Laws of 1815 are clear evidence of the power of property.

Poverty became an important social problem during the Napoleonic wars, as the continental system caused some unemployment in the exporting manufactured goods sector, and poor harvests generated an increase in grain prices and living costs. Many attempts were made to deal with this problem in the spirit of the Elizabethan poor laws. The Speenhamland system, which was widely adopted in the years following 1795, was a relief system that was particularly beneficial to landowners because it produced for them a large supply of cheap labor. The Speenhamland system was a program of wage subsidies designed to raise labor incomes to the level of subsistence. Without this wage subsidy program, landlords might have seen a significant labor movement to the cities, with the resulting increase in rural wage costs. Instead, Speenhamland tended to keep labor immobile and allowed landlords to continue to pay subsubsistence wages.

The Corn Laws of 1815 were not the first tariffs on agricultural imports. Parliament passed Corn Laws in 1791 and revised them many times both before 1815 and after. But the 1815 legislation shows the power of landed interests even after the structural changes of the industrial revolution were well under way. The Corn Laws regulated grain importation, keeping British prices artificially high at all times. Britain's agricultural sector was highly productive and experienced many good harvests, but population growth exceeded the increase in farm productivity, making imports of food a necessity. (In much the same way, the United States has a large and highly productive petroleum sector, but imports oil anyway because domestic demand exceeds domestic supply.) Artificially high grain prices benefited property owners at the expense of workers and manufacturers. Workers obviously had to bear higher living expenses due to the Corn Laws. Manufacturers saw their labor expenses rise and, because high grain costs absorbed much disposable income, they faced a smaller domestic market for their output.

Industrial capitalists were not impotent in the political economy of the early nineteenth century, but they were no match for the forces of the landed interests. Industry managed to obtain passage of the Combination Acts of 1799–1800, which banned labor unions. But on issues like the Corn Laws, which clearly set the interests of property against those of capital, the landlords always prevailed.

As the principle source of wealth, property was the logical source of government revenue and, in fact, property did bear much of the tax burden. Still, the landlords found ways to pass the burden of government onto others. Tariffs on imported goods, for example, had the double effect of protecting domestic interests and shifting the tax burden onto the working classes. Even taxes on property, however, were fashioned to burden property as little as possible.

The residential property tax was an important source of revenue in eighteenth-century Britain. But the tax was not levied on the value of residential property, in part because of the difficulty of assessing such a value accurately, in part because of the predictable corruption that was inherent in such an assessed tax, but also because the tax would have fallen heavily on property. Instead, to avoid corruption, the residential property tax was assessed according to the number of windows—a window tax. The rich had more windows than the poor and middle class (especially after a period is allowed for the poor to purchase boards and nails), but the tax was probably still regressive and fell harder on lower incomes relative to their income or wealth than on higher incomes.

These examples illustrate the fact that prior to the Industrial Revolution— and indeed until the 1830s—landed property held the critical position in British political economy. Property was the dominant economic force that shaped Parliament and influenced government policies.

As the nineteenth century wore on, the cumulative impact of structural change became noticeable. The landlords were still important, but their economic significance was shrinking relative to newly emerging groups. Industrial capitalists and city financiers were now gaining economic clout. The center of gravity of the creation of wealth was shifting from the rural estates to urban factory towns, out of the hands of the traditional elite and into the pockets of Catholics, Jews, and Dissenters from the Church of England. There is no stable equilibrium when political power resides in the hands of one group while economic power is shifting away.

Pressure for reform took many shapes: letters to the *Times*, bills in Parliament, and scholarly debate and intellectual essays. Very proper, very British. But it is a mistake to ignore the role that public violence and the threat of violence played in British reform. Victorian "society" may have been high-toned and genteel; but taking the center of gravity according to population density, it was poor, crude, and not uncommonly drunk. The rough neighborhoods of factory towns were never very safe; and hard times, crystallized by the increasing specialization of labor, were a recipe for public protest and violence.

The working classes did not achieve direct political representation during the Victorian era, so violence and the possibility of disruption were sometimes their only way to influence policy. Even after 1829 and the advent of Robert Peel's modern police force (the members of which were nicknamed "bobbies," after him), the threat of civil violence was never completely out of the minds of parliamentary leaders.

This is the context from which to view the reform legislation of the 1820s and 1830s. Over the course of a decade, Parliament passed a number of bills that brought the forces of law into line with the economic pattern that had been etched by fifty years of structural change. List making always means oversimplifying, but here is a list of important dates and actions in the reform period:

1824	repeal of Combination Acts
1829	Catholic Emancipation Act
1832	Parliamentary Reform Act
1833	Factory Act
1834	Poor Law Relief Act

The repeal of the Combination Acts in 1824 reflected the rising influence of the working classes and allowed for workers to organize, within limits. Of more immediate importance, however, was the Emancipation Act of 1829. Legislation dating from the reign of Henry VIII had attenuated the rights of Catholics and Dissenters. They could not hold office or participate in government without renouncing their religious beliefs. (Even professors at Cambridge were required to pronounce the Church of England's shibboleth.) Catholics and particularly Dissenters grew in numbers and economic importance, forcing Parliament repeatedly to suspend official discrimination for a year at a time. Compounded pressures (and the possibility of violence in Catholic Ireland) induced the government to propose the Emancipation Act in 1829, opening Britain more fully to economic and political entrepreneurs.

After the Emancipation Act it could be said (although not with complete accuracy) that Parliament represented property irrespective of the religious views of its owners. But this was only a small improvement when Manchester and Leeds, big important factory towns, completely lacked representation in Parliament. (Meanwhile some tiny towns, seats of propertied interests, had multiple members of Parliament.) The Reform Bill of 1832 corrected this imbalance. Parliament still represented property, not population, but property was now sifted with a coarser screen; so that industrial entrepreneurs, financiers, and some members of the middle class gained political voice.

The Reform Bill weakened the influence of the landed interests, but it did not strip them of their political power. The Reform Bill did, however, alter Parliament's balance of power, making further reform possible.

Sometimes the most important item on a list is the one not there, the missing element. This is the case with the reform acts previously listed. The key reform movement of the period failed to influence legislation directly. This was the Chartist movement. The Chartists sought adoption of a "People's Charter," or listing of specific reforms aimed at improving the political and economic lot of the working classes. This was an intensely popular movement, designed to appeal to the masses with the consequent threat of insurrection and mob violence. Their charter was never adopted by Parliament, and the movement died out in the 1840s; but it would be wrong to say that the Chartists did not influence the reform movement. The Factory Acts, which provided for the inspection of factory work conditions, and the Poor Law Relief Act may have owed their success in pat to the Chartists. (But the Factory Acts may also have been property's revenge on the industrialists.) Even the Corn Laws were eventually repealed.

Structural Change and Tax Reform

The role of taxes in the saga of Victorian structural change and fiscal crisis will be examined in the next chapter, but any discussion of the political economy of structural change is incomplete without at least a quick look at the important tax reforms of the 1840s, which so clearly reflect the political and economic forces of the period. We must, therefore, take the risk of getting ahead of ourselves a bit in order to examine the income tax of 1842 and the repeal of the Corn Laws, in 1846.

A constitutional statesman, according to Walter Bagehot, is "a man of common opinions and uncommon abilities."[19] If we accept Bagehot's definition, then Robert Peel, the central character in this story, was a constitutional statesman. Robert Peel clearly had uncommon abilities. Peel twice served as prime minister in the 1830s and 1840s and played a key part in reform legislation in the first half of the nineteenth century.

Whether Peel had "common opinions" is an open question because many of his actions were bold, but clearly his opinions were shaped by the "common" forces of the changing political economy of the time. As a member of Parliament, Peel knew his duty to represent the interests of property. As founder of London's police force, he knew the problems of mob violence and the social problems of the growing urban population. He knew from personal experience the structural changes taking place in Britain. Peel's grandfather had been a mill worker, and in the course of three generations the Peels rose to be mill owners, property owners, and influential legislators. It was impossible for Peel to ignore either the growing legions of urban workers or the increasing economic importance of the industrial capitalists.

While all of Peel's political biography is fascinating, we are most interested here in the tax reforms enacted by his second Conservative government, which was elected in September 1841 and dissolved in July 1846.

On assuming office in 1841, Peel found himself facing a fiscal crisis. The national debt was still very large, and debt servicing costs were still high; and he faced the prospect of a series of budget deficits that would make fiscal problems worse. At the same time, the long tariff list, a major source of revenue, was distorting trade patterns and imposing great burdens on urban workers and their industrial employers. According to the influential theories of Adam Smith and David Ricardo, unfree trade and a large national debt were both great evils that should be avoided. Peel's problem was to eliminate one evil (the tariffs) without falling deeper into the clutches of the other (public debt).

The pressure to eliminate tariffs was intense and came from two sides. On one hand, the domestic economy was suffering from the remnants of the panic of 1837 and continued depression. On the other hand, the tariff list was proving to be a disappointingly static revenue source. The government had attempted, but failed, to increase revenues from tariffs by raising rates in 1840. Adopting a "supply-side" approach in 1841, they tried to increase revenues by cutting the tariff rates. This experiment also failed. Tariffs appeared to be the ultimate inelastic tax source. Besides, many tariffs produced little revenue but still required complex and costly administration.

Influenced perhaps by common opinion, Peel sought a path out of this economic maze in the form of the Income Tax of 1842. Peel's budget of 1842 eliminated or reduced rates on over half the items on the tariff list (although not on the grains subject to the Corn Laws nor on items such as sugar and tea, which were taxed for their revenue-raising potential only). Duties on raw materials, manufacturers, and semifinished goods were all reduced. To replace this substantial revenue loss, Peel revived the income tax, which had last been collected in 1815.

Peel's famous budget speech of 1842 shows the pressures he was responding to:

> I propose that, for a time to be limited, the income of this country should be called upon to contribute a certain sum for the purpose of remedying this mighty and growing evil [the national debt] . . . for the purpose of not only supplying the deficiency in revenue, but of enabling me with confidence and satisfaction to propose great commercial reforms, which will afford a hope of reviving commerce and such an improvement in the manufacturing interests as will react on every other interest in the country; and, by diminishing the prices of articles of consumption, and the cost of living, will, in a pecuniary point of view, compensate you for your present sacrifices; whilst you will be relieved from the contemplation of a great public evil.[20]

To understand this bold stroke, we must understand how despised the income tax was. It was called "the most unpopular tax that was ever introduced in

England."[21] The income tax had been imposed during the Napoleonic wars and was only accepted then because it was clearly the last resort of a desperate nation. The income tax was barely tolerated before Waterloo because, without its sturdy revenue base, Britain's ability to finance the continental wars and its own defense would have been seriously undermined. The income tax had been quickly repealed, to popular approval, as soon as the Treaties of Vienna in 1815 brought war to an end. Perhaps only Peel, newly elected and with a strong working majority in Parliament, could have succeeded in reimposing the income tax. Even then, he proposed it as a temporary emergency tax, not as a permanent feature of British fiscal culture.

Peel's Income Tax Act was nearly a carbon copy of the income tax of 1806 (and set the pattern, in many important respects, for the current British income tax). With many tariffs reduced and the income tax enacted, Peel had accomplished a major redistribution of the tax burden. The working classes saw their tax burden fall, since they were hit hardest by the many tariffs and excises. Landowners and financiers, who were little affected by duties, saw their burden rise. Industrial entrepreneurs paid more tax than before; but free trade was in their best interests, so the promise of higher profits encouraged their support for the reforms.

Peel's free trade budget of 1842 was successful. Lower tariffs did in fact stimulate the economy and the income tax brought in even more revenues than had been anticipated. But the Corn Laws remained a problem. Grain prices were still very high, creating discontent and unrest among the working classes. Repeal of the Corn Laws was the logical action, especially given the great revenue-raising capacity of the income tax, but Corn Law reform meant a direct confrontation between the emergent interests of the industrial sector and the still-powerful interests of the landlords. Capital and industry versus property.

The Reform Act of 1832 had ended property's hegemony in Parliament. But such was their residual influence that even fourteen years later, Peel's Conservative government could not calmly contemplate an assault on property's sacred cow, the Corn Laws. It took a crisis among the lower classes to motivate the government. Nature supplied this crisis in the form of a potato crop failure in Ireland. Famine, food riots, and mob violence would have been the expected result if the Corn Laws had remained in effect.

With the income tax providing steadily rising revenues and the Irish famine threatening, Peel was in a position where he could do little but act to repeal the Corn Laws, whatever the political consequences. The political outcome was dramatic. The forces of property could not stop repeal of the Corn Laws, but they were potent enough to force Peel and his government to step down.

Adoption of the income tax and repeal of the Corn Laws illustrate the nature of political economy during a period of structural change. Structural change causes the distribution of income and wealth to shift, and eventually the political structure changed to reflect the new reality. Eventually, economic policies also adjusted to reflect the interests of the new power groups. The struggle over the Corn Laws shows us the potential flexibility of government institutions, how they can bend and change to accommodate structural change.

But this episode also shows how inflexible these institutions can be and how long it can take for government policies to reflect the facts of economic life fully.

The Failure of Victorian Britain

All the events and trends that we have observed in these pages fail to prepare us for the failure of the Victorian economy in the last quarter of the nineteenth century. The years from 1873 through 1914, which Crouzet divides into the Great Depression and a period of slow growth (the *belle époque*), saw Britain slide from the first rank of the industrial nations. Other countries—Germany, the United States, even Sweden—not only caught up with Britain, which might have been expected, but accelerated past her, an unexpected event. Maddison chooses 1890 (about the start of Crouzet's *belle époque*) as the key year when Britain surrendered leadership to the United States, but this date is of course arbitrary. The bright promise of the great exhibition of 1851 was not to be fulfilled.

Among economists and economic historians there is almost complete agreement that Victorian Britain failed.[22] There is considerable disagreement, however, as to the causes of the failure or whether there was anything that the British could have done to prevent it.

Britain's "failure" can be viewed from two perspectives, a macro view looking at the British economy overall relative to its industrial competitors and a micro view focusing on British experience in some of the key industries. Tables 4.1–4.3 present data that illustrate the macro events.

Table 4.1 compares the pace of British economic growth with similar growth rates in other countries. Tables 4.2 and 4.3 show the cumulative result of these growth differentials on industrial production and income.

Britain had never achieved the high growth rates that are expected of industrial economies in the twentieth century, but table 4.1 shows that in the last quarter of the nineteenth century, other nations did. The average growth rate of Britain's GNP during the period 1870–1913 was 2.2 percent, a good perfor-

Table 4.1. Annual Average Rates of Economic Growth in Selected Countries, 1870–1913 (%)

Nation	Real GNP	Real GNP per Head	Real GNP per Labor Hour
United Kingdom	2.2	1.3	1.5
Germany	2.9	1.8	2.1
France	1.6	1.4	1.8
Sweden	3.0	2.3	2.7
United States	4.3	2.2	2.4
Average of 10 European countries	2.4	1.4	1.8

Source: Francois Crouzet, *The Victorian Economy* (New York: Columbia University Press, 1982), p. 377, table 66.

Table 4.2. Shares of Total World Industrial Production (%)

Nation	1870	1913
United Kingdom	31.8	14.0
Germany	13.2	15.7
France	10.3	6.4
United States	23.3	35.8

Source: Francois Crouzet, *The Victorian Economy* (New York: Columbia University Press, 1982), p. 378, table 67.

mance by British standards. Yet this rate of overall economic growth fell below the European average and was much lower than the growth rates attained in Germany, Sweden, and especially the United States.

As a result of slower overall growth rates, the British standard of living (as measured by real GNP per head) also grew at a slower rate than other industrial nations. The third column of table 4.1 shows that the increase in productivity in Britain was very low, only an average of 1.5 percent per year; while Swedish productivity increased almost twice as fast. The industrial world was experiencing a "second industrial revolution," as we will soon discuss, and Britain failed to adapt to the changing world.

Growth rates can be deceptive because differences that appear to be very small (and are small for a given year) are, in fact, very important and create large differentials over time. Table 4.2, for example, shows how small differences in growth rates, compounded over a generation, create a startlingly different world. In 1870 Britain was clearly the dominant industrial nation, producing almost one-third of the world's total industrial output. Germany and the United States together roughly accounted for another third, with all other nations combined producing the final one-third of industrial items. By 1913, however, the United States had assumed Britain's place in the first rank. Britain had slipped behind Germany in terms of total share of industrial production.

Britain's "failure" is not proven by its slipping industrial market share. We would expect Britain's share of output to decline as other nations caught up with Britain's early lead. What is important is that Britain's slower growth

Table 4.3. Estimates of Per Captia Income Levels
Measured in Constant 1970 U.S. Dollars

Nation	1870	1890	1910
Great Britain	904	1,130	1,302
Belgium	738	932	1,110
Denmark	563	708	1,050
Germany	579	729	958
France	567	668	883
Sweden	351	469	763

Source: N. F. R. Crafts, *British Economic Growth during the Industrial Revolution* (New York: Oxford University Press, 1985), p. 54, table 3.2.

caused it to be surpassed in industrial production, losing the early lead legacy of the Industrial Revolution.

Germany, Sweden, and the United States overtook British industry; they were soon enjoying living standards near the London level, as table 4.3 shows; and were by 1910 fast approaching the point where the trend lines cross and Britain was overtaken by this measure as well. Two world wars and a Great Depression would bend and distort the growth lines; but by 1950 and still more by 1960, the event would be history. The slow growth rates experienced by Britain persisted and compounded mercilessly over long decades to bring the final result.

While Britain as a whole was being overtaken by other industrial economies, this was not true in every sector of the economy. Britain retained its lead, for example, in the service sector in general and in the areas of banking, insurance, and transport in particular.[23] Indeed, in finance and shipbuilding Britain was the world leader. These success stories are service industries that are more closely linked with commerce and international trade than with manufacturing itself.

In fact, what was happening was that Britain was beginning to take its place within a developing world economy. Britain had been decidedly outward-looking throughout the nineteenth century; it was perhaps even the so-called workshop of the world in the early years of the century. As the rest of the world changed, however, Britain's place within it was beginning to change. Industry was giving way to finance, commerce, and shipping as Britain's international comparative advantage. Although industry had been, and would continue to be, important, the emphasis had shifted.

This change took place not because Britain gained new advantages in finance or commerce but rather because she lost her comparative advantage in industry to other countries. Another wave of innovation swept the industrial world in the 1880s and 1890s. New methods were found to produce old products, and new industries were developed along fresh lines. These were, first, the new electrical and chemical industries and, later, automobiles. There is abundant evidence that Britain had the physical resources necessary to update technology and to enter new industries.[24] The evidence is, however, that the opportunity was missed. The terms that seem best to describe British industry during this period are "rigid" and "stagnant."

The second industrial revolution, which Britain largely missed, differed from the first in important ways. The first industrial revolution was a long, slow process, driven by an expanding population, growing infrastructure, and broad-based innovation. The innovations were incremental changes in existing technology, often initiated by workers and craftsmen on the shop floor using only a little capital and alot of ingenuity. Compared to a full-scale research and development program, these early innovations could be considered amateurish tinkering. But they existed, and they worked — which was the important thing in a world where change and growth were unexpected and unlikely events.

.   The innovations of the second industrial revolution were fundamentally different. New products and processes did not happen just by chance (although it would be unwise to understate the influence of chance and luck), they were the product of scientists and engineers working in their laboratories. Knowledge of science and applied science acquired through years of study replaced intuition and ingenuity learned through practical experience as the critical resources of growth and change.

Britain's pattern of trade reflected the fact that its industry remained static in a very dynamic world. In 1913 Britain's comparative advantage was found in the industries of rail and ship transport, textiles, iron and steel, and spirits and tobacco — mature industries built on hundred-year-old technology (and often built in hundred-year-old factories). The comparative advantage of Germany and the United States, on the other hand, were in the quickly growing fields of chemicals, electricals, industrial equipment, and automobiles.[25]

It should not be thought that Britain was untouched by the scientific revolution of the late nineteenth century. It is clear that individual entrepreneurs in Britain experimented with the techniques, processes, and products that were also being developed in Germany and the United States. But these industries did not catch fire in Britain the way they did elsewhere and did not develop sufficiently to have an aggregate impact on the British economy.[26] Thus, Britain's overall comparative advantage remained in the old industries (textiles) and the new services (finance, shipping), but not the new-emerging industries.[27]

British goods had no clear market advantage in the industrialized economies, so Britain shifted its trade towards the middle range of countries: not Sweden, Germany, and the United States, but Spain, Italy, and Latin America. Hobsbawn characterizes the late-Victorian pattern, perhaps too strongly, as follows:

> The British economy as a whole tended to retreat from industry into trade and finance, where our services reinforced our actual and future competitors, but made very satisfactory profits. . . .
>
> Britain, we may say, was becoming a parasitic rather than a competitive economy, living off the remains of world monopoly, the underdeveloped world, her past accumulations of wealth, and the advance of her rivals. That, at all events, was the view of intelligent observers, only too keenly aware of the country's relative loss of momentum and decline, even though their analysis was often defective.[28]

Any effort to catalog all the theories that attempt to account for Victorian Britain's decline is necessarily doomed to failure. Too many people have suggested too many theories for us to deal with them all.[29] A few ideas seem to stand out and warrant a more-than-cursory examination in the light of our new economic data for this period.

We can usefully divide these theories into two lists made up of (1) "general theories," which attempt to explain the universal phenomenon of economic decline (and use Britain as a specific example of a general law), and (2) "special theories," which attempt to explain the decline of Victorian Britain alone. In the group of general theories we can place the interpretations of British economics in terms of the work of Joseph Schumpeter and Mancur Olson. In the group of more narrow "special" explanations, we can include theories that deal with overcommitment, imperfections in the capital markets, the British educational system, and assorted "cultural factors" that account for Britain's failure to participate in the second industrial revolution.

A Schumpeterian interpretation of Britain's decline can be constructed based on his famous notion of long technological cycles in growth (and the process of "creative destruction" that goes along with technological change). Schumpeter conceived of growth as being driven by technological change (only partially true in Britain's case). Growth is fast initially, as the pace of technological improvement is rapid, then slows down as businesses experience diminishing marginal returns to innovations that are essentially variations on an earlier theme.

Slow growth replaces fast growth and the economy eventually stagnates until a rash of new products and processes appears. This happens eventually, but not until the safe profit on marginal improvements in existing technology falls low enough to warrant the higher risk inherent in research and development on new and untried products and processes. The cycle of innovation and growth then begins to repeat itself. At the end of each long cycle, new technology overtakes older processes, the creative destruction of old factories makes way for new ones.[30]

The Schumpeterian theory of technological cycles fits many aspects of our story, particularly the progress of the second industrial revolution following the first. What it does not explain, however, is why "creative destruction" did not happen in Victorian Britain. Britain appears to have remained with the mechanical innovations of the first industrial revolution (and the slow growth inherent in mature technology) while Germany, Sweden, the United States, and other countries took up the chemical and electrical innovations of the technological revolution of the 1890s.

Thus, while a Schumpeterian interpretation explains why Britain's growth was slow and why the growth of the newly innovating economies was so much faster, it is by itself an incomplete theory of Victorian failure. Schumpeter's model may prove useful, however, when we supplement it with specific reasons, cultural or otherwise, for the peculiar behavior of British entrepreneurs.

Mancur Olson developed a more complete general theory of the phenomenon we are concerned with in a book called, appropriately, *The Rise and Decline of Nations*. Olson's theory is based on the existence and growth of "structural rigidities" — social and economic institutions that become increasingly inflexible over time. At the heart of Olson's analysis is the conflict between the general interest, which benefits from change, and special interests, which are potentially threatened by any alteration in the status quo. Here is a simplified version of Olson's model of rise and decline, with specific examples from our present discussion inserted in parentheses.[31]

Over a period of time, the most cohesive and concentrated special interests (propertied landlords, members of the Church of England) tend to organize to increase their share of society's resources. Because these special interests represent but a small fraction of the total population, they can be the gainers even if society loses overall, so long as the policies and institutions that are adopted

(Corn Laws) provide specific benefits to them that exceed their share of the social loss. (Landlord's increased profits from the Corn Laws easily exceeded the loss they themselves suffered due to the impact of higher grain prices on their cost of living.)

Left alone, an economy will tend to accumulate more and more special interest groups, which will become progressively more and more rigid as they seek to preserve their share of the social pie. Eventually, then, the economy becomes very inflexible and unable to deal with change, technological or otherwise.

It takes a really large and unusual event to break up the accumulated rigidities in an economy, but such events do happen (Napoleon and the drastic necessities of the Napoleonic wars). With interest groups at least temporarily broken up, the economy is much more flexible and able to undertake fundamental change (the social reforms of the 1830s and 1840s). Change is widespread (the pattern of industrial innovations in Britain in the early nineteenth century), and the whole economy grows.

Eventually, however, new special interests slowly begin to accumulate, introducing new rigidities that slow the pace of innovation and growth. A "distributive" economy results, where the payoff to special interest efforts to gain a larger share of the existing pie exceeds the potential profit from innovation to increase the pie's total size.

It does not require much effort to turn the last paragraph into a serviceable account of the failure of Victorian Britain. For Britain, the years after 1815 — and especially after 1850 — were marked by little in the way of dramatic events that would weaken the hold of existing special interests. There were wars, but they were smaller than the Napoleonic campaigns, were thousands of miles away, and therefore did not shake up the pattern of British interests in any significant way. (Indeed, they may have increased the hold of these interests on the economy.)

Germany, Sweden, and the United States also had strong interest groups; but each of these countries experienced a major national event in the second half of the nineteenth century. The United States Civil War, for example, shattered the prior pattern of interest group development, especially in the South, but everywhere else, too. When peace was restored, the people and goods were more mobile and the U.S. economy was more flexible and able to adapt to change. Innovation and faster growth in the United States was duplicated in other nations; and these nations began to gain on Britain, the world's stable but sluggish economic leader.

Olson's analysis is more robust than the Schumpeterian model in accounting for the events of Victorian economic history. But to make Olson's theory stick, we must come up with his structural rigidities — the institutions that would have prevented change in Britain.[32]

It is easy to pick out events and institutions for the years before 1850 that could correspond to Olson's picture. War, technological innovation, and, perhaps most importantly, the social strains caused by the rapid growth in population account for the breakup of property's rigid institutions. The Reform Act and repeal of the Corn Laws have obvious interpretations in this light.

We are left with the question, What were the structural rigidities that prevented innovation and slowed growth in the years after 1850? The answer to this question brings us to the list of "special theories" of Victorian Britain's failure, which we can view either as stand-alone explanations of Victorian trends or, perhaps more usefully, as examples of the structural rigidities that fit Mancur Olson's model of economic decline.

The special theories that have been developed to explain Britain's relative decline cover a wide range of characteristics that are peculiar to British industry and society in the nineteenth century. The "overcommitment" thesis, for example, takes the once-popular view that Britain was cursed in the long run by its "early start."[33]

Overcommitment is the notion that the slow growth late in the nineteenth century resulted from Britain's inexperience in dealing with structural change. After a very long period of economic and social stability, Britain experienced rapid structural change and reacted to it as if it were a unique event, not an ongoing process. Resources moved to new places in the economy, then took root again, counting on a return to the old stability in a new status quo. The roots went too deep — overcommitment — and Britain was unable to branch out as the process of structural change continued into the 1890s and later.

One problem with the overcommitment hypothesis is that it fails to provide a firm reason for the Britain's increased rigidity as the nineteenth century progressed. This difficulty can be overcome if we divide the sources of growth and change into two segments: growth from increased population and growth from other factors (improved technology). Britain seems to have been very successful in coping with change due to population growth. Workers were mobile and flexible, and there was no major change in this pattern over time. British industry, on the other hand, seems not to have been very flexible regarding major technological change at any time in the nineteenth century. Marginal improvements in products and processes were rapidly adopted, to be sure; but major changes, which would require large capital investments, were uncommon at any time in the nineteenth century (with the exception of canals and railways).

A working hypothesis is, then, that Britain was always overcommitted (not the best term in this context, but an adequate one) to existing technology and capital and never overcommitted on the labor side. British growth slowed as the driving force of structural change and economic growth changed from population increases earlier in the nineteenth century to the scientific applications at the end of the Victorian era.

Both of these overcommitment hypotheses have much in common with Olson's model of structural rigidities. They differ, however, in that they do not view the economy's rigidities necessarily to be the result of interest group action. Other sources of rigidity must be found. This search for sources of inflexibility leads us to special theories of slow growth based on problems in Britain's capital markets, its educational system, and its overall culture.

Some scholars hold that Britain's financial system denied industry the resources that it needed to modernize. The evidence for this is that not much capital flowed through the City of London to innovating and modernizing firms. The funds that did flow through the City tended to go to fund the government debt and to finance the construction of canals and railways in foreign countries. British capital exports, guided by the City's distorted markets, starved British industry of the funds it needed to participate in the second industrial revolution.

There is a good deal of circumstantial evidence assembled against this hypothesis. Britain had enough capital available to fund both its domestic industries and foreign investments at the same time. A careful search of the City fails to find any formal barrier to industrial finance; indeed British innovations in industrial finance are cited by some, such as Rosenberg and Birdzell, as reasons for Britain's early lead in manufacturing. Finally, economic historians find that funds seem to have gone where the return was highest, just as theory predicts if markets are efficient.

The evidence arrayed against the special theory of imperfect capital markets is substantial, but it is premature to render a verdict on this matter. Let us wait until we have explored the role of British public debt in the next chapter before dismissing this notion completely.

Another special theory is that the British educational system was rigid and did not adapt to the increased need for scientists and engineers. (Indeed, many argue that Britain still underallocates resources to science education.) Britain therefore underinvested in human capital in general and in scientific human capital in particular.

Britain's educational system is peculiar and was firmly established at a relatively late date. (Mandatory schooling became effective in the 1880s and 1890s, although irregular patterns of school attendance were common long before.) The three Rs of elementary education were widely available; but the three Rs were all that most people needed, since most industrial jobs at mid-century could still be performed by illiterates.

Education after elementary school followed one of two paths: to the workpace and whatever on-the-job training was available, or to the university, with formal classes. Neither of these routes was likely to lead to an understanding of applied science.

Technical training at the workplace concentrated on existing technology. A bright worker, tutored by a foreman or entrepreneur, would gain a working knowledge of technical processes and perhaps an intuitive feel for the science involved. But there would be little exposure to abstract notions. Innovations would never start with a clean slate but always involve incremental improvements of existing technology. Technical training, such as it was, therefore encouraged the kind of industrial development that, according to Schumpeter, leads to slow growth.

Higher education in Britain did not compensate for the weakness in technical education. British colleges based their curricula on the successful models provided by Oxford and Cambridge. They were small (with limited total enrollments) and traditional. The educational elite therefore studied theology, philosophy, the classics, John Stuart Mill's political economy, and some history. (If you were lucky enough to attend Toynbee's famous lectures, you even learned about the Industrial Revolution.) Students did not learn science, however.

Britain's educational system kept science out of the hands of entrepreneurs and workmen. Germany's schools, on the other hand, gave scientific knowledge to those who could best use it. Crouzet concludes,

> A society has the educational and scientific system which it desires, and the contrast which has just been underlined was the result of differences in demand, which arose out of Great Britain's early start in industrialization and the efforts of Germany to catch up. In England, the Industrial Revolution occurred spontaneously at a time when there was no true educational system. . . . Innovations were then the work of practical men or else of amateurs. From this sprang a powerful tradition of indifferences or even hostility to education, and to technical or scientific education in particular. . . . So even when industry became more and more science-based, the man who had been trained on the job continued to be preferred to the one who had received a theoretical education.[34]

This brings us to the matter of British culture and the special theory that cultural factors contributed to the Victorian decline.[35] The problem with British culture might be best described as the dilemma of traditional values in an upwardly mobile world. On one hand, Britain benefited from individuals' ability to move up in its economic and social ranks. Workmen could hope to become foremen, foremen could aspire to be shop owners. Shop owners might own factories. Entrepreneurs and managers could reasonably hope to gain property and mix with men of old wealth. Money could even lead to nobility.

The existence of realistic upward mobility was an important positive incentive for British workers and entrepreneurs, while class lines in France made hard work and risk taking less desirable. This social flexibility was a boon to the early development of the British economy.[36]

While mobility among social and economic classes was relatively free, the attitudes within each class were relatively fixed. The proper behavior of men of property, for example, was well defined by centuries of practice. As entrepreneurs advanced to high social rank, the nouveau riche sought acceptance by assimilating the attitudes of old wealth and property. These attitudes were distinctly different from the risk-taking behaviors that had created entrepreneurial wealth in the first place. Britain's willingness to innovate was bred out of its entrepreneurs as they ascended the class scale. Factory owners were the sons of innovative workmen; their sons became lawyers.

Traditional values within each economic or social class became a shibboleth that retarded the progress of scientific industrial change. Entrepreneurs sought acceptance by acquiring the horsey tastes of estate owners.[37] At the same time, however, they imposed on the upwardly mobile classes below them their own set of values—the fear of science and education (which they did not themselves have) and the value of practical experience (their route to the top).

These traditional values froze British industrial culture in time. If each class undertook its practices and attitudes in its own narrow self-interest, then these are Olson-type structural rigidities.

Looking back over this account of Britain's rise and decline, the thing most notable to the modern reader is what is *not* found — the role of government. No contemporary discussion of economic problems would be complete without some significant reference to government as either the cause or the potential solution to whatever dilemma is posed. But no important theory of government's systematic influence on British economic growth exists. In particular, public debt and taxation (except tariffs and the wartime income tax) play no really major role in this story. Government sometimes reacts, but it does not take positive action.

The reason government's economic role is all but ignored is easy to guess. The nineteenth century was, for the most part, the era of laissez-faire. Government's economic role had been defined by Adam Smith and his invisible hand of self-interest. Smith's philosophy was influential, and government did not seek opportunities to participate actively in economic events.

If the conventional wisdom calls for minimum government interference, if government officials themselves espouse this philosophy, and if legislative actions do not display the activist fiscal politics that we accept as part of the post-Keynesian world, it is easy to believe that government had negligible direct impact on the British economy. No theory is necessary to explain the cause and effect when no cause is suspected.

Yet modern economists realize that government policies can have many indirect and unintentional impacts of people, firms, and the overall economy. Indirect causes can have indirect effects. In particular, the patterns of government borrowing and taxation can have a relatively large cumulative effect on the economy over a period as long as a century.

Therefore we can ask the questions, How did British taxation and public debt affect structural change in Victorian Britain? How did these policies contribute to the industrial rise and eventual decline of the British economy?

5

The Odious Tax
and the Standing Miracle

In damp subterranean caverns, drops of water, each containing a minute trace of minerals, fall from the stone ceiling and hit the stone floor. In the short run, all we have are drops. In the long run, however, the trace minerals can accumulate and gradually reach down from the ceiling (stalactites) and up from the floor (stalagmites), forming sturdy stone pillars. When we think about the forces of nature, we generally think first about explosive volcanoes or fierce storms; but nature also works slowly, one drop at a time.

There is a lesson here for students of government finance and public policy. When we think of the forces of government (and how government can influence the private economy), we usually think first of the overt and intended policies that seek to bring about some visible change in the way the world works. So we look at regulations, tax incentives, subsidies, and expenditure programs when we seek to see the hand of government at work. But government influence can also be subtle and delicate, nearly invisible for the moment but capable of mighty effect, whether intended or not, as the years accumulate and compound drop after drop.

Victorian Britain was the avowed embodiment of "laissez-faire" economics. Government in nineteenth-century Britain followed the teachings of Adam Smith and sought to minimize its interference in the work of the invisible hand of the marketplace. British government intended to have little influence on the day-to-day actions of its private economy. It is my thesis, however, that the British system of public finance contributed to the ultimate decline of Victorian Britain in the sort of indirect, unintended way just suggested. British public finance was certainly not the cause of the economic stagnation of the late nineteenth century, but I will argue that the patterns established by government finance logically contributed to this economic stagnation in a significant way.

An important factor in the decline of Victorian Britain was its persistent inability to invest in new processes and new products, especially in the last quarter of the nineteenth century, despite high potential profits from such investments and an adequate supply of resources to invest. British public finance contributed to this problem in two ways, through its system of public debt and through its system of taxation. Both debt and taxes exerted subtle unintended influences on the pattern of investment in Britain, with eventual dramatic impact.

The tax side of the story is relatively straightforward to anyone familiar with modern tax policy. Parliament in the 1840s faced a fiscal crisis; several years of growing peacetime deficits, combined with the need to cut import duties, forced Robert Peel's government to propose an income tax to generate revenue. Adopted as a temporary measure, Peel's income tax became a permanent feature of British public finance.

The income tax was flawed in many ways, but perhaps its most important imperfection was its failure to account for the cost of new investment correctly. As we will see later, repair of existing equipment and processes enjoyed a substantial tax advantage over investment in new capital. This bias against new investment was not intended but grew out of the imperfect understanding of the concepts of income and capital that prevailed at the time. The British tax system thus accidentally discriminated against the types of investments that would have allowed Britain to modernize its industry and compete more effectively with Germany and the United States.

The effect of Britain's public debt on its economic growth experience is more complex. Britain's financial system was amazingly modern and sophisticated, but its growth and development was shaped by public sector debt more than by any other factor. Government debt established deep channels through which finance flowed smoothly. The pattern of public finance subtly shaped the pattern of private finance, too. This resulted in an unintended bias in the British financial system that contributed to Victorian Britain's decline.

Like people everywhere, the Victorians looked for success where they had found it before. This tendency, combined with the particular pattern of British taxation and public debt, conspired to deny resources to the sectors that needed them in the last part of the nineteenth century.

Life Before the Income Tax

Taxation in Britain in the period before the Napoleonic Wars is hard for modern observers to take seriously. The economic role of government was relatively limited in this period; so its tax needs were small, especially since public debt was an easy alternative to taxation in case of emergency. Most nondefense government functions arise when the population becomes urbanized, and Britain was still relatively rural. Many modern government functions were performed through the forces of tradition and the social customs of the manor.

Peacetime government had modest cost, so Parliament could finance its activities through a variety of customs and excise taxes. Some bizarre excises were imposed, including taxes on female servants, pleasure houses, race horses, hair powder, dogs, clocks, and armorial bearings.[1] Often these taxes were meant to accomplish a social goal as well as generate revenue. A land tax existed and provided the government with a stable revenue base. But because Parliament represented property's interests, it proved politically impossible to increase land tax revenues when need arose.[2]

New taxes were imposed to pay for the war in America, including a tax on inhabited houses and a variety of related excises that together were called the "assessed taxes." William Pitt (the Younger) established a centralized administration for these assessed taxes in the office of the Commissioners of the Affairs of Taxes, which was responsible for uniform assessment of household tax burdens. But still the biggest burden fell on consumption, not on wealth or property, inspiring Samuel Johnson to define *excise* as "a hateful tax levied upon commodities." Seligman provides this accounting of British revenues:

> In 1792, just before the outbreak of the French war, out of a total tax revenue of about seventeen and a quarter millions sterling, the land tax yielded only two millions and houses and establishments only one and one-quarter millions. Almost the entire remainder came from customs and excises. Taxes on articles of food and drink were responsible for nine millions. Taxes on manufactured articles—primarily soap, candles, leather, printed goods, glass, and drugs—yielded about one million. . . . Direct taxes played a very slight role.[3]

Taxation became a more serious business when Napoleon's armies forced Britain to raise large armies and larger sums in her own defense. The long war with France (1793–1815) forms the critical period in the development of both the tax and debt aspects of British public finance.

Prime Minister Pitt found Britain's tax system inadequate to the demands of the wartime budget. Although public debt would turn out to be an important factor in wartime finance, government bonds at first appeared an unlikely alternative to tax revenues. British *consols* (bonds, from *consolidated annuities*) fell in price each time Napoleon's armies advanced on the continent. There seemed to be no alternative but to increase taxes.

Pitt's budget speech of 1797 presented a radical proposal, the so-called triple assessment, which Pitt termed "a general tax on persons possessed of property commensurate as far as practical with their means."[4] The triple assessment was a tax on consumed "property" (as listed in the books of the assessed taxes) a progressive tax aimed at forcing men of property to help pay for its defense. (Pitt noted that "Assessed Taxes are often eluded by men of large property" but that additional revenues would be "forthcoming at the solicitation of self-interest and self-defense.")[5] Probably only Napoleon's long shadow made Parliament reluctantly agree to Pitt's plan.

The basic idea of the "triple assessment" (or the Aid and Contribution Act of 1798, as it was officially known) was to increase tax collections through a progressive surcharge on the assessed taxes. This was accomplished, first, by dividing taxpayers into three classes according to the types of property owned. The first group included wealthy people, as evidenced by their ownership of carriages, man servants, and so on. The middle group lacked carriages but owned luxury items such as watches and had houses with windows (a window tax was included among the various assessed taxes). Finally, a third group was provided for the poorest taxpayers.[6]

The triple assessment was an attempt to spread the burdens of war according to ability to pay. Although imperfect in this regard, the assessed taxes approximately achieved Pitt's goal of taxing discretionary income. One writer noted that "expenditure is taken as the criterion of ability, and, considering how few there are in this age of luxury who do not spend as much as they can afford, it must be allowed to be the best criterion that could be discovered."[7]

The 1798 law provided for voluntary contributions in addition to mandatory payment of the tax (on the logic that some wealthy people, having little of the particular types of properties subject to the assessed taxes, would wish to contribute more than their legal minimum to the kingdom's defense).

Perhaps the most important issue regarding the triple assessment involved the difference between income and capital, an issue that will reappear in various forms later in this narrative. The triple assessment attempted to tax income by taxing a list of expenditure items that had conveniently been assembled under the assessed taxes. Income, however, was a fairly abstract notion to men of the eighteenth century. Income, a flow, was not so concrete as capital (or property), the accepted source of income.

In a world where property and capital were the tangible measures of ability to pay, even a perfect tax on income would be misconstrued to be an inferior attempt to tax capital. If income from trade and income from property are taxed equally, for example, this implies a differential tax on "temporary," working capital versus "permanent," fixed capital. The "differentiation" problem was made worse, of course, because the triple assessment did not perfectly tax income and because of its differential treatment of the three classes of taxpayers (which suggested to some differential treatment of three types of capital).

There were plenty of flaws in the triple assessment, but its biggest problem was that it was relatively easy to evade. Pitt was appalled by the "shameful evasion" and "scandalous frauds" that his big tax hike produced. Pitt had projected total revenues of £6 million (£4.5 million from the tax and £1.5 million through voluntary contributions). Actual collections totaled just £4 million—only £2 million from the tax itself but an amazing £2 million more in voluntary contributions! People were willing to contribute toward the defense of the kingdom, as the unexpectedly large contributions showed; but they were afraid to establish a record of high tax payments, perhaps for fear that the "triple assessment" would be tripled again and again as the war progressed until a truly crushing tax burden resulted.

The triple assessment is best seen as an unsuccessful compromise between a consumption tax and an income tax. As a source of revenue for war, it was not successful; but it did pave the way for the more comprehensive tax reforms that followed.

An "Odious" Tax

Pitt was convinced that a broad-based tax, like the triple assessment, was required to finance Britain's war effort. The problem with the triple assessment was not, as his critics alleged, that he had gone *too* far towards taxing income but that he had not gone far enough. By taxing income only indirectly, through selected expenditures, Pitt had made it too easy to avoid the tax (by not purchasing assessed items or by concealing their purchase). Pitt's proposals of 1798 (like most of the other income tax reforms of the war years) were aimed first at tightening enforcement and administration to increase tax revenue and only then at achieving equity and efficiency. The result was "the tax that beat Napoleon."[8]

Pitt's proposal was for a wartime tax on all income from whatever source derived, including both labor and capital income and income from government bonds. Pitt's tax was opposed primarily on three grounds: (1) that its enforcement would require "inquisitorial procedure," (2) that by taxing all income equally it unfairly failed to take into account the different sources (types of capital) that produced the income, and (3) that the existing system of indirect taxes was a better choice than this direct tax. Of these objections, perhaps the strongest involved Pitt's scheme for equal taxation of what many people viewed as unequal sources of income. It was inequitable, Pitt's critics said, to treat as equals "a widow who lived only on a pension with . . . a person whose capital brings him the same income by way of interest" or "a man who had £1,000 a year arising from capital and the man who gained the same annual sum by a profession or business."[9]

It is clear from the debates that Pitt was a skilled orator and no mean political economist. He understood the principles of his tax scheme and argued persuasively in its favor. To counter the criticism that it was unfair to tax all sources of income equally, for example, he argued, "What does the new tax do? Are they not left in relation to each other precisely as they were before? The tax creates no new inequality. The justice [and] injustice remain precisely as they were. To complain of this inequality is to complain of the distribution of property; it is to complain of the constitution of society. . . . To think of taxing these two species of incomes in a different ratio, would be to attempt what the nature of society will not admit."[10]

Pitt also argued that the burden of collecting such large revenues from indirect taxes such as the excises would be grossly inefficient, perhaps even impossible. And only dishonest men would oppose strict enforcement of the tax laws. These arguments carried the day and the act of 1799 cleared Parliament. The income tax was unpopular; but it was clearly billed as a war tax and Admiral Nelson's recent successes in the Mediterranean might well have encouraged many people to think that however onerous it might be, the period of income taxation would be brief.

The income tax remained in place until 1802, when the Amiens Treaty ended the French wars (or, more accurately, interrupted them). Lord Addington, Pitt's successor as prime minister, declared the income tax to have been wisely conceived for wartime emergency but too heavy a burden to be borne in peace. The tax was repealed, and its records destroyed.

While the income tax did contribute to the needs of Britain's wartime treasury, it proved to be less than a fiscal cornucopia. The new tax had yielded about £6 million in each of the three years it was collected, or about 50 percent more than generated by the triple assessment with the voluntary contributions.

This £6 million yield was much less than Pitt had expected; his estimate of £100 million of income taxed at 10 percent led him to anticipate revenues of £10 million.

The income tax failed to live up to its revenue estimates because it proved too easy to escape the tax by squeezing through the loopholes. The child allowances had caused a suspicious burst of "official" population growth; taxpayers suddenly found themselves with many more children (all age six or more to gain the maximum tax advantage). The British had all suddenly fallen deeply into debt, judging by the great deductions for interest paid. This condition was suspect, given that interest payments deducted so greatly surpassed interest income declared. Although my sources do not mention it, it is probably safe to assume that life insurance premiums — also tax deductible — experienced an "official" rise that would have astounded the companies that supposedly received them.

The problem with Pitt's income tax, as with his triple assessment, was enforcement. There were too many returns to audit and, in any case, the newly appointed general commissioners lacked procedures and authority to undertake detailed audits of private records even if they had had the time and inclination to do so. Pitt had wanted to tax all income equally, but his machinery of tax administration made this goal impossible.

The faults of Pitt's income tax gained renewed importance in 1803, when war with France flared again, and Lord Addington was forced to call for another income tax to replenish the Treasury's coffers. Predictably, the "tax on property and productive industry," as the 1803 income tax was called, was designed to eliminate loopholes and strengthen administrative enforcement. In the place of a general declaration of income, the new law provided for detailed accounting according to an outline or system that still defines British income taxation.

The most important change in the 1803 income tax was adoption of the administrative principle of "stoppage at the source" of income as a means of limiting tax evasion. Employers were responsible for paying the tax on their workers' wages. Tenants paid the tax on their landlords' rents. And so forth.

Under this rule, income is taxed as close as possible to its source, leaving to markets and private contracts the task of shifting the tax burden where it belonged. Under the old income tax, for example, interest on debt was deductible and interest income was taxed, creating two opportunities for tax fraud. Taxpayers overstated their interest expenses and understated their interest earnings. Under the 1803 income tax, however, no allowance was made for interest expenses in calculating taxable profits. It was assumed that the borrower would pass some of this tax burden back onto the lender in the form of reduced interest payments. Thus, the net effects would be the same for interest payee and payer, but with less tax evasion overall.

"Stoppage at the source" was not the only tax reform included in the 1803 law. Rather than a single tax falling equally on all income, the 1803 law provided for a series of taxes that fell unevenly on different sources of income, which were to be explicitly enumerated under five schedules. Schedule A taxed income from landed property. Schedule B's target was the profit from tenant farming.

Schedule C taxed profits, annuities, and income arising from public investments, such as stock in the national debt. Schedule D was a catchall, put in place to trap income not taxed elsewhere in the law. Finally, schedule E taxed income from "public" offices, defined so as to include what we would normally think of as private activities, such as businesses and corporations.[11]

While tax exemptions were still provided for those with low incomes, other deductions and abatements, such as the child allowance, were eliminated.[12] The ranks of the enforcement officers—the general commissioners—were supplemented by new "additional commissioners," and tax enforcement was tightened up generally.

A basic tax rate of 5 percent (one shilling per pound) was applied against taxable income under the 1803 law. So successful was the law in "stopping at the source" tax on income that would otherwise sneak away through loopholes that the yield of the 1803 tax at a 5-percent rate was nearly equal to the revenues of Pitt's 1799 tax at 10 percent. The rate was increased to 6.25 percent in 1805. Revisions adopted in 1806 substantially strengthened the income tax and increased its rate back to the 10-percent level of Pitt's tax. The result was an increase in revenue to over £12 million in 1806, rising to almost £16 million, an enormous sum, at the end of the Napoleonic Wars.

It is important to understand that this income tax, which was conceived in an emergency and invented in great haste, was a really modern tax and a substantial intellectual and practical achievement. In its form and intent, the 1806 tax is the father of Britain's current tax system. And although the British tax is different in form from the U.S. tax institutions, anyone familiar with both the U.S. and British income tax will sense their underlying kinship.

The income tax proved a powerful fiscal weapon in the long war with France. By itself, the income tax produced a total of £80 million and financed about one-third of the total cost of the war, a significant contribution from a new and unpopular institution. The measure of its unpopularity may in fact be gauged by its success in extracting tax revenue from an unwilling British public. Seligman reports the mixed emotions that many had regarding this device:

> The City of London, which had prided itself on contributing to the repeal of the tax in 1802, held a public meeting in July 1803. . . . Some extremists declared that if the income tax were necessary to save the country, it would be better to have the country go than to endure the tax. But others said that it would be wiser to declare part of one's income to the income tax commissioners than to give up all to Napoleon.[13]

Taken in its final 1806 form, the British income tax was a successful tool and was widely recognized as such in Europe. It was meant to be a simple tax that fell on all income at its source. The British found, however, that simplicity is complex. The tax schedules and cases became complicated as they tried to deal with all possible cases and possibilities. The result was a law that was "so complicated as to be unintelligible" according to a critic of the period.[14] This comment indicates at least that unintelligible taxes are not exclusively a twentieth-century institution.

The Income Tax Retired

Peace came in 1815, and Parliament quickly repealed the income tax. Wellington's Waterloo victory and the subsequent Treaties of Vienna were political death to the income tax. Men of wealth who would barely tolerate income taxation as an alternative to conquest by Napoleon wasted no time railroading its repeal once victory was final.

It should be noted that Britain's government did not give up the income tax revenues willingly. Attempts were made to reduce, water down, or alter the income tax but still to retain it as a powerful fiscal tool. Parliament would have none of this, however, and even ordered that all the records of the tax be destroyed, to make reenactment that much harder. (The originals were destroyed, following Parliament's order; but the copies that had been made systematically over the years were saved.)

People (particularly men of wealth, who paid income taxes while their low-paid workers did not) disliked the income tax because it was burdensome, hard to avoid, and exposed them to "inquisitorial" tax commissioners. Government officials liked the tax because it raised a good deal of revenue and because it was an elastic source of funds, growing with the economy. These two characteristics of the income tax are significant, but there is another aspect of this tax that we should note here.

Britain's experiment with income-based taxes (including the triple assessment and the income taxes that followed) lasted from 1797 through 1815. These years span most of the Napoleonic Wars, but they were also a period of substantial economic growth and structural change in Britain.

The income tax probably did not play a large part in the structural changes that Britain experienced during the war years. We have already cataloged the factors that contributed to economic change, including population growth, technological change, and the dislocations of the war itself. But it would be wrong to dismiss completely the contribution of tax reform to structural change on the margin during this period.

The income tax replaced (at least to some extent) the assessed taxes and was itself replaced in 1815 by excises, especially the agricultural tariffs contained in the Corn Laws. A comparison of these three tax institutions—the assessed taxes, the income tax, and the Corn Laws—provides clues to how the income tax contributed to economic growth.

The most important property of the income tax, from this perspective, is that it was a broad-based tax that at least attempted to apply uniform rates on different sources of income. In economic terms, we could say that the income tax tried to be a neutral tax, with few distortions that would misallocate labor or capital. (The tax was not actually free from distorting effect, as we shall soon see; but it was in fact *relatively* neutral, given the pattern of capital formation that prevailed at this time.) The income tax did not provide incentives for investment in cotton mills as opposed to wheat farms, but taxing them equally did not prevent the flow of capital and labor from rural village to urban industrial centers.

The income tax alternatives—the assessed taxes and the Corn Laws—can best be characterized by their relative *non*neutrality. The assessed taxes, for example, fell mainly on expenditure, which was therefore discouraged. This tended to promote preservation of the status quo, since economic change (in whatever form) generally involves additional (taxed) expenditure. Parliament, in the control of the landed interests, developed the assessed taxes as an alternative to a rise in the land tax; so it should not be surprising that profits arising from land were favored over other activities. The assessed taxes, imposed at rates high enough to generate the revenues that the income tax produced, would have greatly distorted the flow of economic resources during the Napoleonic Wars and would have reduced the degree of structural change that took place.

The Corn Laws—as imposed in 1815 and modified several times over the years—were a series of taxes and "trigger price mechanisms" designed to protect agriculture in Britain. The landed interests profited from the war years, which limited competition from continental farms. Had they possessed clear foresight, they might have viewed peace as an opportunity for a surge in agricultural exports. Britain, free from invasion and the accompanying devastation, was in an ideal position to provision the recovering European nations. The legislative goal of the landed interests might intelligently have been to seek Parliamentary influence to keep continental markets open and free from import restraints.

The Corn Laws took the opposite strategy; feeling threatened by the potential of foreign competition, the landed interests taxed foreign grain to give themselves a near monopoly on the rapidly growing domestic market. (A trigger price mechanism was used in some years to make tax-free imports of grain available, but only when bad harvests caused domestic prices to rise to extraordinary levels.)

Taxes such as the Corn Laws distorted the process of structural change in several ways. Obviously, the protected industries enjoyed greater profits than they otherwise would, promoting investment in these sectors over others. Second, high food prices tended to increase the wages necessary to attract workers to manufacturing jobs, thus reducing profits and growth in these areas. A third effect is that limits on British imports from the continent had the indirect effect of also limiting European purchases of British manufacturers. Overall, the imposition of tariffs high enough to replace income tax revenues would have led to huge distortions in some specific markets and reduced economic growth overall.

Perhaps Britain would still have experienced its industrial revolution if either the assessed taxes or the Corn Laws had been substituted for the income tax during the critical period when it existed. But it is likely that the degree of structural change would have been less, and the rate of economic growth lower; and Britain might not have triumphed in war. By being neutral (at least in intent), the income tax sought to "leave them as you found them" (in Seligman's words). In a world of uneven taxes biased against economic development, this was just what the doctor ordered.

The Corn Laws were enacted both to protect British agriculture and to provide the necessary revenues for the expanding government sector. The increased urbanization of the growing population was forcing government to take on a larger role in the economy and in society, and this meant more and more taxes; and even then, the national debt remained large and hung like a sword of Damocles over a nervous Parliament. Taxes — import tariffs and domestic excises — sprouted on every convenient base. The *Edinburgh Review*, beacon of Adam Smith's laissez-faire philosophy, complained in 1820 of

> Taxes upon every article which enters the mouth or covers the back or is placed under foot. Taxes upon everything which it is pleasant to see, hear, feel, smell or taste. Taxes upon warmth, light and locomotion. Taxes on everything on earth or under the earth, on everything that comes from abroad or is grown at home. Taxes on the raw material, taxes on every fresh value that is added to it by the industry of man. Taxes on the sauces which pamper man's appetite and the drug which restores him to health; on the ermine which decorates the judge, on the rope which hangs the criminal; on the poor man's salt and the rich man's spice; on the brass nails of the coffin and the ribbons of the bride; at bed or board, couchant or levant, we must pay. The schoolboy whips his taxed top; the beardless youth manages his taxed horse with a taxed bridle, on a taxed road, and the dying Englishman, pouring his medicine, which has paid seven percent, into a spoon which has paid fifteen percent, flings himself back upon a chintz bed, which has paid twenty-two percent, and expires in the arms of an apothecary who has paid a license of one hundred pounds for the privilege of putting him to death. His whole property is then immediately taxed from two to ten percent, besides the probate judge's fees demanded for burying him in the chancel; his virtues are handed down to posterity on taxed marble, and he will then be gathered to his fathers to be taxed no more.[15]

This tax system was supported by Parliament, which in the 1820s was still constituted so as to represent the interests of property exclusively. The Corn Laws increased landlord profits; while the various other excises fell on the rich and poor alike but according to their relative consumption expenditures. The tax burden on the landed interests was therefore relatively light.

Three groups in particular opposed this tax system: the manufacturers, the "economic liberals," and the working classes. Manufacturers, as already noted, saw in the Corn Laws and other excise taxes only higher wage costs. To the extent that food and other necessities were taxed, the domestic population had less discretionary income with which to buy the new items of mass production. Lower grain imports from abroad meant lower exports of manufacturers. Manufacturers had growing economic clout; but their influence in Parliament was not great, at least not until the Reform Bill of 1832 restacked the deck.

The manufacturers opposed the Corn Laws and excises because it was in their own narrow private interest to do so; the followers of Adam Smith and David Ricardo, preaching the tenets of "economic liberalism," opposed these taxes as a matter of public interest. Free trade maximized national welfare, according to Smith and Ricardo. The Corn Laws distorted the invisible hand of the market and violated the law of comparative advantage. David Ricardo, who was himself a member of Parliament for a time, opposed indirect taxes, advocating direct taxes on both income and capital in their stead.[16] The intellectual movement that advanced the ideals of economic liberalism was a potent force but, like the manufacturers, it lacked the votes in Parliament to carry out its program.

The urban working class had the most reason to oppose the British tax system because it was on their backs that the burden fell most heavily. Workers' interests were not reflected in government institutions. Several attempts were made to organize workers to act in their group interest, notably trade unions and the People's Charter movement. These met with only limited success, however.

The only advantage the workers possessed in the economic conflict with the landlords was their sheer numbers. These numbers counted for little at the ballot box (they couldn't vote), but mattered a good deal more in the streets. The fact that the economy was depressed – a burden that fell heavily on the masses – did not help matters. Mob violence and mass protests increased. The threat of insurrection did not escape the notice of the wealthy, who probably still carried in their minds images of the French revolution. (It is instructive that part of Robert Peel's early reputation derived from his 1829 organization of London's efficient police system to control street crime and violence.)

We have already seen that the Reform Bill of 1832 redefined Parliament, making it representative of population, not just property. Suffrage was not universal (there was still a means test that disenfranchised most workers), but manufacturing interests were now much better represented in the legislature. The Catholic Emancipation Act of 1829 similarly opened Parliament to men who were not members of the Church of England – not only Catholics but also the many Protestant Dissenters, who included among their number an abundance of entrepreneurs and laissez-faire intellectuals.

The new Parliament reflected the emerging interests of the British economy. Reform of the old laws grounded in the interests of property – specifically, restoration of the income tax and repeal of the Corn Laws, as well as reform of the Poor Laws – was now possible.

Peel's Income Tax

In 1842 Robert Peel's government proposed its famous free trade budget, which reduced or eliminated a wide range of tariffs. To make up for the lost revenue, Peel reinstated the income tax, an action he did not take lightly.

The income tax was never popular – indeed, Peel was no fan of it himself. But neither was he a fan of a rising national debt. Peel had little choice but to recall the broad-based tax that had proved itself such an effective money spinner during the French wars. The situation Peel faced in 1842 has been characterized this way: "Matters had come to a crisis. The panic of 1837 had left behind it a wake of long-continued distress; the new poor law was unpopular; the Chartist agitation was acquiring new momentum; and the Corn Laws were becoming increasingly unpopular. For the last five years there had been a repeated deficit in the budget."[17]

Peel's choice of the income tax solved two problems. First, it allowed him to reduce tariffs and excises, an action that found favor with manufacturers and intellectuals and took some steam out of the worker protests. The revival of the income tax is remembered mainly because it is seen as a progressive reform, in the spirit of the times. But the income tax was also a practical choice because it solved the fiscal crisis problem of small but persistent deficits, which the then-existing tax system could not. (The Victorians were almost compulsively concerned with fiscal balance, as I will explain later, so that even relatively small deficits were treated very seriously.) There is some evidence that the British excise tax system had hit the "bend" in its Laffer curve; that is, tax revenues were maximized and any increase or decrease in tax rates would fail to increase tax revenues. Only a new tax could generate more tax revenue in the short run.

The income tax would raise enough revenue, by Peel's calculation, to shift the budget from deficit to a £2 million surplus. These funds could be used to retire public debt. It is a good thing for Peel that the income tax could solve so many problems at once. This allowed him to argue to each group according to its interests, citing finance benefits here, commercial gains there, and philosophy somewhere else. The Property and Income Tax Act of 1842, which imposed the income tax for a period of just three years, passed Parliament with a majority of 106 votes.

Peel's income tax was act 1 of a two-act melodrama that has already been briefly summarized elsewhere in this narrative. In act 1 the income tax was revived, and many excises were reduced. But the Corn Laws remained. It took the multiple crises of 1846 to pry the landed interests loose from this shield. With social pressures growing in any case, the crop failures in Ireland brought the kettle to boil. Famine and poverty would result if the Corn Laws remained. The income tax's unexpectedly large revenues (£5 million instead of the expected £3.25 million) made elimination of the Corn Laws and loss of their income possible. Peel acted, and it was the end of Peel.

The Corn Laws and Peel both disappeared, but the income tax remained. It was renewed repeatedly, for short periods each time, always with the promise that it was a temporary tax and not a permanent burden.

The income tax of 1842 modified the 1806 law in only two significant ways, expanding the low-income exemption to relieve the burden on urban workers and tightening enforcement. Otherwise, the tax was really unchanged; indeed, "the only thing original in the scheme is its introduction during a time of peace."[18]

The 1850s and 1860s were a period when the income tax was repeatedly criticized, studied, and modified. A plan to end the income tax had to be dropped because its revenues were too important (especially during the Crimean War) and the alternative of excise taxes too unpopular. Seligman explains that the Parliament put up with this tax "not because it loved the income tax more but because it loved the indirect taxes less."[19]

This was a boom period for Britain, and the income tax proved so productive that its rate could be repeatedly reduced. Low rates were felt to be important to the tax's economic success, not just to its political acceptability, as we might suspect. Ursula Hicks explains that "The economic effects of personal income tax impinge on both the willingness to save and the incentive to work. The Victorians . . . were particularly anxious to keep the income tax low because they relied on personal savings as the chief source for increasing capital formation—savings which would either be lent on the stock exchange or directly invested in the family firm, then the typical form of business organization."[20]

Even when the tax had become an accepted feature of the fiscal landscape, however, it remained controversial. Two issues reappear again and again. The first problem was the difficulty of guaranteeing equal taxation, given the strong propensity of people of all classes to cheat in their declarations. John Stuart Mill despaired the "present low state of public morality."[21]

The second issue was the problem of taxing different types of income (temporary versus permanent), or income derived from different types of capital equally. There was a great disagreement regarding how to tax incomes equally and whether an equal tax on all income in fact imposed equal burdens on different sources of income. The argument that "the only way to tax all income equally is to tax some income more than others" sounds both foolish and vaguely Orwellian, but modern economists know that truly defining income is not a simple matter.

Even the best political economists of the time did not yet have a firm grasp on the concept of income and its relation to the concept of capital (at least insofar as these notions apply to taxation). But Ricardo was correct when he wrote that "taxes are not necessarily taxes on capital because they are laid on capital; nor on income because they are laid on income."[22] The issue was muddied by the form of the income tax itself, which was partly determined by its historical evolution from the assessed taxes at the end of the eighteenth century.

John Stuart Mill was a vigorous advocate of differentiation. He called for lower taxes on unfunded income (e.g., labor income) and higher taxes on funded income (capital income) based on the notion that (to state it roughly) funded income is perpetuated by the capital that created it, while the basis for unfunded income disappears as soon as income is created. Mill argued for consumption taxes, which would tax consumption from income equally, however the income was earned.[23] The advantage of a consumption tax in Mill's eyes was that it spared saving. Mill thought it unfair to tax both income that is saved and the interest that saving earned. He therefore favored a consumption tax because of its improved equity (despite the fact that he himself advocated higher income taxes on capital income).

A tax that favors saving over consumption tends to promote capital accumulation, a fact that Mill does not seem to have considered but that plays a central role in the modern tax policy debate insofar as capital accumulation is linked to economic growth. At the same time, an income tax that falls heaviest on capital income tends to discourage capital accumulation and therefore hinders growth. Mill, the preeminent economist of the age, advocated both tax policies. This shows, I think, that there was not a profound understanding of the relationships between capital and income and between capital and growth.

There are two points worth underlining and highlighting in this discussion. First, there was a good deal of confusion about what the income tax was supposed to tax: Was it income, or was it capital? Even the tax's name— *property and income tax*—caused confusion. Second, it is noteworthy that the issues that dominated debate were matters of tax equity, the problem of just taxation. Issues of efficiency or the economic effects of the tax did not attract nearly an equal amount of attention. How did the income tax affect resource allocation in Britain?

The Income Tax and Britain's Rise and Decline

I suspect that Britain's income tax played an important role in the country's economic development, a bigger role, at least, than is commonly thought. Taxes affect how individuals allocate resources, at least at the margin; and these major shifts in British taxation had the potential for major effect.

The British income tax was in effect during the Napoleonic Wars and again from 1842 onward through the end of the period under study.[24] Its effect on the economy changed over the years as the world economy experienced structural change. To see this, let me divide the income tax's lifetime into three periods.

The first income tax was imposed during a period of war but also a time of economic growth. The second period began when Peel's tax changes took place—reenactment of the income tax in 1842 and repeal of the Corn Laws in 1846; the years that followed until 1873 were a golden age. Here again, the income tax accompanied economic growth. The third period begins in the Great Depression and extends through the end of the Victorian era. The income tax continued, and at higher and higher rates; the economy declined both absolutely (at least for some years) and, more importantly, relative to its major international competitors. This is the decline of Victorian Britain that was charted earlier in these pages.

Pitt's income tax (as modified over the years) was a broad-based tax that attempted to tax all sources of income equally. As such, it had little impact on the allocation of resources between consumption and saving, agriculture and industry, or other competing uses. As Hicks has noted, "In Victorian times it was . . . argued by economists that income taxes were to be preferred to outlay taxes, not only on distributional grounds, but because they implied no disturbance to consumption or production."[25]

Schumpeter put it another way, describing the goal of Victorian taxation as "to raise revenue . . . in such a way as to deflect economic behavior as little as possible from what it would have been in the absense of all taxation ('taxation for revenue only')."[26]

This relative neutrality is important because the alternative taxes during this period would have shifted resources away from the emerging industries and back into the primary sectors of the economy. Thus, the income tax contributed to the early emergence of British industry.

A similar argument can be made regarding how Peel's income tax (as modified over the years) affected the British economy during the years 1842 through, say, 1873.[27] Peel, by removing the excises and tariffs and replacing them with the 1806 income tax, replaced a very biased tax system with a relatively neutral one. The tax system no longer stood in the way of the efficient allocation of scarce resources, and it is not surprising that the economy picked up. The income tax by itself did not cause the Victorian boom of this period; the income tax alone was not that large an influence on the economy. Rather, the tax reforms that Peel instituted, taken as a group, removed a cork that had prevented the British economy from growing (and had been the cause of a good deal of social tension).

So far, I have given the income tax partial credit for Britain's periods of economic growth even if this credit is of a stingy, typically economic kind—the tax did not cause the growth, it just did not hinder it, as the other taxes had. This leaves me the task of explaining the third period, when Britain lost its lead. What impact did the income tax have on the events of these years?

The income tax did not change significantly during or after Britain's Great Depression of the 1870s, so I cannot claim that a change in the tax pushed the economy from rise to decline. But the driving force of economic development did change at about this time; and a fatal flaw in the income tax—an accidental nonneutrality—magnified all the British biases against change discussed earlier. As a result, the income tax tended to lock the British economy into the patterns that had been developed earlier in the century. The tax acted as a barrier to the changes that would have allowed Britain to retain her lead. The structural changes that I am talking about here are, of course, the development of new industries based on modern science and technology and the changing structure of international comparative advantage that followed. Electrical, chemical, automotive, and other industries grew significantly in Germany, Sweden, and the United States but failed to develop in Britain. These modern industries are alike in at least two respects: first, they involve a more systematic application of science and technology than did the textile mills on which Britain's Industrial Revolution was based; second, these new technologies were significantly more capital-intensive than were the smaller-scale factories of earlier years. The late 1880s therefore saw a shift from trial by error to scientific research and development and from labor-intensive to capital-intensive production.

How did the British income tax treat capital-intensive industry relative to the earlier business technologies? In answering this question we will discover that the income tax inadvertently imposed a higher burden on capital-intensive production systems, giving older-style technology a tax advantage that artificially increased its relative return, prolonged its use, and helped freeze the pattern of British industry in this critical period.

A modern economist who wants to know how a tax system affects capital formation looks first for the tax treatment of depreciation expense. Assuming that the tax rates on different types of investments contain no bias — an assumption that largely holds for the British tax — then how or whether depreciation is used to compute taxable profits pretty much determines whether capital-intensive investments bear the same, higher, or lower effective tax rates than other investments.

A neutral income tax system would provide for "economic depreciation" as a business cost to be offset against revenues in determining taxable income. Economic depreciation is the true cost to the firm of the wearing out of its production capital over its lifetime.[28]

A tax system that overstates economic depreciation, through systems of accelerated depreciation for example, provides capital-intensive investments with a tax incentive in the form of relatively lower taxable profits and therefore a relatively higher effective posttax rate of return, which encourages this type of development as compared to other types that use less capital. On the other hand, a tax system that understates the cost of capital consumption artificially inflates taxable profits for capital-intensive industries and therefore discourages investment in these sectors by reducing the effective after-tax rate of return. A tax system that allows true economic depreciation to be treated as a business cost is neutral and neither encourages nor discourages capital-intensive investments compared to alternative types of production.

It is significant, therefore, that Britain's income tax did not have any provision for capital depreciation at all; that is, this important cost of capital was completely ignored in the determination of taxable income for the individuals and firms that engaged in investment and production. The British tax system was thus strongly biased against capital-intensive investments of the type that became increasingly important in Germany and the United States in the 1880s and later.

There are probably many reasons why the British income tax did not recognize the cost of capital deterioration. One reason was that the roots of the income tax ran deep — to the Napoleonic era when the capital requirements of industry were extremely modest and depreciation was a relatively unimportant concept. Indeed, Adam Smith's vision of the future, his pin factory, was built on division of labor, not mechanization. But, as we have seen, *nineteenth*-century economic theories would not have provided any enlightened guidance on the depreciation issue, either: Ricardo was ensnared in his labor theory of value, which made only ambiguous provision for capital; and Mill, the leading economic influence for much of the century, had inconsistent views about capital and how to tax it. Guidance on tax policy, especially in the early years, had to come from practitioners, not theorists.

As a practical matter, there was not very much capital used by industry (compared with home production of textiles, for example) in the days when the income tax was being developed. The pace of technological change was not rapid, and the changes that did take place involved modification of existing machinery, not replacing one large lump of capital with another. In this world it would be important to allow for the costs of repair and maintenance in calculating taxable income, but it would not be obvious that depreciation costs were important.

As a practical matter, then, repair costs were what mattered in 1806, not depreciation, and the tax law reflected this fact. But because of the peculiar history of income taxation in Britain, the income tax law in the 1840s, 1850s, and 1860s was pretty much like the law of 1806, even though the underlying economics of industry had changed.

It would be wrong to say that no one appreciated the importance of depreciation, but there certainly was confusion about the matter. Here is an account of Britain's treatment of this issue, based on the records of the Departmental Committee of 1904:

> The question of allowance for depreciation gave them a little more difficulty.
> . . . The acts of 1842 and 1853 allowed the actual cost of repairs, but made no provision for depreciation. The practice, however, gradually became more liberal than the letter of the law, which was interpreted to include renewals; and in certain cases, especially in regard to ships, allowances were made which to some extent admitted of the writing off from profits of certain amounts toward replacement. In 1878 this practice was specifically recognized by law. But the interpretation of the new law was never very clear, although it gradually became more liberal. . . . The concession in the act of 1878 was still further developed by administrative action in 1897. . . . The committee pointed out that no definite steps had been taken by any one to make this matter public, and that most people seemed to be ignorant of it. . . . The allowance for wear and tear of buildings was . . . limited to actual expenditure for repairs. The committee now decided that, in view of the fact that the amount of wear and tear of mills, factories, etc., greatly exceeds that of buildings, the full annual value of the premises so occupied should be allowed.[29]

Although some allowances for depreciation were probably taken in the 1850s and 1860s, they were concentrated in just a few industries (shipping and printing, for example, where the wear on capital was visible and therefore obvious). But even at the turn of the century the tax treatment of capital depreciation was uncertain, uneven, and far from general in application. It was not until 1907 that a reasonably complete system of "allowances for wear and tear" was integrated into the income tax.

Especially after the Great Depression of the 1870s, how the income tax treated capital-intensive investment became, we now know, critical. The British tax system favored the continued use of existing capital in existing industries (through the correct tax treatment of repairs and maintenance), but discriminated against the big lumps of capital needed for the emerging scientific industrial revolution.

It is significant that some industries took advantage of the potential for depreciation allowances before others did. Britain retained its lead over its competitors in the shipbuilding industry, for example, where the reality of depreciation costs were recognized early on. The pace of technological change was rapid enough in shipping that hulls would be outmoded and replaced long before they actually wore out. British shipbuilders and shipping firms were successful in worldwide competition precisely because they kept pace with the innovations.[30] One reason (but not the only one) they could do this profitably was that the tax system allowed depreciation relief and so did not erect a barrier to technological change. As noted above, relatively few industries were so favored by the income tax system. Capital in this sector was taxed appropriately (at least more appropriately than elsewhere), and as a result capital was attracted and the technological lead maintained.

It is also significant that the tax bias increased in the last years of the nineteenth century just when investment in new capital equipment and technology was crucial. Income tax rates, which had been extremely low in the period of Gladstonian finance, crept back up later and became relatively high around the turn of the century.[31] The lack of an efficient system of depreciation allowances was significant but of little practical impact when tax rates were very low, but the tax bias against new industries increased along with the tax rates until it was quite important indeed.

The tax bias against capital formation in British industry tended to freeze the technology and the range of markets in which British firms competed. New processes and new products required big lumps of new capital that were taxed at a higher effective rate than the existing capital of the traditional industries. The tax system thus reinforced and compounded the many other factors that created the rigid structure of British industry during the Victorian decline.

Rise of the National Debt

The practice of funding has gradually enfeebled every state which has adopted it. . . . Is it very likely that in Great Britain alone a practice which has brought either weakness or desolation into every other country should prove altogether innocent?   Adam Smith, *The Wealth of Nations*

A country which has accumulated a large debt is placed in a most artificial situation; . . . it becomes the interest of every contributor to withdraw his shoulder from the burthen. . . . A country which has involved itself in the difficulties attending to this artificial system would act wisely by ransoming itself from them at the sacrifice of any portion of its property which might be necessary to redeem its debt. That which is wise in an individual is also wise in a nation.

David Ricardo, *Principles of Political Economy and Taxation*

I have known some People such ill Computers as to imagine the many Millions in Stocks and Annuities, are so much real Wealth in the Nation; whereas every Farthing of it is entirely lost to us.

Jonathan Swift, *The Conduct of Allies*

Here are opinions, not a bit uncertain, regarding Britain's public debt.[32] Public debt is a bad thing, clearly — perhaps not so bad as plague or high taxes, but plenty bad enough. David Hume found five evil forces in public debt, the fifth being that it created an idle rentier class.[33]

To balance the equation, here are a few words on the other side of the public debt issue:

> Mortimer describes the national debt as the "standing miracle in politics, which at once astonishes and overawes the states of Europe." . . . Pitt in 1786, said he was persuaded that "upon this matter of the national debt repose the vigour and even the independence of the Nation.[34]

Here we find that the national debt is the foundation of the economy and the guarantor of "vigour and even independence." Which is it to be — devil, angel, or both?

The predictable answer to this question is that no single characterization of the national debt can be accurate. Rather, its role and effect changed over time; a theory of the national debt that is correct in one period can be very wrong in another. Or, as Braudel has written, "Public finance makes sense only in the context of the overall economic life of a country."[35] We have seen that Britain's economy changed in important ways during the years covered by this study. It is not surprising, then, that its public debt changed too.

My goal here is to explain how Britain's public debt contributed to the late-Victorian decline. My thesis, as outlined earlier, is that the national debt had an important — but indirect and long-term — impact on the pattern of British investment. As the largest borrower, Britain's government was the most significant force in credit markets, which therefore adapted and established financial channels based on the nature of government borrowing. These channels largely bypassed the important science-based industries that grew up in Germany and the United States, contributing to the rigidity of British industry in the late 1800s. I do not conclude that the channels established by the national debt caused Victorian Britain to be overtaken; this is a very complex event that fits no single-cause theory. But I do think that the financial patterns established by the national debt contributed to the decline.

Monarchs and governments have always borrowed; but for us *public debt* is synonymous with *funded debt* like the Florentine Monte Commune — debt that is backed, explicitly or implicitly, by a stream of state revenues (not the personal guarantee of a head of state). In Britain, the Bank of England was established in 1694 for the purpose of creating a funded debt system. Kindleberger sums up the importance of this event neatly: "The early days of the Bank of England were associated largely with operations in government debt, to transform the chaotic assortment of obligations issued by the English government during its almost continuous wars into funded obligations, widely distributed. Its success has been called a financial revolution that enabled England with a population one-third that of France to defeat it time and again in battle throughout the eighteenth century."[36]

And what a "chaotic assortment" of public debt there was! Straightforward loans seem to have been the exception, not the rule, in part because of the church's long-held prejudice against the payment of interest. Thus, British government finance, reflecting continental practice, included indirect credit instruments such as

- *Annuities*. In return for a fixed payment to the government, an annuity of fixed or life-term (either the lender's lifetime or that of some other party) would be paid.
- *Tontines*. A form of lottery, or crude insurance. In return for a current payment pooled from several parties, the government would provide a return to be divided equally among survivors until all were dead. One advantage of the tontine was that it was "self-liquidating."
- *Lottery loans*. The return on these loans depended on a lottery drawing. Lottery loans were often combined with other types of loans as an incentive to provide funds to the government.[37]

Each type of loan both satisfied a social need (for insurance, risk taking, or converting wealth into an income stream) and at the same time provided a return that one could claim was something other than "interest." These relatively complex financial instruments were for a very long time preferred over simple loans such as the short-term instrument of the Exchequer bill, which was introduced as early as 1696 and paid three pence per day (4.6-percent annual interest on a hundred-pound loan). (Not until 1877 would Walter Bagehot invent the Treasury bill, which paid interest through a discount on face value, just as commercial bills were discounted. The Treasury bill would prove much more popular than the Exchequer bill and soon dominated British finance.)

Consols were created through the refunding operations of 1749. Many forms of debt were collapsed into one fund, the "consolidated annuities" (*consols* for short). Consols were and still are perpetual annuities, paying a fixed nominal return forever—exactly the opposite of the self-liquidating tontines. (The consol was conceived as a type of standardized annuity having infinite life rather than the arbitrary and unpredictable life of a particular person or group.) The introduction of standardized securities simplified the practical matter of floating government debt, and competitive bidding for new issues was soon instituted.

These financial innovations produced what Dickson has called Britain's "financial revolution." The existence of these standardized government securities (called "stocks" in Britain), backed by government revenues and made liquid by the existence of an active market in the city, allowed the government to channel funds efficiently from throughout Britain (and, indeed, from other countries, too) in times of need. Government no longer depended on a few men of wealth for loans, as was still the case in France.

Britain frequently had cause to raise funds through the "stock" market in the eighteenth century because of war. War was perhaps the one near constant of this century: the War of the Spanish Succession (1701–1714), the War of the Austrian Succession (1740–1748), the French and Indian Wars (1756–1763), the American War of Independence (1775–1783), and the Napoleonic Wars (1793–1802, 1803–1815).

Government debt, as Adam Smith suggested, formed the elastic revenue source needed to finance wartime expenditures. The land tax was inelastic and could not be raised. Excises on consumption created their own revenue limits. Money borrowed from the landed gentry and from abroad, particularly from the Dutch, provided Britain with the resources to fight these wars.

War is always costly and Britain's national debt began to grow into a mountain. In 1702 the total debt stood at £12.8 million with an annual interest charge of £1.2 million. At the start of the Napoleonic Wars in 1793 the debt had increased to £244 million, with annual debt servicing costs of £9.5 million. In 1815 the totals had risen to £834 million in debt with an annual interest cost of £31 million.

This huge accumulation of public debt with its attendant interest burden was not accidental or unnoticed, and the epigraphs from Smith, Ricardo, and Swift above suggest the degree of controversy associated with it. On one hand, the debt could be seen to generate the obvious benefits of military triumph and economic prosperity in the short run. It is really not clear that Britain could have mobilized the resources necessary to achieve victory without its efficient national debt.

Economists and moral philosophers were alarmed by this debt buildup; maybe they were *too* alarmed, because while they knew history, their visions of the past did not enable them to see the future. Adam Smith knew that other countries with similar debt burdens had been unable to escape from them. He did not see that Britain's funded debt, built on the Bank of England, was a fundamentally different institution from the public debts of earlier centuries or the French debt system of his own day. Ricardo could not see how such debt could exist without crippling taxes, but he did not count on the economic growth that was slowly transforming the world around him. Jonathan Swift feared the foreign ownership of the debt, seeing it as almost economic slavery, England voluntarily subject to fat, Dutch money men through its debt burden. He did not see that the financial linkage between the English and the Dutch would make for a strong military alliance against Napoleon (although it did not eliminate conflict between the Dutch and the English in the eighteenth century).

The pattern of public debt that developed in this period had an important beneficial property—it established channels of public credit that essentially bypassed the channels of normal business finance. The city financed the public debt, while business was more or less self-financed through far less formal instruments and markets. This contributed to Britain's continued industrial growth during the war period because, as recent studies indicate, the government was able to borrow really large amounts without "crowding out" business investment. Thus, government borrowing did not stifle Britain's "early start" and may well have contributed to the economic conditions that encouraged it.[38] No crowding out of private investment occurred because the financial spheres in which business capital and government bonds circulated were distinctly different and intersected hardly at all.

The national debt was a great warrior, but it did not take well to peace. The interest burden of the debt was a problem. Excise taxes and tariffs were required to make the continuing interest payments, which went mostly to the landed gentry around the kingdom who grew to like the secure flow of rentier income they received. Landlords found "clipping coupons" superior to risk taking or commercial enterprise, just as Hume had predicted.

In hindsight, a more important problem was the effect that the large public debt had on the development of private finance in Great Britain. Paradoxically, the strength and efficiency of the public debt system led to a weak and inefficient system of private finance, at least until the middle years of the nineteenth century. This is a paradox because it seems logical that on observing how successfully the Bank of England could channel resources toward the public interest, Parliament and entrepreneurs would clone other institutions that would similarly mobilize resources for private sector use, particularly in peacetime. But this did not happen.

So important was the national debt, in contemporary view, that its security needed to be protected at all costs. Parliament — which was in the pockets of the landed creditors who held this view most strongly — sought to preserve the integrity of the public debt by granting preferential treatment to the Bank of England. Thus, for example, the Bank of England was for some time the only "limited liability" bank in Britain. Banks elsewhere in London and in the country were partnerships restricted to six partners.

British banks were necessarily small in capital and tremendously risk-averse in lending behavior. Even so, they were prone to financial crisis and collapse. With short-term deposits that could disappear in an instant, these banks could not make long-term loans. In their credit politics, they found it prudent to imitate, in terms of risk, term, and liquidity, the government debts that set the financial pattern of the markets. The banks provided floating capital for commerce, not fixed capital for industry.

The country banks were so weak, in fact, that they often were unable to provide for even the most basic needs of local businesses. Many times, for example, local banks could not produce the coins that firms needed to meet weekly payrolls. Some firms instituted "company stores" and associated credit systems just to overcome this scarcity of small coins.[39]

Britain's banking laws were reformed in the 1840s and in later decades, removing much of the bias against private banks; but the pattern had already been set. Over the course of a hundred years it is not surprising that we should find some exceptions to the rule, but it was generally true that British banks did not engage in large, long-term industrial finance.

I suspect that the biggest factor in the peculiar development of British banks was not legislation (or lack thereof) but rather the great success of the public debt. Exchequer bills and, later, Treasury bills were highly liquid and very secure. They worked for British investors, who tended to go with the pattern of prior success instead of striking out bold new designs. Indeed, banks that tried different designs, making long-term loans, were unusually susceptible to the periodic financial crises, reinforcing the prevailing wisdom that liquidity and security were the key to financial success.

The national debt therefore set the tone and pattern of all of Britain's financial markets. The public debt worked, and because it existed as constant competition to necessarily weaker private sector instruments, it forced banks to mimic its own characteristics.

Throughout the nineteenth century the city's stock markets focused on government debt. Some "public utility" securities were introduced during the canal and railroad manias and the spread of the public corporations late in the century caused increased trading in corporate stock. But London's financial markets, which had developed to trade public debt, remained largely devoted to this purpose.

The Rise of Foreign Loans

There was plenty of capital available for British industry, but it got there (or didn't) in peculiar ways. During the early industrial revolution of 1780–1820, industrial capital largely bypassed the city financial markets. Start-up money was raised through the practice of forming partnerships. Expansion capital came from retained earnings. Only circulating capital, to finance inventories and facilitate trade, was drawn from the financial sector through local banks. As Crouzet has noted, "A bank whose clients may have their deposits back on demand, or after only a brief delay, cannot afford to sink them in long-term investments, which are not quickly realizable and may even be risky, such as loans to industrial enterprises for creating fixed capital or a share in the equity of some other firm."[40]

This pattern of industrial finance became rigid as the nineteenth century progressed. When large amounts of long-term capital were required for the "scientific" industrial revolution of the later Victorian years, there existed no proven institutions to get funds into the hands of educated entrepreneurs. There were plenty of funds in total, but they could not get into the right hands.[41]

It is true that during this period there was a significant increase in incorporations. The records show many firms "going public" and issuing stock. This gives the false appearance that an organized stock market existed to provide investment capital to private firms. Most of this activity involved a simple change in the legal organization of existing firms designed much more to get around the rising inheritance tax than to raise capital for expansion or change.

This inefficient system of industrial finance persisted in Britain until relatively recent times. In 1931, for example, the Macmillan Committee studied British money markets and discovered the "Macmillan gap" that denied funds to many middle-size firms. Very small companies could get adequate finance through old-fashioned financial means: family, friends, business associates, local banks, and so on. And the very largest firms went directly to the city with stock offerings. Most potential new firms fell in the missing middle, however; their needs were too great for traditional means, but they were too small to afford the relatively high costs of issue stock in the city.

The missing middle was important because it is often precisely firms of this intermediate size that develop innovations and so generate growth. The smallest firms lack the resources for innovation while the largest firms sometimes (not always) have vested interests in existing technologies and so may be resistant to change.[42]

In late-Victorian Britain, in particular, the Macmillan gap came at precisely the point in the business structure where heavy machinery was introduced.[43] This was the critical point, given the capital requirements of the scientific revolution.

The problem was that financial institutions could not efficiently distribute the adequate supplies of funds, a type of problem that is not unique to Victorian Britain. In his survey, *A Financial History of Western Europe*, Kindleberger described this situation as resulting from information cost:

> The historical and analytical point . . . is that investors lack costless world-wide knowledge, and in making choices among investment opportunities, scan limited horizons. These horizons shift from time to time, displaced by some striking innovation, event, or bargain. . . . The consequence of limited horizons that change discontinuously is that capital flows take place in deep channels. . . . Unlike water flowing evenly over a broad surface, capital moves like water in sluices or conduits, ignoring or bypassing better opportunities on occasion, because of the high cost of obtaining information about them.[44]

Individuals invested in their own businesses (or those of their close associates) because they had firsthand knowledge of the properties of the risks and returns. They also knew what to expect from government debt. These financial channels were firmly entrenched. Information concerning other investment opportunities was too costly (for the size of the transactions involved) to break out of old channels and divert funds from the entrenched old routes. Kindleberger's "river of finance" metaphor fits the events nicely.

But an examination of the pattern of British investment during the Victorian years, in light of Kindleberger's model, reveals at least one seemingly contradictory trend. While there was no channel to get funds from the city to large-scale industry in Britain, we do observe a deep, strong and growing flow of funds from London to the continent, the United States, Canada, South America, India, and elsewhere.[45] The question is, If British financial markets lacked sufficient information to make informed investments in industrial concerns at home, why did they invest abroad, where information would be even more expensive and risks even less certain?

The solution to the puzzle of Britain's persistent capital exports is that a "striking event" at the end of the Napoleonic Wars diverted part of Britain's financial stream, digging a permanent channel abroad. Once established, this channel carried funds to other countries in flows that pretty much mirrored the patterns and trends at home.

The British government was responsible for the important initial foreign capital flows. The Treasury made substantial loans to Austria during the early years of the war with France. But the striking events that really set British capital flowing across the channel to the continent, which was also induced by government action, were the Baring indemnity loans. The long wars with

France ended in a second Treaty of Paris, which imposed a substantial indemnity on France's new government—payments totaling fr 700 million.[46] Britain's share of the peace settlement came to fr 125 million; Prussia, Austria, and Russia were the main recipients of the remainder. France could not pay; it had no reserves, and its budget was already in the red. Its only recourse was to borrow abroad.

Coming all at once, the French indemnity was a truly "striking event" that attracted the attention of firms in the city, particularly the Baring Brothers finance house. A scheme was put together whereby the Barings would purchase heavily discounted pools of French rentes (life annuities) for resale in Britain. In trading in the city, the initial rentes promptly appreciated, attracting capital from throughout the kingdom. The rush was on, with subsequent issues oversubscribed.

The Baring loans worked. They attracted capital initially because they were similar to familiar domestic investment instruments. But, more important, the French actually repaid the loans, validating the risk of foreign investment. Since the British liked to retrace profitable patterns, the success of the Baring loans established a permanent channel abroad for future loans, most of which also worked though some of them came up losers. Foreign investment also benefited from the fact that many continental financiers emigrated to Britain during Napoleon's wars, bringing with them a shrewd understanding of markets and conditions abroad.

The Baring loans were good investments, in the narrow sense; but they also worked for Britain in a second way, they promoted British exports, thus promoting growth of the textile industry at a critical moment. Funds (often the profits of British export industries) went to the French government, which recycled the money back to Britain, but also to Austria, Russia, Prussia, and the others. Some of these payments naturally returned again to Britain, as payment for British goods, preventing an even greater collapse in trade. Spared the tremendous immediate burden of the indemnity payments, even the French could buy some British items. The loans successfully paid off—for British industry and commerce, for investors who provided the funds, and for the city's financiers, who set up the whole thing. As Kindleberger concludes, "The Baring loan primed the pump. . . . [But it] did more. It recycled French indemnity payments, and it broadened the horizon of English investors to include foreign lending."[47]

British capital subsequently flowed all over the globe during the Victorian era, but while the list of countries that received these funds is long and varied, the pattern of investment was rigid and unyielding, molded on the Baring Brothers successful original form. British capital exports were generally fixed-rate loans, not equity participation. Interest on the foreign loans was often higher than on domestic issues of similar risk—which made sense, given that Britain was capital-abundant, foreign countries capital-scarce, and markets imperfect at equating the various returns. Britons might have earned an even higher return on riskier direct investments in new domestic industries, but they did not wish to assume the added risk.

In form and function, these foreign loans were modeled on the successful financial instruments of the city, which means that they had much in common with government debt issues and traded comfortably alongside them. Walter Bagehot noted the dominance of foreign credit in the 1880s, writing that "The truth is, that the . . . great instruments for transferring capital within a nation . . . have begun to operate on the largest scale between nations. . . . A cosmopolitan loan fund exists, which runs everywhere as it is wanted and as the rate of interest tempts it."[48]

There was generally a link (an important one) between the foreign loans and Britain's export industries. In the 1840s, for example, Britain experienced a railroad boom at home. The growth of the railroads was another "striking event" in financial history. Like the Baring loans, railroads required so much capital all at once that by gravity's force alone new financial arteries appeared. A good deal of the resources for railroad construction was provided by British insurance firms, which did not need the high liquidity of government debt but demanded a high level of security, which railroad investments provided. British industry developed to supply the necessary physical capital (rails, engines, carriages, etc.). When a French railroad boom ensued, British investors, insurance companies, and others, too, were ready and willing to provide the financial backing, which was recycled back to the British manufacturers that exported railroad capital to France.

In the decades that followed there developed similar patterns of exports, of both capital and industrial production, involving other nations on the continent, North and South America, and Britain's scattered colonial possessions. While long-term credit financed public utilities such as canals and railroads, short-term credit flowed abroad to provide the commercial liquidity necessary to the success of other British industries, such as the textile trade.

While British capital helped less-developed countries "catch up," the pattern of these capital exports, so closely tied to existing industries, served to increase the structural rigidities at home. Foreign loans were profitable in several respects, but they dug more deeply the existing financial and industrial streams and broke no new ground.

The fact that British investors could profit handsomely from paper investment — foreign bonds and government debt — contributed to the structural rigidity and bias against risk taking that characterized Britain in the late Victorian period.[49] Families of wealth earned in textiles invested in the past (insurance companies, railroad bonds, and Treasury bills). They did not invest in the future (chemical plants or electrical parts factories).

The point of this discussion of foreign lending is that government debt policy (the Baring loan) combined with the powerful pattern established by the national debt served further to deepen the channels of British finance, moving credit through the city in rather fixed ways. These deep channels bypassed important sectors of British industry. Thus, public policy regarding debt contributed in unintended ways to the Victorian decline both directly and in more subtle ways.

Fiscal Crisis and the Balanced Economy

> A business firm grows and attains great strength, and afterward perhaps stagnates and decays; and at the turning point there is a balancing or equilibrium of the forces of life and decay.
>
> Alfred Marshall, *Principles of Economics*

This relatively brief look at structural change and fiscal crisis in the Victorian economy opened with the Great Exhibition of 1851. The Victorians themselves saw 1851 as the midpoint of a century that had seen Britain grow into a position of economic dominance, a trend they expected to continue. Instead, we now look back at the midcentury as a turning point, a time when the forces of growth and decline just balanced and would soon tilt the other way.[50]

Britain had adjusted successfully for the most part to the structural changes of the first industrial revolution. British institutions had evolved to support the new social and economic structure. The tax system and the national debt are two of the many institutions that contributed to this successful adjustment.

Like everyone else, the British sought to repeat patterns that were successful in the past. Their institutions began to freeze in place and become increasingly rigid. This is not necessarily bad in a stable world. Many social and economic institutions have remained basically unchanged for centuries because they successfully solve problems that have not changed in any important way.

The "second industrial revolution" with its emphasis on big capital and modern science was an unexpected event. New institutional patterns would be needed to maintain the Victorian lead. So rigid were Britain's social and economic institutions that they largely prevented the necessary structural change from taking place: "Newton's cosmos created a model for government, economy, and society. If balance among opposing forces sustains order in the universe, might the balance principle also provide the means of maintaining order in society?"[51]

Balance was an important notion to the Victorians. They sought a balanced and ordered society and economy. A balanced budget was a necessary element of this overall social equilibrium in the compulsive era that began with Gladstone:

> On the budgetary side Victorian policy insisted that the Chancellor must always plan for a balanced budget, save in the most severe emergency.[52]

> Budgetary balance was the perfect compromise between individualism and collectivism. . . . Hierarchy agrees to limit its appetite (or at least pay its bill), and individualism to pay more, provided the budget remains balanced.[53]

Gladstone established a fiscal equilibrium at midcentury that provided Britain with a balanced budget for the remainder of the Victorian era. Property and industry, town and country, rich and poor were balanced within this fiscal structure.

Balance is desirable, but once it is established, equilibrium can become an undesirable compulsion. It is like the man who has reached his "ideal" weight and, once there, is terrified at the thought of gaining a pound or losing one, for fear that he will uncontrollably inflate or wither. When balance dominates obsessively, change can be impossible, even change to a different and perhaps more desirable equilibrium.

So obsessed were the British with fiscal balance that they were troubled by the national debt even during the years when they were systematically able to reduce it. This may seem strange to modern readers, who take for granted the existing stock of national debt and focus on the annual deficit or surplus as the indicator of fiscal balance. For Victorian political economists (or some of them anyway), the very existence of a national debt was in and of itself a fiscal balance problem. To them, fiscal balance could not be restored by a simple balanced budget, or even a small surplus. The problem was not solved until the national debt itself was eliminated. Given an understanding of this attitude, the amazingly strict discipline of Gladstonian public finance is easier to accept.

Britain's obsession with fiscal balance may have contributed to its growing rigidities. Any major change in taxation, expenditures, or the nature of public debt threatened to throw the entire system out of balance. So the British adopted institutions that worked — or seemed to — and resisted change. British public finances provide evidence of this tendency. The following account suggests the compulsive attachment to balance that characterized British public finance and stymied structural change:

> Despite limited spending and steady revenue growth, the threat of budgetary deficits continued to haunt politicians. No political leader of the 1850s, '60s, and '70s could ever be certain that revenue would be adequate to balance the budget. Year after year at budget time, always offering profuse apologies to the public for failing to repeal the income tax as Peel had promised long ago, England's finance ministers deferred risk by retaining it a few years longer.[54]

The Victorians' belief in the notion of balance and equilibrium was so strong that virtually any imbalance or threat of one could panic them. The assumption seems to have been that their fiscal balance was an unstable one that could keel over and crash at any moment. Marshall described equilibrium as an apple in a bowl, but the Victorians felt that their budget was balanced on the point of a pin.

When Britain needed an income tax in the 1840s, it fell back on the tax of 1806, despite the significant changes in the economy during these years. Indeed, the 1806 tax fell more heavily on commerce and industry by design, since Parliament was controlled by the landed interests at the turn of the century. Peel's tax reforms at midcentury were adopted by a reformed Parliament that now reflected urban interests but still fell back on the old tax.

The 1806 tax was flawed; the treatment of capital depreciation in particular caused problems. Yet the perceived danger of disturbing fiscal balance discouraged adjustments and reforms and allowed the income tax to remain for years an obstacle to industrial modernization.

In the same way, the basic structure of the finance system in general and the national debt in particular remained rigidly fixed for decades because of the successful balance that had been achieved. Change was so slow! Walter Bagehot, editor of the *Economist*, is credited with the invention of the Treasury bill, an innovation that further increased the liquidity of government obligations by allowing them to trade at a discount, the same as commercial bills. What is amazing in this story is not that Bagehot thought of discounting government bonds — this idea should have been obvious. The important fact is that it took so very long for someone to gather enough influence to cause the city to make this small change in their business.

Victorian Britain found its center of gravity and evolved social and economic institutions to make sure it kept its balance. Without the same rigid institutions, other countries lost their balance and surged ahead. British government did little that openly promoted the early growth or obviously caused the later decline — that is the myth of laissez-faire. But as we have seen, fiscal crisis and public finance in Britain helped form the institutional constraints that hampered structural change and ultimately contributed to the Victorian decline.

6

The American Century
and the American Crisis

In just twenty-five years we have gone from the American century to the
American crisis. This is an astounding turnaround—perhaps the shortest
parabola in history.   Felix Rohatyn

The postwar baby boom generation has witnessed a series of economic and
social changes that accumulating gradually over the short and incomplete span
of their generation, changed dramatically the world in which they lived and
transformed forever the world their children will inherit.

One need not agree completely with Felix Rohatyn's characterization of the
"American century" as the "world's shortest"[1] to sense, feel, and think that the
place of the United States and its citizens within the world has changed, has
deteriorated. U.S. hegemony over the economic and political spheres has been
replaced. No, we are not dominated by others; but we are now dependent on
what other economic powers do. We have become more like the other players in
this great drama, a rude and unwelcome fact to a nation used to the featured
role.

What was the turning point? When did the "American century" end and the
crisis begin? It is hard to resist the temptation to pick a time or event that
divides the boom from the bust. In his influential study of the auto industries
of the United States and Japan, David Halberstam locates a turning point in
the early 1980s, during the recession of the early Reagan years:

> In the first half of this century America had been the most dynamic and
> productive society in the world. Now, in the latter part of the century, its
> strengths were diminished. Manufacturing something, actually producing
> something, had become costly and difficult. Except in the world of high
> technology . . . the actual making of goods had become a burden. . . . Na-
> tions just emerging into the industrial sphere, particularly those in Asia, were
> proving fierce and unrelenting competitors. . . . Money could be put into
> money funds where it sat, making more money than could be earned if put
> into the blue-chip industrial stocks of yore.[2]

It was not that in the early 1980s the economists and bean counters had
taken over from the visionary industrialists and production line manufactur-

132

ers—that had happened years before in the days when bean counter Alfred Sloan's General Motors cars raced ahead of old Henry Ford's Model T. Now it was not the number of beans but the counting itself that mattered.

Leveraged finance—the paper chase that the Medici called "dry exchange"—replaced the worker's wrench and the accountant's ledger as the source of business profits. "Lee Iacocca . . . was not a manufacturer, but a portfolio manager. . . . It was more profitable for him to make money off money—to have Chrysler become, in effect, a financial house, than it was for him to actually produce something."[3]

Detroit, the city that Halberstam uses to symbolize the U.S. economy, awoke like Rip Van Winkle to a world at once both familiar and completely changed. The transformation of the postwar world has been complete, at least in the sense that virtually all aspects of life have been affected, but it has not been sudden. The changes were many and gradual, accumulating over several decades, spanning the globe as world markets expanded and interacted.

Because of the complex and gradual pattern of structural change, it is difficult (and perhaps even misleading) actually to draw the parabola of boom and bust as surely as Rohatyn's periodization or to pick a turning point as precisely as Halberstam. These changes came in small doses, by fits and starts, a day at a time, unnoticed until enough had accumulated to make their shape obvious to sharp eyes. The economy changed as the seasons changed. But unlike the seasons, these changes were unexpected and so took longer to become obvious to eyes that expected endless summer.

Orders of Magnitude

The United States has experienced a very high rate of structural change in the years since World War II. Part of this change is due to the nation's great (if uneven) economic growth. But a good deal of the structural change that we observe derives from a series of "revolutions" in population, technology, finance, and communications, which will be analyzed in the next section.[4]

The economic and social institutions of the United States and many other developed nations have not adjusted successfully to the profound and startling cumulative effects of the normal pattern of economic transformation associated with growth combined with, and compounded by, these additional sources of change and growth. The symptoms of this problem can be seen in the prolonged and persistent fiscal imbalances that have been especially noticeable in the 1980s. This section presents some data that describe the size and scope of the structural changes and fiscal imbalances that the U.S. economy has experienced in the postwar era.

A. G. B. Fisher's theory of structural change during economic growth predicts that as the economy grows, production and employment will shift progressively from the primary to the secondary to the tertiary sectors of the economy. This general pattern of structural change appears when we examine production patterns in the U.S. economy in the postwar era, as shown in Table

6.1. This table shows how the share of gross national product has changed regarding its relative division among Fisher's three sectors.[5]

Production by the primary sector (agriculture plus mining) in the United States increased significantly over the four decades between 1947 and 1987, from $123 billion to over $213 billion in real (1982) dollars. In relative terms, however, the primary sector declined by half, from about 11.5 percent of GNP in 1947 to only about 5.5 percent of GNP in 1987. As table 6.1 shows, economic growth has shifted production to the secondary (construction plus manufacturing) and the tertiary (trades and services) sectors of the economy. It is noteworthy, however, that the share of output flowing from the secondary sector has not continued to rise to absorb resources released from primary production but peaked in the 1960s at a little over 30 percent. While tertiary sector production has continued to grow (and now represents about two-thirds of GNP), secondary sector output has declined in relative terms, to the point where it represented in 1987 a smaller fraction of GNP than in 1947 (26.3 percent in 1987 compared to 28 percent in 1947).[6]

The relative decline in output by the secondary sector is the first disturbing fact we will encounter. It is the first indication that there is more than economic growth at work here; and it is perhaps the first symptom of the inability of economic institutions to adjust to rapid change.

The relative decline of the secondary sector of the U.S. economy is even more significant if structural change is measured, as Fisher first suggested, using employment rather than production data. In terms of jobs, the manufacturing sector has experienced a dramatic decline in the postwar era, from providing over 35 percent of employment opportunities in 1947 to only about

Table 6.1. Structural Change in the U.S. Economy:
GNP Shares, Selected Years 1947–1987 (%)

Year	Primary Sector	Secondary Sector	Tertiary Sector
1947	11.5	28.0	60.0
1950	11.3	29.7	58.1
1955	10.7	30.8	57.7
1960	9.7	30.1	60.6
1965	8.4	31.4	60.1
1970	8.4	27.9	63.2
1975	7.3	25.8	65.8
1980	6.6	25.9	65.3
1985	6.2	26.3	66.5
1987	5.5	26.3	67.4

Note: The primary sector is agriculture and mining; the secondary sector is construction and manufacturing; the tertiary sector is wholesale and retail trades, finance, insurance and real estate services, and services. Sector definitions are not exhaustive with respect to GNP; columns therefore do not sum to 100 percent.

Source: Based on data from President's Council of Economic Advisors, *Economic Report of the President* (Washington: GPO, 1989), table B-11.

18.6 percent in 1987. Table 6.2 shows the fraction of total nonagricultural payroll jobs provided by manufacturing versus the service sector of the economy. It indicates that the service sector is now the home of over 75 percent of all payroll employees (in 1987) compared with about 58 percent of these jobs in 1947.[7]

It is not necessarily surprising that the secondary sector of the economy declined in relative terms over this forty-year period. In fact, Fisher and Engel lead us to expect a shift in this direction as the higher incomes generated by economic growth combine with our evolving tastes and preferences. What makes this trend worthy of our attention is not its existence but its size and speed. This is really a very large relative movement in resource use and production in so short a period of time.

The pace of structural transformation has been rapid in the postwar era, much faster than the rate of economic growth. This tells us that individual workers, investors, and firms in the economy have been forced to change the patterns of their behavior dramatically. The impact of all these changes on the economy, in terms of the effect on fiscal balance, is suggested by the data in Tables 6.3 and 6.4.

Economic and social (but especially economic) institutions legitimize and sustain themselves in part by achieving a balance between and among competing forces. Thus, for example, the political institutions of government achieve a balance between individual and social rights and responsibilities. And the political economy of the government's budget is essentially a balance between the social uses of scarce resources and the alternative private uses. Social and economic institutions are preserved when they successfully keep their balance.

The federal budget has lost its balance, as Table 6.3 makes clear. The politi-

Table 6.2. Trends in Manufacturing versus Service Employment: Nonagricultural Payroll Employees, Selected Years 1947–1987 (%)

Year	Proportion of Jobs in Manufacturing	Proportion of Jobs in Services
1947	35.4	58.0
1950	33.7	59.0
1955	33.3	59.5
1960	30.9	62.3
1965	29.7	63.9
1970	27.3	66.7
1975	23.8	70.6
1980	22.4	71.6
1985	19.7	74.5
1987	18.6	75.7

Note: Division is not exhaustive; columns do not sum to 100 percent.

Source: Based on data from President's Council of Economic Advisors, *Economic Report of the President* (Washington: GPO, 1989), table B-43.

Table 6.3. Measure of Fiscal Balance in the Economy,
Selected Calendar Years 1947–1987
(% of Current-Year GNP)

Year	Federal Budget Surplus	Current Account Surplus	Net International Capital Inflows
1947	5.7	3.8	—
1950	3.2	−.6	—
1955	1.0	.0	—
1960	.5	.5	−.3
1965	.0	.7	−.7
1970	−1.2	.2	−.2
1975	−4.3	1.1	−1.5
1980	−2.2	−2.8	2.4
1985	−4.9	−2.8	2.4
1987	−3.4	−3.4	3.0

Note: Comparable data on net international capital inflows not available for years before 1960.

Source: Based on data from President's Council of Economic Advisors, *Economic Report of the President* (Washington: GPO, 1989), tables B-79, B-102.

cal and economic institutions of the federal government have progressively failed to balance competing resource demands. This imbalance is dramatic in the United States, but many other developed countries face a similar imbalance. This suggests that there may be larger forces—those of structural change—at work here.

The economy has also lost its balance with respect to the international economy. Table 6.3 shows that the current account of the United States has slipped from surplus to deficit. The current account, which is dominated by international trade flows but also includes payment of investment income, shows roughly the net impact of international transactions on current national

Table 6.4. Net U.S. International Asset Position in Billions of Current Dollars, 1980–1987

Year	U.S. Assets Abroad	Foreign Assets in U.S.	Net U.S. Asset Position	Net Position (% of GNP)
1980	607.1	500.8	106.3	3.8
1981	719.8	578.7	141.1	4.6
1982	824.9	688.1	136.9	4.3
1983	873.9	784.5	89.4	2.6
1984	896.1	892.6	3.5	.0
1985	950.3	1,061.0	−110.7	−2.7
1986	1,017.4	1,340.7	−269.2	−6.3
1987	1,167.8	1,536.0	−368.2	−8.1

Source: Based on data from President's Council of Economic Advisors, *Economic Report of the President* (Washington: GPO, 1989), tables B-1, B-106.

income. As these figures show, the international economy has gone from having a relatively large positive impact on national income in 1947 (3.8 percent) to a large negative impact (-3.4 percent of GNP in 1987). The large current account imbalance of 1947 is understandable in light of the nature of world adjustment to the end of World War II. The almost equally large imbalance of 1987, however, suggests that the United States is facing an adjustment problem of its own of nearly the same magnitude.

The substantial international imbalance between the United States and the rest of the world can be seen in two other ways. The last column in Table 6.3 shows a measure of net international investment or capital movements for selected years. These data show that the United States has been transformed from a source for international capital to a net recipient of funds from abroad. In the 1980s these international capital inflows have been very large, amounting to 3 percent of GNP. This is equivalent to the idea that on net, 3 percent of all domestic goods and services were purchased with funds borrowed from abroad. This is not necessarily a fatal imbalance, but an imbalance it is and a sustained one.

The massive inflows of funds from abroad in the 1980s have reversed the long-standing international investment position of the United States. Table 6.4 shows that the United States had a net asset position of $106 billion in 1980, which means that U.S. persons owned $106 billion more of foreign assets than foreigners owned of U.S. assets (land, stocks, bonds, etc.). Between 1980 and 1987 this position suffered a stunning reversal. By 1987 the United States was a net international debtor (in the accounting sense of foreign debits' exceeding foreign credits). This is another indicator of the large extent of fiscal imbalance in the U.S. economy.

There is much that can be (and will be) said about these changes and imbalances. The point to be made here is that these structural changes are too large to result from routine economic growth; other forces are at work. Our social and economic institutions have not been able to cope successfully with these large changes, as indicated by the fiscal imbalances we have seen.

Sources of Change in the American Economy

The United States entered the postwar era as the leading economy and the strongest economic force in the world. This, according to Paul Kennedy's analysis, explains why the United States was also the leading and strongest political and military force at this time, despite the long-standing U.S. propensity to look always inward, not abroad, and avoid foreign entanglements.[8] The United States assumed fully the mantle of the leading industrial economy during the Second World War, with all the associated rights and obligations. But the United States had in fact become the world's leading economy fifty years before.[9] The United States overtook Britain in economic terms in the last decade of the nineteenth century, if not earlier. The vast human, technical, and natural resources of the United States achieved their great productive potential in the hands of U.S. capitalists. British entrepreneurs at this time remained stuck in the ruts of an earlier age, caught in the waning age of textiles and railroads while the world moved ahead to electricity and the age of the automobile.

It is the nature of growing economic systems to change, but the changes that the United States experienced in the decades after World War II were different by several orders of magnitude from those generated by growth alone. Some of the changes were short and sharp, obvious in this if not in their ultimate consequence. Other changes were small and subtle—tiny shifts that built and compounded over the years, too small to make the news on any given Thursday but greater in their total impact than a year's worth of headlines.

The forces that created the postwar boom and bust were like the forces that created the Industrial Revolution of the eighteenth century in the respect that no single dynamic determined the course of economic history; patterns of economic development and structural change can be explained only as the complex interaction of several trends. In the historiography of the Industrial Revolution these trends are called "revolutions," which is therefore the term I will use here. The postwar era was marked by revolutions in population, technology, finance, and communications. Together these forces created the "American century" and the "American crisis."

The Population Revolution

The "baby boom" of the 1950s (and the subsequent baby bust) is the most obvious and arguably the most significant revolution of the postwar era. It is also the event that is most clearly a "revolution" in the proper sense, a true reversal in direction rather than an oblique change in course or a sudden shift in speed.

The birthrate in the United States had long been falling from the high rates of the nineteenth century. The crude birthrate in 1870–1875, for example, was 40.8 births per thousand of population; but it had fallen to about 30 births per thousand by the turn of the century and was lower still, about 23 births per thousand, in the 1920s.[10] The overall rate of population growth was also slowing during these years—but by a smaller amount due to migration and a falling death rate.

This falling fertility trend was sharply punctuated in the 1930s by a baby bust. The crude birth rate fell suddenly to about 18 per thousand population and remained at this low level. The Great Depression of the economy was mirrored in a great population depression, which was not reversed in any significant way during the war years of the 1940s.

Given the secular decline in the birthrate and the sharp drop in births of the 1930s, the baby boom of the 1950s was truly revolutionary. The crude birthrate jumped by almost one-third, from about 18 births per thousand in the 1930s to over 25 births per thousand in the late 1950s. The birthrate remained above the secular trend until the middle years of the 1960s.

The baby boom was a remarkable, unexpected event. It was not anticipated that population growth would remain in the 1950s at the very low rates experienced in the 1930s; an increase in fertility would be needed to return the birthrate to its downward-sloping, long-term trend line. But the baby boom went far beyond any adjustment to trend, creating a surge in the supply of people and in their demand for resources.

A baby bust followed the baby boom; the crude birthrate in the 1970s dropped nearly by half, from about 25 births per thousand population to less than 15. This "bust" may in fact have represented a return to the long-term trend in fertility. It is hard to look at a picture of the crude birthrate over the last century without sensing that the long-run trend line was regained in the 1970s after three decades or more of anomalous behavior. But if the recent baby bust was a return to "normalcy," it hardly had that effect on the economy.

As Victor Fuchs points out in his excellent survey, *How We Live: An Economic Perspective on Americans from Birth to Death*, each stage of life carries with it a different set of choices, problems, and needs. How we (both as individuals and as a society) make these choices, how we confront these problems, and how we meet these needs determines how we live. To an important extent, our social system tries to provide institutions that support and encourage us at each state of life, helping us make sound choices, define and solve our problems, and gain the resources necessary to meet our needs.[11] The institutions of government, for example, attempt to provide education for the young, the opportunity for productive work in middle years, and a measure of economic security for the old.[12]

The choices, problems, and needs that people face are such that society is almost always strained to cope with them, even when population patterns are smooth and predictable. The bust–boom–bust population cycle I have just described was not smooth and predictable and has therefore imposed extraordinary strains on the fabric of society and the institutions that are woven into the social cloth.

There are any number of ways to illustrate the impact of the uneven birthrate on the economy. Space does not permit a comprehensive analysis of the situation, but we can gain at least the flavor of the problem by looking at how the baby bust–boom–bust has affected the system of public education (the young), the job market (the middle years), and how it will affect the social security system (the old).[13]

Education is an investment that requires even more investment. It is an investment in human capital because skills and knowledge gained now produce a stream of benefits in terms of greater understanding and higher productivity in the future. Investments must be made to make this investment; schools and libraries must be built, books must be written and published, and teachers must be trained. A very substantial amount of human and physical capital is required by the education system. Such large capital-intensive systems cannot adjust very rapidly to changes in the quantity or type of education produced. Educational institutions, like large ships, are dominated by their own momentum; they cannot turn on a dime.

But turning on a dime is precisely what the U.S. educational system has had to do in the last four decades. In the 1930s and 1940s, for example, the educational system had to adjust to a much smaller population of students with relatively modest goals. The downsizing of the school system was facilitated by the war, which readily absorbed all spare resources (and then some). The lean and spare schools of the forties, built for the scarce children of the thirties, were therefore unprepared for the baby boomers. Very large amounts of resources had to be moved from other parts of the economy and invested in new buildings, books, and teachers to meet the requirements of first primary, then secondary, and then finally higher education. When the baby bust became apparent in the 1970s and 1980s, the problems became how to divert these skilled and productive resources from education, where they were no longer needed, to other areas such as housing, where baby-boomer demands were mounting.

The unexpected changes in the birthrate caused clear and — in retrospect — obvious institutional problems in education. The schools moved from over- to under- to overcapacity. The degree of structural change necessary to accommodate the population bulge was significant and the social cost was high, in no small part because of the expensive long-term investments necessary at each stage.

Another set of adjustments was required as these different population groups began to enter the labor force. First came the depression's baby bust generation, which entered the civilian labor force, for the most part, after World War II. At first the relative dearth of workers was offset by a similar lack of civilian sector jobs, but this changed as the economy adjusted to peace. Soon supply-demand conditions in the job markets, combined with other factors to be discussed soon, helped to push wages and incomes up. The standard of living in the United States began its greatest rise in the 1950s and continued in the 1960s. The "Great American middle class" was created, relatively large in numbers and endowed with greater purchasing power than any similar group in economic history. This group married earlier and had more babies than the previous generation; these were the parents of the baby-boomers.

As the children of the baby boom arrived at working age in the 1970s and 1980s, they found labor supply in excess of labor demand. Predictably, relative wage rates were not so high for these new workers as for their parents and their standard of living was relatively lower. The relative decline in wages was one of several factors that contributed to another significant demographic shift at this time, the dramatic increase in female labor force participation. More and more women delayed marriage and motherhood to enter the job market. While the supply of male workers was rising, the increase in the number of women in the labor force was substantially greater because of the increase in participation rates among females. This put great stress on a labor market that was unready for so great an increase in supply and that had long applied gender-specific labels to many jobs.

Relative wages were depressed by the very large increase in the supply of labor and by the even larger relative increase in the supply of female workers, who were traditionally paid on average about 60 percent the wage for men. They flooded the market for "women's work," finally inducing many employers to treat male and female workers as close substitutes. Cheaper female labor bid jobs away from formerly better-paid men. The result was that while relative wages were held down or fell (particularly compared to the prior generation's experience), the relative wage of male workers was more greatly affected. Men in many occupations began to be paid as women had always been paid. This meant lower living standards and made the one-paycheck household of the 1950s an endangered species.

Society had to create more and new jobs to meet the needs of the members of the baby boom generation as they reached their twenties and thirties. There is no magic formula for absorbing labor supply. All else being equal, greater quantities of labor are absorbed by businesses by assigning them to relatively lower-productivity tasks and adjusting down the relative wage rates according-ly. When the baby bust generation reaches working age, the same dynamic will work in the opposite direction. Fewer jobs and of a different type will be needed. The structure of the economy will necessarily change again.

Retirement imposes another set of stresses and strains, aches and pains, on society. As the baby boom generation begins to age, more and more resources will need to be allocated to the types of goods and services that the aged require and demand. This will cause a dramatic shift in the focus of society, because there will be relatively fewer workers compared to the number of retirees. This means that for a time at least, a rather large fraction of those in the labor force will be employed in the service of their parent's generation: supplying them with medical and nursing home care, for example.

The institutional structure of the economy will eventually shift far off center as it tries to balance the needs of the large elderly population against the smaller but highly compensated human resources of the baby bust generation. The dynamic will continue but reverse as the baby-busters themselves enter their retirement years.

In summary, the baby bust–boom–bust has created an environment where stable and long-lasting institutions, including public sector institutions like education and private sector institutions like the labor market, attempt to adjust to an uneven pattern of population and labor force growth. As the patterns of demand and supply in the economy shift and shift back, tremen-dous resource movements follow. A good deal of the structural change we have observed in the postwar period derives from the population revolution alone.

The Technology Revolution

It is everyday common sense to think that the United States and the world have experienced (and are still experiencing) a revolution in technology. Clearly, technology has changed with respect to our everyday lives. Ordinary people in the industrial countries now come into daily contact with relatively sophisticat-ed devices such as optical scanners, videocassette recorders, and a variety of computer-monitored items installed in automobiles, heating systems, commu-nications devices—the list goes on and on.

With our daily lives so filled with new gadgets and high-tech toys, it is natural for us to suppose that business and industry have adopted new tech-nologies to an ever greater extent. It is natural to suppose that we are living through a technology revolution. Britain's (first) Industrial Revolution was mechanical — machines replaced or augmented people in the production process. The second industrial revolution, late in the nineteenth century, was electrical and chemical. New processes and products based on scientific advances formed the thrust of this revolution in production. Given this background, it seems natural to suppose that the current revolution is somehow based on electronics in general and computers in particular.[14]

This commonsense understanding of the technology revolution is right, and it is wrong. It is clear that there has been great change in the technology that U.S. citizens use at work and at home; you see this every time you start your car. But the real revolution has not been in the invention of new products and processes so much as in their much more rapid diffusion within the economy and across international borders. The speed within which innovations move through the world economy is the real "revolution" in technology and therefore the most important cause of the rapid technology-based structural changes we have observed.

One way to think of the technological revolution is to look at the process of technological change as a series of three steps. The first step is investment in research and development, which provides the seed resources necessary for technological change. The second stage is innovation, where new or improved products or processes take form as marketable products. The third stage is diffusion, where innovations in products and processes are adopted by domestic and foreign firms. This is the stage at which most of us actually come into contact with technological changes.

The United States is the leading economy in the first stage of this complex process. The amount of real resources that the United States economy allocates to research and development is very high — over $100 billion in 1982 dollars or about equal to the total research and development (R&D) expenditures of Japan, West Germany, France, and the United Kingdom combined.[15] Of this total for the United States about half is supplied directly by private industry, and about half is funneled through the federal government to R&D projects undertaken by universities and private firms.

Almost two-thirds (64 percent) of the United States' national R&D budget is devoted to development of existing ideas and processes, while 22 percent goes to applied research and just 14 percent to so-called basic research. The United States devotes many more resources to R&D than do other countries, but it also uses those resources differently than do other nations. For one thing, a great deal of the basic research in the United States is focused on military or national defense projects (such as Star Wars — the Strategic Defense Initiative). Almost zero of Japan's research budget goes for defense-related projects.

The United States has been overtaken by other countries at the second stage of the technology process: innovation. It is admittedly difficult to measure the extent of innovation directly; we are always forced to fall back on imperfect indirect measures of innovation, such as number of patents granted.[16] In recent years the number of patents granted to United States-based innovations has fallen behind patents granted to foreign firms, particularly Japanese firms.

Thus, while we spend more on R&D (the first stage), these resources generate fewer marketable innovations (the second stage).

The diffusion of innovation is really the critical stage of in the technology process. This is the stage where innovations are incorporated into a variety of actual products and processes. This is therefore the stage where visible structural change in the economy begins.

The pace of the diffusion of innovation has increased dramatically in the postwar years and particularly in the past decade. Diffusion is more rapid in three respects:

1. Innovations are now more quickly applied to the specific products and processes for which they were developed.
2. Innovations are now more rapidly spread to other products and processes.
3. Innovations now spread more quickly to foreign firms and markets.

There are specific causes and consequences to each of these aspects of more rapid technological change.

Technology is often embedded in capital, either physical or human. Technological change is often associated with changes in this physical or human capital. But technology embedded in a very large and costly capital component is often resistant to change. Incremental change is sometimes impossible within large fixed capital structure, and wholesale change in this capital is economical only so long as the change in technology is worth the cost of the capital in which it is contained. The result is that some technologies are frozen in place by their capital component.

In this context, the more rapid adoption of innovation by industry reflects the fact that many innovations now have a relatively smaller capital component and so can find wide use more quickly. But it is also true that much innovation and development has focused on products and processes that are outside the main "production line" that is so capital-intensive. This speeds the development and diffusion. In short, computer technology has been quickly diffused because of where and how it is used: in design, in research itself, and in information processing. Diffusion of computers into the actual production process—robotics—has been much slower in part because of the capital cost and the problem of integrating new capital into existing output structures. In summary, technology is now more quickly put into practice because of where and how it is used.

The second aspect of the technology revolution is that innovations are now more rapidly diffused to related fields. Laser disk technology (to use a popular example) was quickly applied to video reproduction (video disks), computer data storage (CD-ROM disks), audio reproduction (compact disks), and into products that combine these and other applications. To a great extent this increase in the rate of diffusion is a reflection of the higher relative emphasis on development versus research. It is also a consequence of the increased competition in the high-technology sector of the world economy, where many firms seek the rapid payoffs from new discoveries through spin-offs and development.

Finally, innovations are now more rapidly diffused throughout the world economy than before. There are many reasons for this change. The growth of multinational firms is one explanation; technological diffusion within the firm is now more likely to take place through international technological transfer not limited to a single country or market. Even where firms are not multinational, many markets are. The United States earns a substantial surplus in trade in "services" through the licensing of U.S. technology to foreign firms.

The increased speed of international technological diffusion is perhaps best seen through the shortening of the international "product cycle," a concept developed by Raymond Vernon. The product cycle refers to a pattern of production and trade that is most common for innovative, labor-saving, high-technology goods. The cycle is that the product is initially developed in a country to meet domestic needs, then produced at home and sold both at home and in other similar high-income countries. In the final stage production is moved abroad, to low-cost producers, and the item is imported into its original home market. Home-grown technology is diffused abroad in the last two stages of the product cycle.

The product cycle, once relatively long on average, has now shortened to just a few years or, in some markets, a matter of months. Innovations now rapidly spread among the developed nations and from them to less-developed countries.

The rapid diffusion of technological change means that resources now move more quickly from place to place within the economy and around the world. Structural change is accelerated; but more than this, its focus has shifted to areas where the impact of changing technology has been greatest.

One important side effect of this process is the increased focus on short-run profit. Resources increasingly flow into areas that are experiencing rapid technological change. But because change is so rapid in precisely these areas and because competition is intense, new products and processes are likely to have a short economic half-life. They will be quickly overtaken by newer developments. Returns therefore must be realized quickly. Diffusion within product lines must be rapid. Firms must innovate, develop, reap the returns, and move on to begin the cycle again.

The postwar technology revolution is like earlier "industrial revolutions" in that improved products and processes are a driving force for structural change. But the emphasis of the degree and speed of diffusion makes this "revolution" different in important ways from those that went before.

The Financial Revolution

Finance is critical to any dynamic and changing economy. Most people think of the problem of finance in the simplest of terms: the problem of getting and keeping the money that a person, business, or government needs to buy what it wants to buy. And this practical aspect of finance is important. But for the present it is more important to consider the social function of finance, which is to direct and lubricate the flow of scarce resources from one use to another. Stocks, bonds, loans, bills, notes, bank accounts, and all the rest are essentially boats that carry resources from one place in the economy to another by way of certain regulated and well-defined canals.

Finance has become a much more prevalent and important part of daily life in every sector of the economy during the postwar period. Innovations in financial markets have been a critical factor in the vast, shifting pattern of structural changes that we have observed. It is thus appropriate to talk about a financial revolution in the years since World War II.

The most important factor in the financial revolution has been the increasing reliance on debt to finance personal, business, and government activities. The increased emphasis on debt has led to innovation in the financial markets, which has been very rapid in the last decade. The need for greater liquidity to deal with this debt has produced a greater securitization of financial instruments and a greater reliance on financial intermediaries. As financial markets have expanded beyond their early postwar bounds, there has been a progressive liberalization of regulation of financial affairs within the industrial nations, and a globalization of financial flows among nations.[17]

Writing in 1980, Harvard finance professor Benjamin Friedman found that

> The single development in the American financial markets since World War II that has been most striking . . . has been the rise of the private debt economy. Individuals and especially businesses have almost continually increased their degree of reliance on debt in relation to their basic nonfinancial activity. Corporations have relied more on both negotiated loans and market debt issues, in comparison to equity. . . . Individuals have relied more on mortgage credit . . . and consumer credit to finance their ownership of durables and even current consumption. As a result, the indebtedness of the American economy's private sector has risen substantially.[18]

Throughout the postwar period up to the late 1970s, according to Friedman's study, the total outstanding debt of United States nonfinancial borrowers had remained relatively stable at about 150 percent of gross national product. But while the government's share of this total had declined after the Second World War, the private sector's share increased. Private sector debt rose from about 50 percent of GNP in the 1950s to about 100 percent of GNP in 1978, a very significant change in behavior.

One explanation of the growth of the "private debt economy" during this period is that the supply of credit was roughly constant (as a fraction of GNP) and the decreasing public sector share had the impact of "crowding in" private sector debt. Lower relative levels of public sector debt reduce interest costs and increase the quantity of credit that the private sector assumes.

The trend toward falling public sector and rising private sector debt experienced a sharp reversal in the decade of the 1980s. The trend of higher private debt continued, but the relative decline of public debt was halted and reversed. Writing in 1988, Friedman noted that "The sustained rise in federal debt in relation to income . . . is unprecedented in our history. . . . In the 1980s, the federal debt ratio is not only rising but rising just as fast as it had fallen in the previous three and a half decades after World War II."[19]

The rapid rise in public sector borrowing and the sustained increase in private sector borrowing was not matched in the 1980s by an equal increase in domestic savings, from which loans could be made. In fact, private savings rates fell in the 1980s as U.S. citizens made the choice not to save for the future but to borrow to consume now. The money to fill in this credit gap came from abroad. The United States quickly became a net debtor nation after many years of net creditor status. The critical influence of the rising public debt on the economy will be explored in more depth in a later section.

It is difficult to establish an unambiguous cause-and-effect relationship for the several aspects of the financial revolution; it is perhaps most correct to state that the various changes in the financial markets fed on each other and accelerated their mutual growth.

The increase in private sector debt, for example, resulted in a need for greater liquidity than was available within the highly regulated financial system of the 1950s. This resulted in a series of financial instrument innovations, such as money market funds and NOW accounts, which answered the call for increased liquidity but tended to fall outside the bounds of the regulatory structure. Unable to put the jinni back in its financial bottle, regulations were liberalized, which stimulated greater innovation in financial instruments and allowed the globalization of financial markets.

Soon financial markets became broad enough to make increasing specialization possible among financial intermediaries, which further reduced the transactions costs of finance market activities. Deregulation increased competition among financial intermediaries, who suddenly had a powerful profit incentive to reduce their costs. The force of falling costs began to drive market growth in addition to other factors.

Financial markets are now much more efficient, in the sense that they can now connect borrower and lender at a lower resource cost. Financial intermediaries are now more specialized, they trade a wider range of specialized financial instruments and, because of the standardization of securities, there is a greater degree of liquidity available. These are all healthy developments.

The downside of the financial revolution is that the economy is now much more highly leveraged (and, therefore, perhaps riskier) than at any time in the postwar period (and any time of prosperity in our history). Efficient financial markets have smoothly and speedily shuttled resources from one use to another, but it is not altogether clear that the resulting distribution and allocation is desirable. In general, funds have flowed from relatively poorer countries (Japan and Germany, but also less developed country (LDC) debtor nations) to richer ones (the United States) and from use in investment and production to the growing trend of public and private consumption.

Some of the effects of the financial revolution are clear and concrete; others are more subtle and abstract, but not necessarily less important. One subtle impact is the growing cultural influence of financial concerns and ideas. The values and priorities generated by and for the financial markets have slowly seeped into the structure of everyday life; it would be foolhardy to conclude that these financial influences have not altered the real structure of the economy.

David Halberstam, in his book, *The Reckoning*, makes a strong anecdotal case for the proposition that the culture of finance has replaced the culture of production in U.S. business, to the economy's detriment. Halberstam notes that

> Gradually the companies began to respond to what [Wall] Street wanted . . . in order to compete for capital. As the companies changed their style, so too did they — almost imperceptibly at first — change their purpose. It was no longer enough simply to make a good product at a solid profit; now more and more the object was to drive the stock up. . . . Inevitably that preoccupation with the stock forced old-line companies to make short-range moves designed to make the present look good at the expense of the future. Research and development were chopped back because they were expensive and cut into profits and hurt the way the company looked on its books. . . . Without anyone's realizing it, the maneuvering room within American capitalism was becoming more and more restricted.[20]

The financial revolution therefore contributed to a series of major economic changes — in international financial status, the pattern of consumption and saving, the distribution and allocation of resources, and the values and priorities that guide everyday decisions.

The Communications Revolution

It is difficult to think about the communications revolution separately from the three patterns of change already discussed. But perhaps the most important point about the revolution in communications is that it has tended to magnify the other structural changes of the postwar era.

The communications revolution is all about information and its use. The years since World War II have seen the role of communications change in the U.S. economy in several important ways. The scope of the communications field has widened dramatically. More types of information are now available to more people packaged in more ways in more different media and at a lower cost. These facts have spurred change and accelerated innovation in virtually every field.

Perhaps the most important feature of the communications revolution is its creation of international, and in some cases global, markets and firms.[21] Communications costs and imperfections represent a limiting factor in the production and distribution of resources. The problem of inefficient communication between buyers and seller, borrower and lender, employee and boss tends to restrict the range of actions that risk-averse people undertake. Ignorance and uncertainty are information problems that limit us.

It is now possible to gather, distribute, and receive a much wider range of more detailed information about the world at a relatively low cost. Anyone with a personal computer and a modem, for example, has practical access to a continuing flow of fact and opinion from around the world.

With the expanded scope and range of communications has come an inevitably wider range of opportunities and actions. The traditional emphasis on economies of scale (do one thing in a big way) was replaced to a certain extent with the ability to exploit economies of scope (apply a basic principle or innovation in as many profitable products and processes as possible). In fact, much production based on scale economies has now been shifted abroad, as product cycle theory predicts. The future for firms in the United States seems to lie closer to the technology-intensive industries that exploit economies of information and scope.

The communications revolution has therefore had the effect of expanding individual interest well beyond the barriers of the prewar economy. Financial markets are now global, traded twenty-four hours a day. Firms find it economical to spread their activities around the globe since many important decisions can be made efficiently from a different time zone, given the rapid flow of information. Although it is too soon to proclaim the existence of the "global village," as some have done, it is too late ever again to think that nations or markets can be clearly and cleanly held apart. The ability to bounce signals off satellites and pick them up on the receiver dish in your backyard make true islands of economic activity rare indeed.

The communications revolution has had a dramatic effect on structural change in the economy, speeding the other forces at work and increasing the amount of information available to decision makers. As much as anything else, improved communications have made possible the global economy and, with it, the problem of global imbalances.

More Than the Sum of the Parts

The total impact of these four revolutions—population, technology, finance, and communications—has been greater than the simple sum of the parts. Together they produced a rapid and dramatic structural transformation of the United States. The change was so great in total as to overwhelm the ability of economic and social institutions to cope with it. Like other great changes, however, it has come over a long-enough period of time that cause and effect are muddled in the daily news and the debate over policies and current events.

The domestic and international fiscal imbalances discussed earlier in this essay are symptoms of the magnitudes of these changes and problems, but they do not completely define them.

The baby boom's rapid and uneven increase in the size of the U.S. population generated an initial strain on the economic system. More and more jobs had to be created to absorb this increase in the work force. The parents of the baby boom generation came to expect a constantly increasing standard of living. The baby-boomers inherited this expectation. To fulfill this expectation, however, the relatively sudden increase in the work force had to be matched by an increase in saving and investment; without increased investment to raise productivity, the ranks of additional workers would be doomed to lower-productivity (and therefore lower-paying) jobs.

The baby boom has been the greatest challenge to the "American dream." The baby bust generation, born in the hard times of the Great Depression, had to create a more productive world for their legions of children if they wanted to bequeath to them a rising living standard.

The technological revolution of the postwar years was timely, given the challenges the United States faced. In theory, technological advances were the key to the puzzle of how to provide a steadily rising standard of living for a much larger population. Without technological change, the parents of the baby-boomers would have had to sacrifice their family's living standards to save and invest, to provide much more human and physical capital for their children's generation than they had inherited themselves. With improved technology, however, a smaller current sacrifice could still generate the kinds of productivity increases in the future that would be needed.

Technology was the answer; there was even an important historical precedent for the belief that the "American dream" of rising living standards could be sustained through technological change. Britain's Industrial Revolution was not just a revolution in manufacturing technology, as many now suppose, but a serendipitous confluence of "revolutions" in population and production. The rate of population increase experienced a spurt in the early nineteenth century that while different in nature from the postwar baby boom, was still significant and a potential threat to average living standards. But Britain's birth boom was met and equalled by advances in technology and productivity throughout the economy. Agricultural productivity increased, providing food for many new mouths that were appearing. Improved technology in manufacturing and elsewhere in the economy provided jobs for workers who left the land.

The issue of how average workers fared in the Industrial Revolution is far from settled (and will not be settled here). There is good evidence to suggest that workers did not experience higher living standards (at least in the first generation or so) as a result of the technical advances of the 1800s. But it is not clear that their living standards fell very much either, which is the important point in this discussion. Without technological change on the farm, at the workshop, and in transportation, it is very likely that Britain's population boom would have caused average living standards to tumble to a bare Malthusean subsistence level.

Technological change helped preserve Victorian living standards, but the reality was more complex than this. Other factors also conspired to Britain's benefit. Because Britain's advances were not quickly adopted abroad, the British enjoyed an export boom. The growing export market created income and jobs for the rising work force. In a closed economy — or one where the advance of technology was quickly adopted by foreign firms — Britain might have had to rely more on its home market. Under these conditions, wages might have been bid down by the higher labor supply and living standards might have deteriorated, even with improved technology.

The technological revolution in the United States has generated a great deal of structural change in the economy, but it has not obviously succeeded in preserving the "American dream" for the baby boom generation. A recent study of the prospects for U.S. living standards concluded that the experiences of the baby boom generation and its children are unlikely to repeat the dramatic increase in living standards that the previous generations achieved:

> At first glance, rising incomes look like a bonus: If future generations could earn as much as today's middle class, it would be quite good enough. But post–World War II America has relied on steadily rising incomes to ease the frictions that arise in society: frictions among regions and among income classes, friction between generations and friction between workers in rising and declining industries.

> It is reasonable to forecast that today's young college education worker will earn more than his college educated father by a modest amount. But the future of today's young high school educated worker is less certain unless the country returns to very rapid economic growth. The kind of upward mobility implied by these projections is significantly less than the kind of mobility that was taken for granted in the 1950s and 1960s.[22]

There are many theories for this failure to recreate the desirable results of the Industrial Revolution, but it is possible to explain much of the problem in terms of the particular circumstances that the United States has faced. The technological revolution has accompanied a population revolution, just as in the British experience, but the change in population has been uneven — bust-boom-bust — in the United States, not a simple increase, as in the British case. (Living standards improved in the British case once the surplus of workers was absorbed.) Significantly, we have also experienced simultaneous revolutions in finance and communications that combined with the other events have weakened the U.S. economy and make the "American dream" that much harder to achieve.

Britain's persistent rise in population served to keep wage rates relatively low in agriculture and industry (or at least prevented any trend toward increase). The bust-boom-bust cycle of U.S. population growth, however, created a different dynamic in the job market. Workers from the Depression era were in relatively short supply in the 1950s and especially the 1960s and were able to bargain for relatively high wages. (The growth of unions in the private sector during these years is at least a weak indicator of the supply-demand imbalance in the labor market.) These workers, of course, were able to earn higher wages in part because investments in better technology and in human capital kept their productivity high. Labor costs in the United States became relatively high and inflexible.[23]

The baby boom generation inherited these labor market conditions, which made labor-intensive goods more expensive than in many other countries. This reduced the beneficial impact of the technological revolution. New products and processes would not necessarily generate more jobs in the United States if these technical advances were offset by higher wage costs in the United States. The U.S. comparative advantage began to move out of manufacturing, where middle-class living standards had previously been determined, and toward the sectors where technology's impact was the greatest and the markets where wage rates were lower or more flexible. The United States began to specialize more in high technology goods and services, where technical advances more than offset high wage rates. At the same time, jobs were also created in services and in the South and the West, where traditional union influences were often weaker and wage rates more competitive.

High labor costs inherited from the baby bust generation gave firms a powerful incentive to implement their technological advances abroad, not at home.[24] The fact that other nations soon began to gain on the United States in terms of research and development, the heart of technological change, made matters worse. The revolutions in finance and communications accelerated the trend toward job creation abroad.

The communications revolution significantly reduced the cost of multinational enterprise. Firms can now more efficiently divide up their various functions, specializing in each area of the world economy according to its special comparative advantage. The revolution in finance, occurring at the same time, made the resource transfers necessary for this division of labor much more efficient as well. Manufacturing capital (and the jobs often tied to it) moved to labor-abundant nations.

Together, the revolutions in population, technology, finance, and communications have made the "American dream"—the expectation of a constantly rising living standard—much more difficult to achieve. But this dream has not died. The notion of a rising standard of consumption remains fixed in the minds of the baby boom generation. While their ability to produce the higher levels of goods and services that they desire has not materialized, their ability to purchase those items does exist, the legacy of the finance boom. The United States has used financial innovation to increase its leverage, using a relatively smaller pool of resources to finance a relatively larger stock of consumer goods.

The result of all this activity is that the United States specializes in high-technology goods (which are sold around the world) and in the consumption of a wide range of goods and services, many of them imported. The rest of the world makes the goods and finances our spending.[25]

Given all these changes, it is not necessarily surprising that the U.S. economy has come unbalanced. Government, a key social and economic institution, has not adapted to changing conditions rapidly enough. The fiscal imbalance, the federal government's growing mountains of public debt, is just a symptom of that imbalance.

The U.S. economy remains unbalanced with respect to the world, as our international payments imbalances indicate. Our standard of material consumption remains above the level that can be sustained.

This analysis helps us understand, in very simple terms, the problems that we face today and their origin in terms of powerful and long-lasting trends in the United States and the world economies. It is unlikely that the causes of the declining U.S. standard of living—changes in population, technology, finance, and communications—can be changed or reversed. The jinni cannot be put back into the bottle. Indeed, given the increasingly international character of all economic and social phenomena today, any attempt to insulate ourselves from these powerful forces would only make our own problem more severe.

This chapter has analyzed the structural changes that have acted on the postwar United States and, to a greater or lesser extent, other advanced, industrial economies. In the next chapter I will discuss how these changes have affected the fiscal institutions of government and therefore how and why we have come to experience fiscal crisis.

7

The Changing Structure
of American Government

No one can question that government's role in the postwar economy has grown tremendously, changed qualitatively, and has affected markedly virtually every aspect of economic activity. . . . The postwar surge of its spending, taxing, regulating, and judging has produced some important accomplishments, but also much to worry us. Not least of these worries is the uneasy and widespread feeling that the juggernaut may be out of control—powered by a dynamic of its own, unrelated to our broad concerns, with results that are as disagreeable to our allies and friends around the world as they are for us. George Shultz

It comes as no surprise that the vast and unexpected structural changes in the postwar economy have had a great impact on the size and shape of government in the United States.[1] The entire government sector of the economy, especially the federal government sector, experienced large and unexpected structural changes in response to the "revolutions" that have swept through the economy in the years since World War II.[2]

It is not surprising, looking back over this period, that the basic structure of government should have changed so much. Government is, after all, a social institution that tends, over time, to adapt itself to the needs and requirements of the economic and social system. When the underlying economy changes, the balance between government and society is temporarily disturbed because governmental institutions take longer to adapt and conform than do the separate individuals that make up society. Structural change in government therefore tends to follow more or less close on the heels of structural changes in the economy and the changes in government necessarily carry some relationships to the changes in the economy.

During the transition, when old government institutions attempt to deal with a changed world, fiscal crisis is likely and mountains of public debt may appear. We have already seen this pattern show up in different ways and at different times—in Renaissance Florence and Victorian Britain. So it is not amazing that we will see it again here. The disappearance of fiscal balance between revenues and outlays in government is a symptom of the underlying imbalance between governmental institutions and the society that supports them.

The relationship between government and society is not a one-way street. Social change alters government, but changes in the institutions of government necessarily alter the payoffs and incentives that confront individuals in society. It is thus the interrelationship between government and the economy that is important for us to understand.

This chapter focuses on the way that the structure of U.S. government in the postwar years has been shaped by the forces of structural change in the economy. The next chapter looks more closely at the other side of the interrelationship, examining how the shifts and movements in the structure of government have impacted the economy and affected its ability to adapt to the emerging, new, world economy.[3]

Structural Changes in American Government

There are many ways to measure and identify the structural changes in government that have taken place in the postwar era, but any analysis of this period must necessarily recognize the following points:

- The size of government has increased. The government share of national income and product has increased dramatically.
- The role of government has changed. This is most easily seen in the changing composition of government expenditures.
- How government is financed has changed. Government now draws *more* resources from the private sector but also *different* resources in the sense that government revenues are drawn from different sectors of the economy.

The increase in the size of government is perhaps the easiest change to document. In nominal dollar terms, federal government outlays increased from just seventy billion dollars in 1954 to over a trillion dollars in 1986. Some of this increase, about a third of it, was due to the simple fact of inflation, which has tended to increase all dollar figures by stupendous amounts. But even adjusting for inflation, the increase in real government outlays has been very large.

Big numbers are sometimes hard to swallow, so it is useful to cut them into bite-sized pieces. On a more personal level, real per capita government outlays increased from $1,639 per year in 1954 to about $3,750 in 1986. This means that even adjusting both for inflation and population growth, the federal government's direct economic role has more than doubled. The federal government commands more than twice as many real resources per person as it did early in the postwar period. The federal government's share of national income rose from about 18 percent in the 1950s to about 24 percent in the 1980s.

Money outlays are just one measure of government's influence, of course, and there are other ways that the growth of government can affect the economy, as through regulations, legal rulings, and the many off-budget aspects of government finance—such as loan guarantees—that do not appear in these figures. The shift toward a larger role for government is both a reflection of the structural changes in the economy and, in fact, a structural change itself. It would not be ridiculous to add a fifth "revolution"—in government—to the previous section's list of four forces of change.

That government does more and uses more resources now than in past years is clear, but what government does and how it uses these resources has changed just as significantly. Perhaps the best way to see this structural change is in the changing balance between national defense and domestic programs within the budget.

In 1954 the share of the federal budget allocated to national defense was 75 percent greater than the share going to domestic programs, which includes social security, education, transportation, and a long list of other payments and transfers. (The exact budget division was 59.2 percent for national defense and 34.2 percent to domestic programs.) The important place of national defense within the federal budget in the early postwar years reflected the role of the federal government and the position than the United States held in cold war foreign affairs. Defense was the government's first priority, and the United States was the key defender of the noncommunist world.

In the 1980s we became accustomed to news of the "defense buildup," but the fact is that the share of the budget going to national defense has trended down during most of the postwar period. In the 1980s, for example, national defense accounted for about 25–27 percent of federal government outlays. While this is much more than in the late 1970s (when defense expenditures were only about 23 percent of federal outlays), current levels of defense spending levels are still far lower than in the early postwar years. The role of the federal government has shifted from the external problems of national defense towards the internal problems of the domestic economy, from public use of private resources to a redistribution of private resources within the population.

The rise of federal outlays for nondefense programs has not been uniform; social security benefits and net interest payments account for the bulk of the increase. Together, social security (about 27 percent) and interest payments (over 13 percent) account for over 40 percent of the federal government budget or nearly 10 percent of the GNP.

What these two budget areas have in common is that they essentially redistribute resources from one group in the economy to another rather than divert private resources for public use. Social security is a program that transfers resources from workers to retirees and their dependents. The payment of net interest tends to transfer resources from taxpayers to the government's growing list of creditors. There are other things that these two budget categories also have in common, which we will discuss in the next section.

Another way to see the relative shift in the federal role from defense towards distribution is by comparing GNP shares. National defense expenditures accounted for over 11 percent of gross national product in 1954; by the 1980s, however, the defense share of GNP had fallen to about 6.5 percent. Meanwhile social security outlays have increased from about 1 percent of GNP in 1954 to nearly 6.5 percent in the 1980s. Net interest payments also rose during this period, from 1.2 percent in 1954 to over 3 percent in the 1980s.

The third major structural change in government is the shift in government finance in the postwar era. Because the government sector has grown, the requirements of government finance have grown proportionately; more and more resources are diverted from the private sector, through government, to other uses.

Two basic trends in federal government finance stand out. First, government revenues have increased, drawing more heavily on the private sector. Second, the composition of federal revenues has changed significantly. In the late 1940s and early 1950s, for example, federal revenues came mainly from personal income, corporate income, and sales and excise taxes. Social insurance taxes were less than 10 percent of federal revenues, while the personal income tax and corporate income tax each accounted for nearly one-third of federal receipts.

By the 1980s this balance of federal revenue sources had changed dramatically. The personal income tax accounts for a larger share of federal revenues, but it is now nearly matched by social security taxes. In fact, it is not impossible that social security taxes will soon become the largest single source of resources for the government.

The rise in social security taxes has been matched by a decline in the importance of corporate income taxes and sales and excise taxes. Only one other revenue source has increased significantly — debt. In recent years approximately 10 percent of federal revenues have come from borrowing, not from taxes.

The Social Context of Governmental Growth

Government's size, role, and structure have changed dramatically in the postwar years and it is clear that many of the changes that we observe are directly related to the four "revolutions" discussed in chapter 6 — the forces that produced structural change in the underlying economic system. The purpose of this section is to analyze the connections between structural change in government and these powerful winds blowing through the economy.

The increasing size and changing role of the federal government in the United States are largely but not entirely the result of the increasing size and scope of social insurance within the economy. To understand why government has changed so much therefore requires a solid understanding of social security.

The Changing Role of Social Security

The social security program, as conceived and implemented in the late 1930s, was a "social insurance" scheme of limited size and scope. Not all workers were covered; taxes and benefits were small in both absolute terms and relative to current amounts. Social security grew into the massive system of today through a series of discrete choices and events.

Social security's importance to the economic system began to expand significantly in the 1950s, when the baby boom generation was in diapers. The private economy was expanding at this time, moving away from the production patterns of wartime, moving toward the consumer economy that was soon to come. Much of this expansion, as already noted, was financed through private debt; both businesses and individuals borrowed more heavily than in the past.[4] More workers fell under social security coverage, providing a relatively larger and deeper pool of funds with which to pay retirement and disability payments. The baby bust generation of workers in the 1950s, with high real wages, was not burdened by high social insurance taxes while they established their claim to future benefits.

Given the fiscal balance of the 1950s, it became possible to expand the scope of social insurance in the United States in the 1960s. The most important innovation was Medicare, a medical insurance program for retirees. Medicare costs were initially relatively low, but they soon began to expand as the population of retirees began to grow and as the cost of medical services increased (due both to rising health care prices overall and to program incentives that unintentionally encouraged health care providers to increase charges).

The decade of the 1970s was the period when social security benefits were increased dramatically, to meet the rising perceived needs of the elderly population and to compensate for rapid increases in the price level. Although social security was not originally conceived as anything more than supplemental retirement income (to fill gaps in pensions, savings, and transfers from children), the retiring baby bust generation began to demand greater benefits. Retirement payments in fact increased very rapidly during this period; some of the increase was intentional on the part of Congress, but some was the result of a flawed system of indexation in the mid-1970s that caused social security benefits to rise much faster than the price level for a time. By the end of the 1970s social insurance benefits (including Medicare) were much higher, and social insurance taxes were also very high.

Social security retirement benefits represented a very high proportion of the preretirement posttax income of many households in the economy. (This is called the "replacement ratio".) Many families were able to retire with little or no reduction in living standard, although this was not true for a significant fraction of the retired population.[5]

The comfortable social insurance fiscal balance of the 1950s and 1960s disappeared in the decade of the seventies. This first became apparent during the stagflation of the late 1970s, when high inflation rates accompanied slow (and sometimes negative) real growth rates for the economy. These macroeconomic conditions caused significant temporary imbalances in the social security trust funds. Slower economic growth meant lower tax receipts, while rising prices continued to push up the indexed benefit costs. The problem was solved, temporarily, through the expedience of higher taxes; but the problem was not really solved and would appear again and again in the years to come.

Significantly, the social security funding "crisis" of the Carter presidency was the first real indicator of the major fiscal imbalances to come. While this fiscal crisis was taken very seriously at the time, subsequent events showed that the "solution" that was adopted missed the point, treating the symptoms of fiscal crisis while not addressing the underlying causes.

The most important dynamic in the development of the social insurance system in the United States has been demographic — the bust–boom–bust sequence of the population revolution. The baby bust generation of the 1930s earned high real wages in the 1950s and 1960s. These wages easily absorbed the modest costs of social security benefits at this time. This desirable balance encouraged the broadening and deepening of benefits. Higher benefits were not only possible, they were important to this group, who, unlike their parents' generation, had borne the expense of raising and educating a large number of children and, consequently, had acquired a larger stock of debt.

Demographic trends were favorable for the workers of the baby bust generation, but the balance turned against their children. Social insurance costs had increased so much in the 1960s and 1970s that even the very large numbers of baby boom workers could not support the retired population without bearing the burden of very high social insurance taxes. Even then, they were left with the problem of their own retirement, which could not reasonably be financed, at prevalent levels, through taxes on the much smaller baby bust generation of their children. We will return to this problem, and its solution, in the next section.

While population was the principal driving force behind the growth and development of social security, it is important to note the contributions of the other "revolutions" of the postwar era. Technological advances were important in at least two respects, for example. First, the advance in technology in the 1950s and 1960s helped build the high real wages of that time, which encouraged the seemingly modest (but ultimately very costly) expansions of social insurance. But technology was also directly responsible for rising social insurance costs. Medical technology advanced perhaps faster than in other parts of the economy. The quality of health care improved dramatically, but costs rose as well. The elderly lived longer and were healthier, but the cost of their medical care, which increasingly fell on Medicare, was the fastest-rising component of the price index.

The financial revolution also contributed to the growth of the social security system, although in a very indirect way. The growth of financial intermediaries and the securitization of finance created an atmosphere where financial contracts and obligations slowly began to replace other types of contracts and obligations within society. (This is a grand generalization and so is necessarily too simple, as well as impossible to prove; I offer it as a working hypothesis.) Broad and deep financial markets allowed parents to save more efficiently through financial assets, not relying on direct or indirect support from their children in old age, as had been the previous typical case. Changes in the tax laws unintentionally encouraged this trend by granting tax relief to some of these savings programs, generally on the condition that the saving be directed toward retirement use.

Parents became more and more able to support themselves in old age (with social security's assistance in many cases), in no small measure because of the development of financial instruments that allowed them to provide for themselves better in their retirement years. Soon this became the expectation: parents were responsible for themselves in old age. But old age is fraught with uncertain contingencies, and it is not clear that the more structured contracts of the financial markets are necessarily more efficient in dealing with the range of old-age problems than is the more flexible social contract among family members. Government, in the form of social insurance, found itself increasingly obligated to deal with problems that had once been the responsibility of the family. Social security grew in part as a result of this trend.

The Relative Decline of National Defense

The social security system grew in every sense in the postwar years: in nominal dollars, in real terms, as a proportion of GNP, as a fraction of the federal government's revenues and outlays, and on a population-adjusted basis. The decline of the federal government's role in national defense, while dramatic, is more complex. What I want to emphasize here is the relative decline of national defense in the federal budget, from over 50 percent in the 1950s to less than 30 percent in the 1980s and, as a fraction of GNP (another relative measure), from about 8–10 percent in the 1950s and sixties to about 5–7 percent in the 1970s and 1980s. This relative decline, however, does not mean that defense spending has fallen in any absolute sense. Indeed, national defense has increased throughout most of this period in nominal and real dollar terms.

There are many "noneconomic" theories or explanations of the relative decline of the United States' national defense role (in the sense stated above). Some argue a "post-Vietnam syndrome" that relates the decline in defense outlays to the military failure in Southeast Asia. Vietnam, according to this view, has made the United States and its leaders less willing to rely on military actions, given the painful lessons of vulnerability that were taught in the jungles of Southeast Asia.

Another "noneconomic" theory relates the decline in emphasis on defense to an easing of the cold war, particularly in relations with the Soviet Union and the People's Republic of China. Diplomatic relations with these countries have improved overall (although not at every turn); these improved conditions have made possible a number of weapons treaties and other signs of cooperation, which has made a lower level of defense possible. This theory is not completely "noneconomic," however, because many observers would argue that the Soviet Union has become more cooperative precisely because its own economy is so weak. The Soviet economy can no longer support prior levels of defense spending, forcing them to seek cooperative solutions. Less defense spending by the Soviets has made possible the relative decline by the United States, this argument goes.

But Paul Kennedy has suggested in his book, *The Rise and Decline of the Great Powers*, that one need not resort to noneconomic stories to explain economic events. Kennedy's book develops the thesis that relative power in international affairs is based on the relative strength of a nation's economy. Kennedy argues that

> the historical record suggests that there is a very clear connection in the long run between an individual Great Power's economic rise and fall and its growth and decline as an important military power (or world empire). This, too, is hardly surprising, since it flows from two related facts. The first is that economic resources are necessary to support a large-scale military establishment. The second is that, so far as the international system is concerned, both wealth and power are always relative and should be seen as such.[6]

As we have already seen, the combined and compounded effects of the "four revolutions" of the postwar era have contributed to the relative economic decline of the United States. Although the U.S. economy remains strong in an absolute sense and U.S. living standards are high in the absolute, both our economy and our living standards have declined in relative terms. This is true in at least two senses. Our living standards are falling relative to those of other developed countries because their growth rates exceed ours. And our living standards are falling relative to the expectations and experiences of recent years, that is, the experiences of the baby bust generation that has now reached retirement age.

According to Kennedy's thesis, at some point the relative decline of the U.S. economy renders the level of power and influence that was achieved in the early postwar years unsupportable. The declining emphasis on national defense within the federal budget is both cause and effect of this economic dynamic.

The relative decline in defense spending in the United States makes it tempting to argue that the United States has adjusted its military commitments to match its shrinking economic power base. But Kennedy does not think this adjustment is complete, or even well under way. The United States still allocates a relatively high fraction of its national product to defense uses, which may be contributing to our slow rate of growth and the fiscal imbalances we are experiencing. Kennedy argues that

> The task facing American statesmen over the next decades, therefore, is to recognize that broad trends are under way, and that there is a need to "manage" affairs so that the relative erosion of the United States' position takes place slowly and smoothly, and is not accelerated by policies which bring merely short-term advantage but longer-term disadvantage. This involves . . . an appreciation that technological and therefore socioeconomic change is occurring in the world faster than ever before; . . . that the economic and productive power balances are no longer as favorably tilted in the United States' direction as in 1945.[7]

If Kennedy is correct, even the trend toward the relative decline in national defense expenditures that we have observed over the postwar era is not necessarily sufficient to compensate for the relative decline in U.S. economic power. Military spending may still be too great, given the economy's relative standing. The powerful dynamic of structural change in the world economy may, therefore, lead to even less emphasis on defense spending in the federal budget.

The Increased Role of Domestic Programs

Much of the rise in outlays for domestic programs can be explained simply by the surge in social security costs and benefits in the postwar era. But not all. Domestic spending increased its budget share overall during these years, even excluding social insurance. While there are many specific reasons why particular programs were implemented, funded, or cut, the broad trend toward more governmental attention to domestic matters is strongly related to the structural changes we have observed in the underlying economy.

The population has had perhaps the greatest influence on domestic spending. As the baby boom generation has moved through its life cycle, it has, at each age and stage, imposed additional burdens on government and the economy. It is obvious, for example, that the bulge of children that flooded schools in the 1950s and 1960s imposed higher costs on governments (state and local perhaps more than federal governments, however). It is clear that a higher population of school-age children induces greater government outlays for school-related programs. It is not always so clear or obvious that the baby boom bulge, as it leaves school, continues to increase government costs, but this is because the adult baby-boomers placed demands on many different government programs, not just one, all of which are stretched and strained by the increase in their client groups.

As adult baby-boomers take jobs and form families, for example, they put increasing strain on transportation systems, roads, and bridges. The infrastructure of urban areas, most of which it has fallen to government to produce and maintain, has come under increased pressure due to the population trends. Domestic spending has had to increase to meet these needs. The frequent breakdown of the urban infrastructure in many areas, however, indicates perhaps that domestic spending has not in fact risen enough to balance the increased demands being put upon it. This suggests that the trend toward greater emphasis on domestic programs will continue and perhaps accelerate in the future, driven by the population-based force of structural change.

As important as population growth pure and simple has been to the growth of domestic programs, it may not have been the most powerful factor influencing this trend. One of government's most important functions is to deal with social costs, costs that society bears that do not wholly or clearly arise as a consequence of any individual action. The broad forces at work in the postwar economy have generated high social costs, which in turn have increased the need for domestic programs.

One way to track some aspects of structural change in the postwar era is to follow the movement of jobs and industries as they attempt to adjust to changing world economic conditions. In very simple terms, we have seen that jobs have moved geographically within the United States (rust belt to sun belt, east to west), jobs have moved from manufacturing to service sectors, and jobs and industries have tended to move abroad as businesses have become increasingly global in their outlook and structure.

Each of these changes in the structure of production and employment has been efficient, in the global sense; but in each case it is true that some people — some workers, businesses, communities — get left behind because they are unwilling or unable to adapt to the needed extent. These forgotten suffer poverty to at least lower-income levels, less wealth, and in the case of workers unemployment or underemployment.

Since the New Deal of the Great Depression (and not excluding the less-generous Reagan years), government has had difficulty ignoring the problems of poverty and unemployment. This is especially true when poverty festers and boils up in crime, drugs, and violence. Some of the increase in spending on domestic programs in the United States is clearly due to the breadth, depth, and duration of the dislocations we have experienced.

We may not have paid great attention to this trend in the United States, in part because our economy has been relatively strong and in part because the problems have accumulated and changed slowly over a long period of time, but that does not mean that the cumulative effects are trivial. One need only look at Western Europe, where the dislocations have been deeper and broader, to see the effect that structural change can have on unemployment and the domestic programs that pertain to it.

Changes in the Federal Tax System

The principal changes in the federal tax system during the postwar period are that taxes have risen overall, both in absolute dollars — real terms, and as a fraction of national income. The relative importance of the different taxes that make up the federal revenue base has changed; personal income and social insurance taxes make up a greater share, while corporate income and excise taxes have fallen dramatically as a source of government revenue.[8]

The rise in the overall tax burden is easy to explain, given the analysis of previous sections. Higher social insurance costs growing out of the structural changes in the economy are a clear explanation for the rise in the earmarked social insurance taxes. At the same time, outlays for other domestic programs have also increased more than the relative decline in defense spending. The costs of these new and expanded government programs have required higher taxes overall and, as we have noted, higher income taxes in particular. What remains to be explained is the link, if any, between the structural changes in the economy and the changing composition of the federal tax burden, social insurance taxes aside.

The realignment of the federal tax burden is most directly explained by two trends: the growth of the personal incomes of the "baby bust" generation of workers in the 1950s and 1960s and the profit decline in the U.S. corporate sector in the 1970s and 1980s. Both of these trends were shaped and influenced by the economy's rapid structural change during the postwar era.

It is perhaps not surprising that personal income taxes increased dramatically in the postwar period, given the dramatic increase in living standards enjoyed by the baby bust generation that came into the workforce in the 1950s.

High productivity and high wages, products of the population and technology revolutions, allowed this group to enjoy improved material living standards at the same time that their federal income tax burden increased. But the explanation of the income tax's increased importance in the federal budget is a little more complex than this.

The federal income tax had been a levy that fell on the "elites," not the "masses," before the Second World War.[9] Given the size and role of government in the 1920s and 1930s and the other revenue sources then in use, the personal income tax was designed to fall on the highest-income groups only. Average workers bore little or none of the tax burden due to relatively high personal deductions and exemptions. The tremendous revenue requirements of World War II, however, changed all this. Tax provisions were modified to include workers generally in the tax base. This changed forever the basic nature of the personal income tax.

The wartime tax changes were significant because a tax on elites could not have grown to finance the enlarged role of government in the postwar years. Absent the war's legacy of a mass income tax, Congress might have chosen a European-style system of consumption taxes, such as the value-added tax. And this might have happened in any case; there was tremendous pressure to cut back the income tax at the end of World War II similar to British desire in 1815 to retire their wartime income tax. The forces of the executive branch, empowered in tax policy by the necessities of the war, resisted the urge to cut the income tax, however. The sudden revenue requirements of the Korean War, which soon appeared, strengthened the grip of the income tax on the public purse.

John Witte, in his history of the income tax, cites the "importance of inaction" of the Eisenhower administration in the area of tax policy.[10] The Internal Revenue Code of 1954 went essentially without change for eight years. The broad-based income tax became a permanent fiscal fixture. As the economy grew in the 1950s and 1960s, so did the income tax.

The institutional structure of the income tax was therefore ideally positioned for a period of government growth. The broad-based income tax became a revenue machine when combined with the changes in the underlying economy, which generated economic growth and rising living standards overall during the decades of the 1950s and 1960s.

The growth of personal income tax collections accelerated in the 1970s due to the influence of inflation. The high and rising inflation rates of the 1970s increased income tax receipts over and above any growth in the underlying economy due to the problem of so-called bracket creep. The effects of inflation pushed nominal wages and incomes into higher and higher tax brackets. Zero and even negative real capital gains were taxed at high rates, given that it was the unadjusted nominal gain that fell subject to the tax code, not the real return. The result was another burst of growth in the personal income tax.

While personal income tax receipts were growing in absolute and relative terms, the corporate income tax was becoming a hollow shell. On the outside, the structure of the corporate tax remained, like some well-preserved stone fortress, tall and forbidding. But the appearance is deceiving, because during this period the corporate tax was becoming increasingly irrelevant as a source of federal revenues. Corporate tax revenues fell in nearly every sense in the postwar era; tax receipts fell in real dollars, as a percentage of GNP, and as a fraction of total federal revenues.

The easiest explanation of the disappearance of the corporate income tax is political — wealthy corporations gained special tax preferences from Congress to reduce the effect of high tax rates on their activities. This easy explanation is applicable to a few specific industries that benefited most from tax preferences, but it is far from the whole story here. The biggest factor in the decline of the corporate income tax, according to recent research, is the declining profit rate of corporations themselves.[11]

The corporate profit rate, which averaged nearly 11 percent in the 1960s, fell by a third to about 7 percent in the 1970s, and fell again to about 5 percent in the first half of the 1980s.[12] With this kind of dramatic decline in the base of corporate profitability, it is not surprising that corporate tax revenues declined in relative terms as well.

The declining profits in the corporate sector of the U.S. economy was a reflection of the impact of the structural changes that were taking place, especially in the 1970s and 1980s. It was in this period that the financial and communications revolutions were beginning to be felt at the corporate level. Competition by foreign firms became more intense. Foreign investment and technological transfers abroad also increased. The domestic firms that largely make up the corporate tax base were caught in the middle of the structural change process, and their lower profitability rates indicate the stress they experienced.

There is one more trend in federal taxation in the postwar period that is worthy of note but has not yet been discussed. This is the tremendous growth of tax expenditures in the federal budget. Tax expenditures are nonuniformities in the tax system, specific sources or uses of income that are singled out for preferential tax treatment. Many people call these nonuniformities "loopholes" — especially when they are used by other people.

A tax expenditure is the logical equivalent of a direct subsidy or expenditure payment by government. Suppose, for example, that there is a uniform 50-percent tax on all income, regardless of source or use. Now suppose that a tax expenditure is introduced that makes charitable contributions tax-exempt. A hundred-dollar church donation previously cost the donor a hundred dollars in after-tax income. Now, with the tax exemption, the opportunity cost of a hundred-dollar donation is only fifty dollars. If no donation were made, the hundred dollars would be fully taxed and the potential donor would keep just fifty dollars of it. So, when the hundred dollars is given to the church, the true cost to the donor is only the fifty dollars in foregone after-tax income.

Where does the other fifty dollars come from? The answer is that the fifty dollars that the donor gives is matched by an implicit fifty-dollar subsidy or expenditure by the government that takes place via the tax system. The donor's fifty dollars is matched by the fifty dollars that would otherwise have gone to the tax coffers.

The name *tax expenditure* derives from the tax law's ability to mimic direct expenditures or subsidies through the nonuniform treatment of certain activities.[13] If the government wishes to transfer funds to churches, for example, it can use the tax law, as already noted, as a substitute for a direct payment or a direct subsidy to donors.

The most important difference between a tax expenditure, as defined here, and a direct subsidy or direct expenditure is that because the tax expenditure is implicit and not direct, tax expenditure "payments" need not appear in the budget as an expense of government. The tax expenditure is revenue left uncollected and, like an invisible man, casts no shadow in the debits and credits of the federal budget.

The federal government began to calculate a tax expenditure "budget" in the 1960s. According to these calculations, tax expenditures have tended to grow faster than federal budget outlays overall. Tax expenditures were equal to about 20 percent of direct government outlays (4.4 percent of GNP) in 1967, for example, but had increased to nearly 35 percent of federal outlays (8.4 percent of GNP) by 1982.[14]

The growth of tax expenditures is significant in several respects. First, it reinforces the trend, already noted, toward growth in government in general and growth in domestic programs in particular in the postwar period. If we take tax expenditures into account, the trend toward a greater domestic role for the federal government is even stronger than previously appeared. It is a fact that in some areas of domestic policy, such as the development of natural resource deposits and, to a lesser extent, housing subsidies, the tax expenditure allocations completely dwarf the amount of outlays provided directly through the budget process.

The increase in the burden of the personal income tax is also more dramatic in light of the growth of tax expenditures. The proliferation of tax preferences slowly reduced that tax base of the personal income tax, but tax revenues increased anyway. Tax expenditures also contributed to the decline of the corporate income tax, although Auerbach and Poterba maintain that over half of the decline in recent years can be attributed solely to declining profitability.[15]

What accounts for the growth of tax expenditures in the postwar years? The tax expenditure "budget" swelled for two reasons: increased use of existing "loopholes" and the introduction of additional nonuniformities in the tax system. Funds poured through existing loopholes at a faster rate due to the incentive effect of the higher tax rates that applied to unsheltered income and profits. In other cases, new tax expenditures were created due to the political economy of Congress, which favored payment through "invisible" tax expenditures over visible direct subsidies and outlays as the size of the visible budget became more and more of an issue.

The growth of tax expenditures was also affected by the structural changes in the economy. As the economy changed, for example, we know that the financial sector became more and more important. As resources were rerouted within the economy, they sought the highest posttax return. The existence of tax expenditures tended to funnel funds to places like real estate and commercial property, where tax benefits were high. The growth of the debt economy increased tax expenditure losses, too, since interest payments are deductible from both personal and corporate income taxes. But the rise of the mountain of private debt in the postwar years was also accelerated by this tax treatment of interest, so together the financial revolution and the existence of these tax preferences were mutually reinforcing.

Finally, tax expenditures grew in part as a result of pressure from the sectors of the economy that suffered most from the effects of structural change. The declining industries sought relief and, perhaps, a temporary competitive advantage through special tax treatment. In fact, it is not unreasonable to view these tax expenditures as classic examples of Mancur Olson's theory of structural rigidities, where existing interest groups sacrifice economic growth for the overall economy in order to preserve and protect their established interests through subsidies and advantageous regulations.

As the tax expenditure budget grew, however, the bases of the corporate and personal income tax shrank. There was less and less income to tax to finance growing federal outlays. As a result, nominal tax rates had to be increased to relatively high levels to generate the needed revenues. High tax rates made tax expenditures even more valuable and so encouraged greater loophole leakages. Tax expenditures induced higher tax rates, which caused even greater use of tax expenditures and even higher tax rates in another mutually reinforcing dynamic.

This process was particularly distressing to those individuals and businesses that did not make high use of tax preferences and so were left paying the high tax rates. These included some of the most important growth sectors of the economy (although some growth sectors did benefit from tax expenditure provisions).

The Rise of the Public Debt

> The sustained rise in federal debt in relation to income that our new fiscal policy has brought about is unprecedented in our history. Apart from the wars that every schoolchild recognizes and the Depression that every grandparent remembers, we have always experienced declining government indebtedness. But with a fiscal policy centered on large across-the-board tax cuts, and no real desire in any quarter to cut the core programs . . . that dominate the government's spending, increasing indebtedness through both peace and prosperity has become our national policy.
>
> Benjamin M. Friedman, *Day of Reckoning*

The last and perhaps most significant trend in the federal government in the postwar period is the growth, in a relatively short period of time, of a mountain of federal government debt. Benjamin M. Friedman, in his excellent book *Day of Reckoning*, puts the debt issue in its proper perspective.[16] The rise of the federal debt is significant because it represents an important break with past fiscal practice in the United States.

The fact of budget deficits is not a radical departure from twentieth-century standards of government behavior, but past deficits have been either small (in peacetime) or the result of extraordinary worldwide events. It has been the norm that the federal debt (and its interest burden) has declined as a fraction of national income during periods of prosperity. This long-standing trend was been reversed within the past decade, with no end to the growing debt problem clearly in sight.

Friedman, however, goes beyond the usual sterile statistical descriptions of the debt problem to focus on its social implications. In forsaking the principle of fiscal balance in the 1980s, Friedman says, the federal government has

> violated the basic moral principle that has bound each generation of Americans to the next since the founding of the republic; that men and women should work and eat, earn and spend, both privately and collectively, so that their children and their children's children would inherit a better world. . . . We have broken with that tradition by pursuing a policy that amounts to living not just in, but for, the present. We are living well by running up our debt and selling off our assets. America has thrown itself a party and billed the tab to the future. The costs, which are only beginning to come due, will include a lower standard of living for individual Americans and reduced American influence and importance in world affairs.[17]

Friedman's anxiety over the United States' mountain of public debt is, and should be, shared by most economists and policymakers, but this common concern has had little effect on the situation. The debt continues to grow. Later sections of this essay will address the economic effects of attempts to deal with the debt and the ultimate consequences for the U.S. economy of the permanent debt burden that has been created. The present problem, however, is to understand the fundamental forces that produced our debt mountain after long years of fiscal balance. The forces of structural change that have appeared repeatedly in this analysis are also important elements of the rise of the federal debt.

The public debt is a critical indicator of fiscal balance — the balance between government outlays and revenues. As we have seen, both outlays and revenues have risen dramatically in the postwar era, but fiscal balance was maintained for the most part until the late 1970s. Outlays and revenues both increased, driven by the structural changes in the underlying economy. Why did the two growth rates begin to diverge? Part of the answer to this important question rests on differences in how the forces of structural change affected the costs of domestic programs versus the economic base available for taxation.

As we have seen, rising social insurance benefits and increases in domestic programs have been the largest source of the growth in federal outlays, and pressures to increase spending in these areas have actually increased in recent years. Social insurance costs have accelerated because they are driven by the powerful engine of demographic change, which has grown stronger and stronger over time. Domestic programs have grown for several reasons, but one important factor has been the rapid pace of structural change in the economy.

The combined effects of revolutions in population, technology, finance, and communications has been to cause resources to shift rapidly and radically from industry to industry and from country to country. The rising cost of domestic programs has been, at least in part, a response to the economic stresses and social strains that the structural changes have imposed on the relatively inflexible institutions of everyday life. Like social insurance costs, the structural forces that have produced the rise of domestic programs have accelerated in the past decade.

As outlay expenses have accelerated, the growth of the revenue side of the budget has slowed; taxes have lagged behind spending programs. This trend is easy to understand when we consider how the tax system developed in these years.

The federal revenue system has evolved into a money machine based on social insurance taxes and the personal income tax. The corporate tax has declined in importance (at least until recently) in large measure because of the structural forces that have depressed corporate profits. Social insurance taxes are tightly tied to worker payrolls and are, in any case, earmarked for social insurance benefits. The income tax is based on personal income; but, as we have already noted, the growth of tax expenditures in the 1960s and 1970s has narrowed that base somewhat. The point is that the job of financing the growth of government has fallen to two taxes that have a relatively narrow combined base that is closely related to the standard of living of average workers.

If living standards, real wages, and the like had grown very rapidly in the 1970s and 1980s (at least as fast as the forces that pushed up social insurance and domestic program outlays), then fiscal balance might have been sustained. However, the very structural forces that were causing federal expenditures to rise were, at the same time, stretching and straining the economic institutions that produce our living standards.

In this context, fiscal imbalance and the mountains of debt are the result of a vicious cycle. Structural changes in the economy cause the increase in outlays, some of which are needed to compensate for the social stresses that result from change. But those same forces also limit the growth of living standards and make existing revenue institutions unable to meet the rising outlay needs. The fiscal crisis that results, as we will see, imposes additional burdens on society and produces even more change, starting the cycle anew.

If the foregoing argument is valid, the rise of the national debt in the postwar period is at least partially the consequence of the forces of structural change and not due to any particular debt-creating legislation or political ideology. Some part of the debt was due to the clash between the unstoppable force of change and the immoveable object of institutional rigidity, but a large part of the federal debt burden derives from intentional policy choices. Much of our current national debt is the legacy of the massive tax cuts of the early Reagan years.

The Reagan tax cuts, embodied in the Economic Recovery Tax Act (ERTA) of 1981, may have been the crucial fiscal act of the 1980s. ERTA's goal, which was the theme of the 1980 Reagan election campaign, was a drastic reduction in the federal income tax burden. The new tax laws were designed to cut income taxes by a total of nearly 25 percent over a period of three years. In addition, beginning in 1985, the income tax was partly indexed, to offset "bracket creep" due to inflation.[18]

The Economic Recovery Tax Act was not intended to create huge deficits. Some people apparently believed in a supply-side "Laffer curve" effect, whereby ERTA's much lower tax rates (a top personal tax bracket of 50 percent, versus 70 percent under old law) would provide such powerful incentives to growth in the tax base that higher revenues would be collected by the lower rates. Not many analysts took this promise seriously, though many were willing to pay it lip service to avoid answering hard questions about ERTA's budget consequences. Others might have believed that the economy, which had operated far below its potential throughout the 1970s, was due for a substantial growth spurt anyway, which would moderate the revenue losses. Finally, others took the need to cut programs to match tax reductions seriously. No one went on record as favoring big tax cuts and big deficits, but the deficits did come.

I believe that the federal tax cut of 1981 was directly descended from California's Proposition 13 tax cut and limitation initiative of the 1970s. Proposition 13 cut California property taxes as sharply as ERTA cut income taxes. More importantly, ERTA and Proposition 13 were similar in their motivation and their intended effects.

The principal motive for Proposition 13, in my view, was the desire to hold on to a standard of living that was visibly slipping away. California in the 1970s was a dynamic and growing economy that benefited in many ways from the patterns of structural change that had emerged. But Californians found it increasingly difficult to hold on to their living standards because of skyrocketing housing costs and property taxes. Simple homes doubled and redoubled in price year after year in California as a relatively inflexible supply of homes collided with a rapidly increasing demand. Housing demand outstripped supply, driven by several forces. California was rapidly gaining population as workers left the rust belt states and headed south and west. At the same time, more and more households were being formed, requiring more housing, as the baby boom generation came of age. There was also speculation—buying to resell a little later at a profit.

The most powerful force behind the rising demand for (and supply of) housing in California, however, was probably the financial revolution that we discussed in a different context earlier in this study. Evolution and revolution of financial intermediaries created enormous liquidity, which the Californians used to drive up housing prices.

It is in this context that Proposition 13 appeared. Rising housing prices were eroding living standards, but there was nothing that people could do about them. They were caught in a prisoner's dilemma that forced them to continue to buy and bid up the prices of their homes. This sent property taxes soaring as well, which added insult to injury. California homeowners might have been *willing* to vote to hold down housing prices (except their own, of course) but *couldn't*. They could, however, vote away the added burden of property taxes. And this they did, through an extremely popular statewide initiative.

Now, it may be obvious to you and me that if you vote for lower taxes, there will be fewer resources to use to provide government services; a vote for lower taxes is a vote for fewer government programs. But the voters of California did not expect this to be the consequence. They wanted lower housing costs; they expected that revenue shortfalls would be absorbed by cutting bureaucratic flab, not touching the muscle of worthwhile programs. They were wrong, of course; and state and local governments reduced service levels, sometimes drastically. But this was unexpected and unintended, as far as many voters were concerned.

Proposition 13 was an attempt by voters to choose a higher standard of living by cutting the cost of government. I think that the Reagan tax program was cut from the same cloth. Voters supported the Reagan proposal in large measure because it was a chance for them to vote to preserve a standard of living that was declining under the obvious burden of higher taxes and inflation but also was strained by the impact of structural change.

Supporters of the 1981 Reagan tax package did not intend to create deficits and alpine debt levels. They intended to reverse or retard the forces that had awakened them from the "American dream" of constantly improving living standards.

It is rude irony that in helping to burden the economy with massive public debt, the 1981 tax cuts ultimately put at risk the very living standards they were supposed to protect. The Economic Recovery Tax Act set in motion a trend that promises to further reduce living standards in the future. In an attempt to offset the effects of structural change, debt-financed tax cuts actually accelerated the long-term pattern of resource shifts within the economy and throughout the world.

8

The New Mountains of Debt

Fiscal crisis exists when the problem of the fiscal balance begins to overshadow substantive decisions regarding the role of government. In fiscal crisis, what government does and how it does it are determined more by the impact of alternative policies on the debt than by goals and needs of the underlying economy.

The U.S. federal government began to experience increasingly severe symptoms of fiscal crisis as the decade of the 1980s progressed. As the economy changed, the government sector experienced persistent and growing imbalances, which slowly came to dominate the legislative process and dictate choices about the role of government in the economy. The Gramm-Rudman-Hollings Act is the most obvious indicator of the depth of the crisis in the federal government. Unable to achieve fiscal balance through normal means, Gramm-Rudman-Hollings provided for arbitrary and automatic budget cuts as a last resort. In passing it, Congress put the problem of fiscal crisis at the very top of the national agenda and at the same time tacitly admitted its inability to make policy in this area.

President Reagan once compared Congress to a drunken sailor, reeling and irresponsible, unable to resist the intoxicating temptation of another shot from the bottle marked "deficit." He challenged the Senate and the House to join him and take the pledge implicit in the Gramm-Rudman-Hollings Act. They did, but with no discernible effect on fiscal balance.

It is not surprising that fiscal balance has not been restored by the policies adopted thus far. Budget deficits in the 1980s were not the result of an inability to resist temptation; they were, as we have seen, the product of several powerful forces that together drive the process of structural change today. This is not to say that today's high mountains of debt were unavoidable. But the forces that created today's debts are larger—and have been acting over a longer time period—than is commonly acknowledged.

The fact of fiscal crisis in government has forced changes in public policies that in turn, now shape the structure of the underlying economy itself. Just as government is affected by structural changes in the economy, so, too, is the economy affected by structural changes in government. The job of this chapter is to examine some of the ways that government, in reacting to fiscal crisis and the new mountains of debt, has influenced or accelerated the pattern of structural change in the economy.

Three aspects of fiscal crisis have had particularly significant impacts on the economy: the growth of the federal debt since the 1970s, the revision of the income tax in 1986, and the reform of the social security system in 1983. The following pages contain case studies of these three events that chronicle their effect on the economy and their impact on the United States' current and future living standards.

Mountains of Debt

The United States has become since World War II a society built increasingly on a foundation of debt. Consumption has raced ahead of production, fueled by the volatile liquidity of the innovative financial services industry. The United States' public debt is both an effect of rapid structural change, as the last chapter described, but also a cause of the vast changes we have experienced.

The growth of the federal government's public debt was at least partly responsible for the financial revolution of the 1970s and 1980s, which has contributed in turn to the growth of private debt and the rapid pace of structural change in the economy. Conservative Treasury bonds, bills, and notes provided the basis for a stream of innovative new financial products and processes through a process that economists call *disintermediation*.

The financial system since the Great Depression had been built on the foundation of solid and secure financial intermediaries. It was expected that most people would place their savings in financial institutions such as commercial banks, savings and loans, or credit unions, which would act as intermediary for their depositors, searching out qualified borrowers for them. The 1930s had taught the lesson of the importance of a stable financial sector; therefore, in the postdepression years a series of bank regulations was erected, backed up by the safety net of federal deposit insurance.

The most important (and controversial) of the banking regulations in the 1970s was the Federal Reserve System's Regulation Q, which governed bank interest rates. In effect, Regulation Q set arbitrary ceilings on the interest rates that banks could pay their depositors, which ranged from 0 percent on checking account balances to nominal amounts (about 5 percent) on savings account balances. Regulation Q put a cap on the cost that banks had to pay for loanable funds. Regulation Q also acted to limit competition for savings dollars. If risk and return were accurately assessed, banks were virtually assured a profit. And depositors were virtually assured security (and a nominal return), which was, after all, the main aim of bank regulation.

Regulation Q pretty much stifled competition among banks and between banks and other types of financial institutions, such as brokerage houses and mutual funds. The pace of financial innovation was sluggish because of the vast perceived difference between the risk, return, and liquidity of different types of financial assets.

The growing federal debt, combined with high inflation, broke down the barriers between financial markets in the 1970s. As inflation rates rose in the mid-1970s, the gap between interest rates offered by regulated banks and those available through direct investment in the financial markets grew. It was no longer a difference of 5-percent versus 6-percent return. Now the interest gap was widening to 5 percent versus 9, 10, or 11 percent. The difference in return was suddenly too great to be ignored, particularly since the risk-return-liquidity profile of a high-interest, short-term Treasury security was effectively the same as that of a low-interest Regulation Q savings account.

The banks began to bleed. Money drained out the tellers' windows and into the money markets. Seizing the opportunity to profit from this flow, Wall Street wizards experimented with new products and services to attract the flow of funds fleeing the banks and thrifts. The Money Market Mutual Fund (MMMF) was perhaps the most successful new product; these funds pooled many small savers' funds and invested them in short-term government bonds. A MMMF could pay market interest rates while investing in government-backed securities, all the while providing the convenience and liquidity of a checking account.

Money market funds were the perfect vehicle for disintermediation. Secure, profitable, and liquid, these accounts introduced a generation to the world of direct financial investment; many of them would never return again to their previous dependence on the traditional old-line banks and savings associations.

The banks were still bleeding pretty heavily, and this created a real liquidity crisis for them because they were saddled with a portfolio of long-term loans and short-term deposits. Soon banks, too, would find it prudent to lend to the government (or its many agencies) instead of lending to private individuals. So government debt became a more important financial asset within the economy in general. In the meantime, however, the banks needed to find a way to compete with the nonbanks that were draining away their deposit base. Just as the pressure to preserve the banking sector in the 1930s had brought on heavy financial regulation, it was now the case that the pressure to preserve the banking sector brought on deregulation, which would allow banks to compete with other financial firms.

Soon banks were offering high-interest money market certificates, which were less liquid than the money market funds but paid a high return and brought back some depositors. Round after round of innovation on both sides of the market followed and the distinction between banks and nonbank financial firms, such as brokerage houses, slowly disappeared.

The large and growing federal debt played an important part in this financial revolution. Without a large supply of high-interest government obligations the disintermediation process would have been slower, and the enormous change in the size and importance of the financial sector accordingly less.

The financial events of the 1970s left U.S. families more liquid and, because of their increased interest income, apparently wealthier as well. Under these circumstances, they could "leverage up" and participate more fully in the consumer society that grew in the 1980s.

If the United States' growing public debt of the 1970s helped break down barriers to change in the financial sector, the much larger deficits of the 1980s went further, forcing the whole economy to change quickly and in radical ways. The financial revolution that gained speed in the 1970s reduced or eliminated the distinctions among different parts of the domestic financial market. The massive buildup of public debt that followed erased the lines that separated the financial markets of the nations of the world. Combined with the other forces at work, this created the dynamic world economy within which the United States would have to exist.

It is a simple fact that the deficits of the Reagan years could not be financed internally. The private sector of the United States had never saved as high a fraction of its income as some other countries, such as Japan and Italy. Now, influenced by the forces of the age and the incentives of the tax and financial system that had evolved, they saved even less and borrowed even more in an attempt to maintain their high standard of living. The 1981 tax cuts, on top of everything else, created more public and private debt than even the innovating financiers could freely fund. The money had to come from abroad.

Charles Kindleberger maintains that credit is like a river; it follows the channel laid down in the past and does not set off in new directions except in exceptional circumstances. An unusual event, such as we have just seen in the 1970s, is necessary to break the channel of domestic financial intermediation. And perhaps an even more unusual event is required to break through the traditional banks and levies that tend to hold credit within its domestic market. Money does not boldly set off into new and uncertain territory, where risk and return are hard to measure, without a very good reason. The huge deficits of the 1980s were an unusual event for peacetime, a very good reason to extend the reach of financial markets around the world.

The real return available on U.S. government debt was higher than that available in Europe or Japan. This positive real interest differential acted like a magnet to pull funds from foreign portfolios, especially in countries where financial regulations still held down legal returns. The international capital movement from Europe and Japan to the United States was large enough and sustained enough to create all the institutions of international finance necessary to make foreign investment a routine and profitable proposition.

Once a deep channel had been gouged out, to transfer credit from the East and the West to New York, there was little cost involved in widening it to accommodate foreign investment in the many other different types of U.S. financial instruments. Foreign investors could trade the stocks and bonds of U.S. corporations just as easily as Treasury bills or notes. To a certain extent the system could even handle cross flows—U.S. investment in foreign financial markets.

The advent of broad and deep international financial markets in the 1980s made it relatively efficient for firms to transfer resources abroad on a scale that would have been hard to imagine only a decade before. There were many barriers to the internationalization of production and marketing—political, cultural, and economic barriers. The international revolution in finance had broken down some of these barriers, however, and weakened others. The financial markets now stood ready to lubricate the flow of resources between and among countries.

The deep, broad, new, international channels of finance were quickly put to use in ways that vastly accelerated the pace of structural change in the U.S. economy. The economic policy of high public debt in an open economy put enormous stress on domestic producers and changed the global pattern of production and consumption, probably forever.

The Smithsonian agreements in 1973 created an international financial system based on mostly market-determined exchange rates. The supply and demand for yen versus dollars was largely responsible for setting the value of the yen versus the dollar. With credit markets pretty well bottled up inside each nation's domestic borders in the early 1970s, the foreign exchange rate was determined largely by patterns in international trade in goods and services. The foreign exchange market was relatively thin and stable, at least compared to later years.

The appearance, in the late 1970s and early 1980s, of a large and active international credit system thoroughly disrupted the flexible exchange rate system. Millions of marks, yen, and pounds flowed into New York to buy stocks, bonds, and other U.S. assets; and each time around, dollars had to be purchased in the foreign exchange market to complete the transaction. The international value of the dollar began to skyrocket as a result of the sudden inflow of finance from abroad.

The dollar's rise began in 1979 and did not peak until 1985. Altogether, the dollar's international value increased by over 50 percent.[1] This meant that United States–made goods became about 50-percent more expensive (due only to the exchange rate effect) in foreign markets, while imported goods became about just that much cheaper in the United States. The United States became an excellent place in which to consume goods but a distinctly unprofitable place in which to produce them.

The dollar appreciation of 1979–1985 gave U.S. citizens a last opportunity to enjoy a very high standard of living. All sorts of imported products were much cheaper than before, and the low cost of imports kept prices of domestic goods down, too. Inflation was low—perhaps artificially low—and the United States' material living standard seemed very high.

Investment spending in the United States remained high during this period, but (as we will see in the next section) little investment went into capital that could produce tradable goods and services. Productive investment by U.S. firms was being channeled abroad, carried along the financial canals on the rising dollar's tide. This foreign investment often embodied the latest technological advance, while the lack of similar investment in the United States created a significant technology gap.[2]

The federal government's big debt had unbalanced both world credit markets and international currency markets. Combined with the other forces at work (changes in technology and communications, for example), the dollar's rise attracted foreign firms to the U.S. market to sell their goods and services, and sent U.S. firms searching abroad for production sites where they could avoid the costly curse of the dearer dollar.

Consumption and production patterns shifted within the United States and between the United States and the rest of the world in response to the dollar's sustained increase. Because an efficient international financial system was developing at this time, these resource movements took place rapidly. The result was to accelerate and magnify the structural shifts that were already occurring.

The 1980s have seen a generation or two of structural change compressed into the span of a single decade. The revolutions in finance, technology, and communications made this change possible and necessary. But the growth of the public debt in the United States is perhaps the most important reason for its being so very sudden and so widespread. The resulting imbalances are huge, and the consequent stresses and adjustment costs are high.

Income Tax Reform

The most important economic legacy of the Reagan presidency is the pattern of debt, structural change, and relative decline that we have just examined. These trends will be long lasting and will affect the living standards of U.S. citizens for several generations. But these results were unintentional, the predictable but still unexpected side effects of policies enacted with good intent. To a great extent, the Reagan years are not ones of action (intentional thrusts of economic policy) but of reaction (last-minute scrambling to deal with fiscal crisis as the economy and economic policy drifted in stormy seas).[3] This was true in every area of fiscal policy but one—taxation.

The Reagan administration achieved political success in the area of economic policy only twice. The Economic Recovery Tax Act of 1981 was the singular success of Reagan's first term and the Tax Reform Act of 1986 was the only political triumph (in economic policy) in the second term. Both policies were designed to achieve populist goals—to reduce the tax burden, simplify the tax system, and make it fairer. And to a significant degree these goals were achieved.[4]

What has come to be most important about the Reagan tax reforms is not their intended goals but their unintended side effects. These side effects have accelerated the process of structural change in the economy and altered the pattern of production and investment in ways that are not necessarily in the economy's best long-term interest.

The most obvious side effect of ERTA was the sudden rise of the federal budget deficit. Not all the increase in government borrowing in the early 1980s was due to ERTA alone, of course. Military outlays rose at the same time that a deep recession depressed tax collections. The Economic Recovery Tax Act's 25-percent across-the-board tax cuts, coming on top of the debt-creating forces already at work, acted to magnify the debt problem. But higher public debt was not the only unintended side effect of the ERTA legislation.

The Economic Recovery Tax Act's biggest direct effect on the economy, debt aside, was to reduce the tax burden and preserve or enhance (for a while at least) the posttax living standards of U.S. voters. Lower tax rates were intended, as well, to provide positive general incentives for production and investment. But lower rates also had the effect of reducing the attractiveness of the many specific tax incentives (tax expenditures) that the tax code had accumulated over the years. A tax deduction for depreciation is worth a great deal to a taxpayer in the 70-percent tax bracket, but it has less value and effect once tax rates have fallen to 50 percent or lower. The political and economic forces that had gained special tax treatment in the first place used the excuse of the 1981 tax reforms to widen and deepen their preferences. The tax expenditure budget increased even as tax rates fell.

The new and more powerful incentives that entered the tax code through ERTA legislation had dramatic impact on the investment patterns in the United States. Some types of investments were taxed at rates much higher or lower than others as a result of the new tax law. The result was an extremely nonneutral tax system where the trivia of the tax code was as important as economic return for making investment choices.

Although the 1981 tax changes (combined with subsequent modifications) were complex in their treatment of investments, it is possible to summarize their effects. Investment in structures was favored over investment in equipment due to the vastly accelerated depreciation allowed for purchases of commercial and industrial buildings. Debt finance was favored over the use of corporate or personal saving; and the more highly leveraged an investment, the lower its effective tax burden.

When combined with the high and unstable real interest rates of the early 1980s, this pattern of investment incentives had the effect of diverting 90 percent of the increase in business investment to just two types of assets: commercial structures and short-lived business equipment (autos and office equipment in particular). Investment in commercial structures surged because the double benefits of highly leveraged debt finance and vastly accelerated depreciation allowances had the effect of producing low and sometimes negative tax rates for this type of investment.[5] Commercial structures could — and did — sit idle for a period and still make posttax sense because of the tax benefits that investors received.

It is interesting to note that investment in commercial structures increased in the 1980s while investment in productive structures did not, even though they received the same tax treatment. In theory, both types of investments should have benefited equally from the new tax code. But theory, in this case, ignores at least two other trends that emerged at the same time. The first, as discussed in the last chapter, was the sudden appreciation of the dollar on international currency markets. The dollar's rise made United States–produced goods uncompetitive compared to the production of foreign firms. The dollar's rise therefore made new productive structures risky or otherwise uneconomic (Who would buy the factory's output?) while commercial structures — stores and of-fices — would still make sense as outlets for imported goods and offices for foreign companies.

Another reason for the investment bias in favor of commercial versus pro-duction structures in the early 1980s was that the production structures are most often erected by the businesses that plan to own and operate them. Such structures contain specific capital and are tailored to a certain product and production process. Commercial structures, on the other hand, are less specific in their design and use and are usually owned by one firm and leased to others. But most importantly, commercial structures can be readily financed by highly leveraged limited partnerships that allow private individuals to gain the bene-fits of tax preferences at relatively low risk.

Such tax shelters, organized to exploit the negative effective tax rates on highly leveraged investments in office buildings, retail space, and apartment houses, experienced tremendous growth as a result of the conditions in the economy and the new provisions of the tax laws. The huge tax benefits that these projects generated dwarfed whatever economic return they could pro-duce. Under the right conditions, in fact, the projects could actually fail, go bankrupt, and still pay back the limited partners' investment through tax bene-fits. The only losers in such a situation would be the banks and savings institu-tions, who provided the "leverage" through mortgage loans, and the taxpayers who financed the project indirectly through the IRS.

The growth of these tax-sheltered investment partnerships was made possi-ble in part by the events of the financial revolution, which had already begun to pull individual saving and investment away from traditional financial interme-diaries. But the tax laws also encouraged and accelerated this trend by boosting the after-tax return on highly leveraged direct investment (through limited partnerships and other organizations) well above that available through more traditional mechanisms.

Investment in business equipment also increased in the first few years after the ERTA legislation, but not uniformly. There was no increase in the industrial type of hardware that comes to mind when the words "business equipment" are spoken — no chemical vats, blast furnaces, turret lathes, or welding frames (or at least no significant increase in these sorts of items). Investment in autos and office equipment increased instead, despite the fact that little was changed in the tax code to favor these types of assets.

What, if not tax incentives, caused the spurt of investment in autos and office equipment? Several factors combined to direct investment funds to this particular end. First, both autos and office equipment are relatively small, general purpose business investments with short economic lives. They are more liquid than turret lathes in a crunch. Second, both can readily be financed using debt, which did benefit from preferential tax treatment. Third, both were part of the technical revolution; new autos and office equipment had important technical advantages (fuel economy, processing speed) over older models. Fourth, due to a quirk in national income-accounting methods, home comput-ers were counted as "office equipment" even if they only balanced checkbooks or blasted video spacemen. Finally, many of the autos and office products were foreign-made and therefore cheaper because of the rising dollar.

The capital "capacity" of the U.S. economy increased as a result of the economic conditions and investment incentives of this period, but in a peculiar and uneven way. Most of the increase in investment in the early 1980s was debt-financed and designed to produce services, not agricultural products or manufactured goods. This investment pattern therefore accelerated the resource movements and employment shifts that were already in progress in the U.S. economy and the world economy.

The 1981 tax reductions lowered tax rates, but they did not truly reform the federal income tax system. In fact, the tax expenditures introduced in 1981 and 1982 made the income tax even more unfair and inefficient. People with similar incomes were often subject to very different tax burdens, depending on how many tax expenditures they qualified for. Rich families might pay less tax than those with far less income. The same story applied to businesses; firms in different sectors of the economy were taxed much differently because of the uneven tax treatment of their business costs, such as depreciation. In some cases firms in the emerging high-technology industries were taxed to subsidize outmoded declining operations elsewhere in the economy.

The tax system was increasingly responsible for directing the economy's investment resources; and it did so poorly. The types of investments made in the early 1980s — commercial property, autos, and microcomputers — were not in themselves a sound base on which to build a growing economy with a rising standard of living.

In addition, the income tax was no longer a responsive revenue instrument capable of financing the costs of government. The growth of the tax expenditure list left less and less to tax. The 1981 tax rate cuts had lost important revenues, but increasing the rates again might not have produced more revenue for government because of the powerful attraction of the tax expenditures.

In this situation, tax reform meant more than mere tinkering with tax rates or deductions. Significant movement toward a flat tax was necessary. A flat tax is one with fewer different tax rates and a larger, loophole-free tax base. Milton Friedman had proposed a flat tax reform in the 1960s. At that time Friedman had calculated that a uniform tax of 10 or 12 percent on all (or virtually all) income would generate sufficient revenue to replace the then-current personal and corporate tax systems. Such a system, Friedman had argued, would be both fairer and more efficient. Families with equal incomes would pay equal taxes. The rich, unable to escape into loopholes, would have to pay more dollars than the poor. Investment decisions would be made based on economic risk and return, not intentional or accidental tax incentives. This kind of tax system would be extremely neutral; it would accommodate structural change without either discouraging or accelerating resource movements in the economy.

Milton Friedman's "pure" flat tax was never much more than an academic pipe dream; but like many such theoretic exercises, it eventually produced some concrete results. The notion of greater equity appealed to some, particularly

Democrats like Senator Bill Bradley and Representative Richard Gephardt, who together forged a modified flat tax that preserved the progressivity of the income tax while broadening the tax base and reducing rates. The dream of more efficiency appealed to others, like Representative Jack Kemp and Senator William Roth. The Kemp-Roth proposal had lower rates and less progressivity than the Bradley-Gephardt plan and differed in many details; but the two packages still had much in common, namely, fewer tax expenditures, lower rates, and fewer tax brackets.

Ronald Reagan recognized the flat tax as the obvious sequel to his successful 1981 tax reduction program. A modified flat tax could have even lower tax rates than the post-ERTA tax laws, thereby at least giving the appearance of a higher living standard. A modified flat tax could also be simpler and promote supply-side growth objectives. Constrained by huge deficits from actually cutting tax collections further, Reagan called for a revenue-neutral tax reform in 1984, assigned responsibility for the details to a Treasury Department study group, and went off to run for reelection.

The tax reform plan that the Treasury produced late in 1984 was an economic theorist's conception of tax reform. Income was defined in the broadest and most complete way in Treasury I, making possible major reductions in tax rates. While Treasury I made great economic sense, it had no political support. The public good of lower tax rates had been achieved by removing all the tax expenditures, which interest groups considered their private property. Clean, pure, and unrealistic, Treasury I did at least begin the process of tax reform, which then gained a peculiar momentum.

Jeffrey H. Birnbaum and Alan S. Murray have described the political process of the 1986 tax reform legislation in their book, *Showdown at Gucci Gulch: Lawmakers, Lobbyists, and the Unlikely Triumph of Tax Reform*. The driving force behind tax reform was a rather negative one, according to Birnbaum and Murray. No interest group wanted its own tax preferences "reformed" no matter how much it might wish other parts of the tax law altered. The traditional politics of special interest was therefore biased against any significant movement toward a flat tax plan. But legislation is made — and killed — by politicians who do not seek out visible ways to offend voters. No group in Congress really wanted tax reform, it seems; but no one wanted to be held accountable for killing tax reform either.

What emerged from Congress, after a long, hard, and uncertain process, was a modified flat tax reform act that was at once more than anyone could have reasonably expected and, at the same time, less than anyone might have hoped for. It accomplished the basic goals set out by President Reagan, or nearly so. It was (almost) revenue-neutral. Tax rates were lower and equity improved. The tax at least appeared to be simpler. Inefficient investment incentives at least appeared to be gone. It was not tax reform pure and simple, but it was tax reform.

The Tax Reform Act of 1986 succeeded in reducing further the burden of individual income taxes in the United States. Most taxpayers got a tax cut; the effect of lower tax rates was greater than the impact of closed loopholes. The maximum tax rate was reduced from 50 percent to about 33 percent. Again, as in 1981, an income tax cut could be used to preserve or enhance living standards, at least for a while. Corporate income tax rates were also reduced, from nearly 50 percent to 33 percent.

On the face of it, Congress and the president had accomplished a feat on the order of the miracle of the loaves and fishes. Both individual and corporate taxpayers received substantial tax rate reductions, yet the income tax was designed to be revenue-neutral (or nearly so), producing almost as much income for the Treasury as the old tax. Alas, this tax trick was accomplished with smoke and mirrors, not divine intervention.

The Tax Reform Act of 1986 did more than just flatten tax rates and expand the tax base. It managed to cut taxes for individuals by shifting a substantial share of the tax burden from individuals onto corporations. Tax rates were reduced for both groups, and tax expenditures limited; but loophole closing was far more thorough in the corporate income tax. The 1986 tax reform redistributed the tax burden between households and business and attempted to reverse the long-term trend of declining corporate tax collections.

There are many unintended side effects that can be associated with the Tax Reform Act of 1986, but by far the most important is the sudden and substantial increase in corporate debt that we have seen in just these few years. The sudden increase in corporate tax burden, combined with elimination of many tax expenditures such as the investment tax credit, forced corporate funds through the few loopholes that were left. The interest on debt was one of the few remaining tax shelters, and corporations and corporate raiders rushed to take advantage of it.

It is important at this point to remember why corporate tax collections had fallen steadily during the postwar years. The most important factor in this trend was the declining profitability of the U.S. corporate sector, which had been caught in the middle of the opposing forces of structural change. The corporate sector did not have much profit to tax, at least compared to the household sector. It is not surprising, therefore, that savvy corporate managers would seek to protect the value of their assets by "going private," taking on burdensome, but tax-deductible indebtedness.

The vast impact of the 1986 tax reforms on the structure of the corporate sector was almost completely unexpected. Economists and policymakers proclaimed the efficiency of the new tax package, which treated different types of investments alike far more than in the past. The differential tax treatment of debt and equity was acknowledged but had long existed; and it was not expected to be as critical as it turned out to be.

The overall effects of tax reforms in the 1980s are that consumers have been able to sustain a relatively high standard of living, fueled by two sets of tax cuts and a variety of consumption-enhancing side effects; more wealth is held in high-return, liquid financial instruments now, ready to be spent; credit is easier to get (credit cards come in the mail every week); spending, in fact, is at a historically high level relative to personal income; and personal saving is very low. The economy looks and feels as prosperous as a Mardi Gras.

The productive engine of the economy has not been maintained and expanded sufficiently to produce the party that is going on outside the factory gates. Investment in the early 1980s was directed to decidedly unproductive areas. The corporate sector, with low profits and large debts, now finds itself faced with the need to adjust to a rapidly changing world but burdened by both higher taxes and heavier debt-servicing needs.

The corporate sector in the United States has not the resources fully to respond to the technical and communications revolutions that engulf the world. Tax and fiscal policy diverts the attention of corporate managers away from what should be their first order of business. At the same time, the channels of the financial revolution are sending resources, technology, and production abroad.

Tax reform in the 1980s has come in response to the problems posed by structural change and fiscal crisis. Rather than solving these problems, or at least contributing to a solution, the tax changes that we have examined have tended to preserve the facade of prosperity while actually accelerating and reinforcing the forces that threaten our future living standards.

The Paradox of Social Security

The social security system entered the 1980s teetering on the brink of insolvency, pulled ever closer to the edge by the fiscal forces of structural change. Social security was designed to be a pay-as-you-go system, with each generation paying taxes to provide for their parents and grandparents, counting on their own children and grandchildren for future support. Unlike a private pension plan, no significant buildup of capital spans the generations. This year's benefits to retirees are paid for by this year's workers.

Pay-as-you-go works best in a stable world with relatively constant rates of population and productivity growth. As we have seen however, the United States and the world have been anything but stable, in this sense, in the postwar era. The bust–boom–bust of population growth, especially combined with the other forces at work in this period, made a successful pay-as-you-go system virtually impossible.

The baby bust generation found it relatively easy to provide retirement benefits for their parents, given their high productivity and the rapid rise in their living standards. The baby-boomers are finding it more difficult to pay for their parents' retirement years because social insurance benefits have increased while the rise in the average living standards of the working generation has slowed or stagnated. Mathematically, it is difficult to imagine how the much smaller baby bust generation of the 1970s and 1980s would be willing or able to finance their own parents' retirement, given current productivity trends, benefit levels, and life tables.

After many false starts, the social security system in the United States was reformed in 1983. The pay-as-you-go system was largely replaced by a program of public saving that provided a means for the baby boom workers collectively to accumulate assets to provide for their retirement benefits. The 1983 reforms were very important because they are one of the most dramatic examples of a major social institution adapting itself to accommodate a new and unexpected pattern of structural change. The social insurance system in the United States is the largest, single, government program in the world. That such a system could smoothly adapt, at least on paper, to major change is amazing.[6]

The paradox of the social security system is that while it has changed its structure to accommodate structural change, this may in fact weaken the program, given that other sectors of the economy are still unbalanced. There may not be any way that the social insurance system by itself can in fact adopt policies to assure solvency in the long run. This illustrates the delicate nature of the interrelationship that exists among social institutions. It is difficult if not impossible for any single social institution to achieve balance when the society that it serves is fundamentally unbalanced itself.

The logic of the 1983 reforms is simple and clear. The way to stabilize social security taxes over the next two generations, given the unstable pattern of population growth, is to abandon pay-as-you-go finance in favor of a system of limited capital accumulation. Beginning in the 1980s, social security taxes were increased above the rate necessary to pay current retirement benefits. The annual surpluses, small at first but larger later, are accumulated along with their compounding interest return. The amount of the cumulative surplus will be huge: perhaps 10 percent of national income by the year 2000, 20 percent by 2010, peaking at more than 30 percent of national income when the baby boom generation begins to reach retirement age in the decade of the 2020s.[7]

In effect, the 1983 social security reforms provide for a form of social retirement saving to supplement both private saving and the ability of future generations to pay social insurance taxes. Annual retirement benefit costs will exceed annual tax collections in the 2020s and the social security trust funds will begin to be drawn down. The trust funds are projected to run dry around 2050 according to the best guesses of today's economists. At that point a social security deficit is possible, or taxes could be increased to return to a pay-as-you-go system. A more likely scenario, however, is that some midcourse adjustment will be made in the future years as more is known about economic and demographic conditions in the post-2020 world.

No institution is perfect, of course; and even on paper bugs remain in the post-1983 social security system. The reforms failed to correct completely a host of problems that have long plagued the U.S. system, which taxes individuals and pays benefits to family units in ways that are not always fair or efficient.[8]

The biggest bug in the 1983 reforms, however, is very large indeed. As radical in nature as the reform package was, it only solved part of the problem — financing future retirement benefits. Paying for Medicare, the hospital insurance component of social security, was not on the 1983 reform agenda.[9] Given its current pay-as-you-go plan, the Medicare program will begin to run very large deficits soon. The demographic imbalance is one reason for Medicare's projected problem (too many beneficiaries and not enough working taxpayers), but the technological boom is even more to blame. One of the greatest successes of the technological boom of the postwar era has been the creation of very complex products and processes in medicine and health care. Doctors and hospitals are now much better able to cope with health problems at every stage of life, but perhaps the most significant innovations affect the very young and the elderly. These benefits, however, have a very high cost; health care costs typically rise faster than just about any other component of the consumer price index. How fast Medicare costs will rise in the future, given the growing aging population and continued improvements in medical technology, is virtually unknowable. It is certain, however, that Medicare costs will rise faster than current taxes are scheduled to increase. Another day of reckoning (probably several of them) therefore awaits us, when a decision will need to be made about how to pay for health care for the elderly.

Balancing social security's retirement budget in the long run does not really solve the problem of providing a stable base of social insurance for today's population so long as so important a program as Medicare remains out of balance. But even ignoring this critical problem, we must understand that the actuarial balance that the 1983 reforms achieved in the social security accounts do not really solve the social security retirement system's dilemma so long as the federal government and the economy remain as they are today, far from their historical pattern of fiscal balance.

The most important problem that the reformed social security system faces, Medicare aside, is that it is very difficult for society completely to avoid a pay-as-you-go retirement system in some sense. Debts and obligations can be shifted back and forth across generations, but retired people use up real resources, which cannot so easily be sent back and forth from past to present to future. As individuals, we save for the future; but this really requires that we transfer real resources to others today and they agree to transfer (different and more) real resources back to us at some point in the future. The transaction makes it possible for us to behave as if we are taking resources and moving it from our present to our own future. But this financial transaction does not really leap through the time barrier, it just mimics the time warp with smoke and mirrors; two exchanges at different times provide the image that substitutes for a movement of resources from present to future. Clever shadows.

Even under ideal circumstances, the reformed social security system involves a measure of the smoke-and-mirrors technology. The logic of the trust fund surplus is that social security retirement surpluses in the next thirty or so years will be invested in U.S. Treasury securities—in government debt instruments. The social security administration will quickly become the federal government's largest single creditor. When social security deficits replace surpluses after 2020, the mountain of Treasury obligations will be slowly cashed in to supplement pay-as-you-go funds. Where will the Treasury get the money it will need to meet its enormous annual obligations (especially in the 2030s and 2040s) to the social security trust funds? The federal government will be forced to raise taxes or sell other government bonds to gain the funds to retire the social security debt.

In other words, the 1983 reforms changed social security from a pay-as-you-go system, with taxes rising steeply to meet increased retirement benefit costs, to a debt-financed system, where the federal government will find it necessary to raise taxes or increase borrowing, especially after 2020, to pay back its obligations to the graying codgers of the baby boom.

Seen in this light, the 1983 reforms may not seem to offer much in the way of reform. It would appear that all that has been changed is the timing of taxes. The pre-1983 system had lower taxes now and very steeply rising taxes in the next century. The "reformed" system raises social security taxes now (to generate the surplus) but requires that income taxes be increased later so that the Treasury can pay its debts to social security trustees. This is true in the sense that social security benefits must be paid by raising some taxes at some point. But there is more than a timing difference here.

In order for the 1983 social security reforms to work, the surpluses in the trust funds must be productive; they must generate a high rate of economic growth. If the huge investment potential of the trust fund surpluses succeed in increasing the rate of economic growth in the United States, then we will have a much richer and more productive economy in the 2020s and 2030s than would otherwise exist. With higher productivity and higher incomes, the next generation will be better able to bear the tax burden and to purchase the new Treasury bonds needed to finance social security.

How can social security trust funds, which are invested in government bonds, produce this dynamic economy and the growth that will be necessary to create it? The logic of the program is that with an increase in social security saving being used to finance the federal debt over the next thirty years, more private savings will be available to finance domestic research, development, education, and investment. Social security "saving" will free up private sector saving for private sector investment, which should produce more rapid increases in private sector economic growth.

If this plan works, it will work because our grandchildren's generation will have much higher incomes than would otherwise be the case. Their higher incomes would be our bequest to them indirectly through our own willingness to bear a high social security tax burden now. But this bequest will not be a free lunch. Along with higher income will come the obligation, more moral than legal, to use their greater wealth to the pay the taxes or buy the bonds that will finance baby boom retirement years.

Pay-as-you-go finance is simple to explain. Trust fund surpluses, however, require a complex chain of cause and effect to make them work. In fact, however, such a system could work by generating more saving and investment in the short run, thereby growing a bigger and stronger economy for future years when retirement costs will be high.

But it is not too severe to say that the social security system, as it now exists, is a bet on economic growth. If investment does not take place and productivity does not increase, the economy of the future will be unable to bear the heavy burden of the mountains of federal debt that we are piling on it.

The social security bet is the right one to make if one is forced to bet. It is foolish to count on luck to pay the future's bills. There is a logical sequence of events, outlined above, that could generate the economic events necessary to pay the future's social security bills. But this said, it is also important to recognize that there is a significant chance that the bet will go badly for all concerned.

The very forces that caused the imbalance in social security in the first place also work against its solution through economic growth. This is true because the imbalance in social security is matched by other kinds of disequilibria in the economy that make it nearly impossible to set social security aright by itself.

The basic problem is whether the increase in social security "saving" will actually result in an increase productive investment. This may fail for at least three reasons that are relevant here.[10] First, the increase in social security saving may not result in an increase in private savings (and therefore private investment) because of increased federal government deficits; that is, higher federal deficits may soak up the social security surpluses, leaving no net addition to the nation's productive stock on which to base future growth. For the social security program to work in the long run, the federal deficit must be stable or, better, a declining drain on the credit markets.

At first glance, it would appear that the worry about sustained and rising federal deficits is a red herring. News reports indicate that the government deficit is moving toward balance, hitting the Gramm-Rudman-Hollings yearly targets (or nearly so) with relative regularity. This is true but deceptive because the Gramm-Rudman-Hollings definition of the federal deficit includes as a revenue item the social security trust fund surpluses. If social security funds are separated, the remaining federal deficit is large — still over $200 billion — and is not declining. At some point the federal budget will certainly be balanced (according to the Gramm-Rudman-Hollings definition) due to the rapid rise in social security surpluses. But this will not tell us anything meaningful about the extent to which federal borrowing is a drain on private savings.

In short, social security surpluses may not significantly increase net domestic investment, broadly defined, if they are only used, in the short run, to finance even higher levels of federal government borrowing.

The second dilemma arises because of the international fiscal imbalance that has become so important within the last decade. The United States is now a net debtor nation, and in the future it will be forced to give up more and more to pay profit and interest returns to the foreign owners of U.S. assets. If this pattern of international indebtedness, driven largely by the federal deficit, continues, a very large increase in U.S. productivity and income will be necessary simply to meet these future foreign obligations. Our legal and economic obligations to foreign creditors will begin to conflict with the political and moral obligations among generations, as defined by the social security system. Future generations, however rich, may find themselves beholden to both foreign creditors and past generations. This is not a true solution to the problem.

Finally, let us assume that federal borrowing stabilizes and falls, so that social security saving really does free up private funds for investment spending. Even in this best-case scenario there is no guarantee that the bet will be won, because high levels of investment spending alone are not enough. We will need high levels of investment spending in productive areas that generate jobs and incomes in the United States. Recent history suggests that there is some risk that this will not happen.

There has been a high level of investment spending in the United States in the 1980s, for example; but, as we have seen, the tax laws and the financial markets have tended to divert these resources from their best uses. The technological and communications revolutions have shortened the product cycle so that new innovations must be created quickly to replace last year's hot products, which are now being produced in some low-wage Third World nation.

In sum, the changing patterns we have seen in the postwar years do not seem to favor the types of events necessary for the social security system to succeed. The 1970s and especially the 1980s have not been years when saving and investment have generated wealth for the United States. Instead, these have been years of consumption and finance.

The bet that society has placed on social security may be the best gamble available, given the structural changes in the economy and the dynamic forces that have been unleashed. But to a great extent the social security system, with its emphasis on surplus, public-private saving, and productive investment, is a bet on the old world—the economy that existed years ago. If that economy had continued, social security would not need to search for solutions today. The changing world of the postwar period both created social security's problems and raised the odds against their easy solution.

Change and Balance

The "American crisis" stems from our inability, as a society, fully to adapt to the revolutions that have swept the world. This failure to adapt is not universal. Some industries and sectors of society have fared better than others. Some groups have experienced at least the appearance of rising living standards, made possible by shifting distributions and debt-financed consumption. Other segments of society have experienced the decline in living standards and expectations more completely.

It is appropriate that this study has focused on the role of government during this period of rapid structural change. Government institutions have played two parts in this story. First, the fiscal institutions of the federal government have been a noteworthy barometer of the changing pressures and forces in the economy. The outlay and revenue sides of government have been affected in different ways (and in different directions) by the forces of structural change. As a result, the federal government slipped slowly, then much faster, into fiscal imbalance. The mountains of national debt that have resulted were not inevitable; but the forces that created them are large—larger than is generally appreciated—and long-term in nature, not just the result of short-term decisions by nearsighted politicians, as we are often told.

Although it was not government's fate to accumulate such a massive debt, it was in fact the fate of government officials to have to deal simultaneously with both chronic fiscal imbalance and the other problems caused by the strong and persistent forces of structural change. At many points, Congress and the president have had a choice: attempt to offset the impacts of structural change on the economy or try to correct the effects of structural change on the fiscal institutions of government.

In the early 1980s, for example, Congress and the president faced growing budget deficits at the same time that a large fraction of the population was experiencing (some briefly for the first time, others more severely) the consequences of structural change on their living standards. The 1981 tax cuts were a choice to try to preserve or improve living standards by the only way directly available to voters and politicians—tax cuts.

The tax reforms of 1986 made the same sort of choice. In the process of reforming the income tax, making it flatter and more neutral in its impact on the economy, Congress and the president also chose to reduce the direct tax burden on households, shifting it onto corporations.

It is significant that the long-term stability of the social security program was apparently considered too important to sacrifice to the short-term interest in higher living standards. In this case the choice was made actually to increase payroll taxes significantly in the short run in order to initiate a process that might logically lead to continued retirement benefits, at roughly current levels, well into the future. It is also significant, alas, that these same reforms failed to address the mounting medical care costs, which seem likely to ultimately overwhelm the importance of the retirement program reforms.

The choices to reduce the income tax burden on households, allowing consumption to rise without an equal increase in the ability to produce, caused the fiscal institutions of government to become increasingly unbalanced. The already-large national debt has grown at an unprecedented pace, in nominal and real terms and relative to national income. It is a cruel irony that this rising debt, created in an attempt to maintain the economy of the past, now threatens to accelerate the relative decline of the U.S. economy. The choices we have made appear to have backfired, with potentially disastrous consequences.

The growing federal debt has speeded structural change. The forces of the financial revolution make the private sector increasingly dependent on debt and increasingly beholden to foreign creditors. The technological and communications revolutions, riding the new international credit channels, have altered the very role of the U.S. within the world economy. Meanwhile, U.S. tax policy encourages corporate debt, not investment, and leaves a legacy of foolish capital accumulation and weakened financial institutions.

What is perverse in this story is that the good intentions of the federal government leaders have, in the end, so thoroughly backfired. The institutions of the private sector have adjusted to structural change faster and better than have the fiscal institutions of government. But the choices and policies of government have had the perverse effect of accelerating and shaping structural change, so that even dynamic private sector actors have found it difficult to accommodate change successfully.

The consequences, private and public, are easy to see. The recent Brookings Institution publication, *American Living Standards: Threats and Challenges*, documents the dismal private sector prospects of the next generation of U.S. citizens.[11] The uncertain future of the social security system (detailed in another recent Brookings volume, *Can America Afford To Grow Old?*) shows that even the apparently sound public choices of the 1983 reforms may not be able to withstand the growing winds of change.

The real issue before us now is the future. How will this drama play itself out? What policy choices are available? What, in short, can we do about the new mountains of debt and their growing effect on the present economy and on the future of the United States.

9

Saddle Points

Early on in their training, mathematical economists come across a curious situation called a saddle point. A saddle point is a somewhat deceptive place; it satisfies all the first-order conditions for a maximum or local high spot, but at the same time it also satisfies all the first-order conditions for a local minimum or low point. In fact, however, life at the saddle point is neither a peak nor a trough. It is literally like the point where you would straddle a Western saddle on a horse—the lowest point on the saddle along the line of the horse but the highest point measured crossways.

Most mountain passes are saddle points. They represent false maximums. The highway's highest point on the road over the pass is typically the lowest point among the surrounding mountains. Once you've reached the summit, you have the opportunity to choose. You descend if you continue to follow the line of the highway; or you can make a sharp turn, changing directions, and proceed even higher, to the true peak of the mountains cut by the pass. It is a place to make choices. Most people follow the highway over the pass, taking the path of least resistance. A few climb higher.

The three economies that we have examined in this book each found themselves at saddle points. Renaissance Florence, Victorian Britain, and the postwar United States reached points where the economic topography of the time began to change. The paths and patterns that led ever higher in the past would soon begin to descend. Following the tried path at the saddle point leads over the hill and down the decline. Making the hard, sharp turn, adjusting the road to fit the new terrain, is the only way to continue to climb.

Renaissance Florence and Victorian Britain stayed the course when they reached their saddle points. Their fiscal institutions shifted into high gear at the summit and speeded their trip down the other side. The question that this chapter sets out to discuss is whether the United States will follow this same path.

Of course the saddle point problem is not so plain and simple for an economy as it is for an individual crossing a mountain range. A hiker can plainly see the lie of the land and know for the most part which way is up and which is down. Even in dense fog, you generally can tell whether you are walking up or down the mountain even if you aren't always sure which mountain.

But the geography of the economy is more complex because our vision is so very limited. The most important features of the landscape — the mountains and the valleys — are shaped by long-term forces of the type I have sought to identify in this essay. But we live our lives a day at a time, paying close attention to the tiny patch of ground we are standing on today. It is difficult really to see the mountains around us amid the more obvious, more immediate problems of the rocky path that lies just slightly ahead. It is hard to see where the saddle point is, when to change directions, and which way to go. This is particularly true because the way we "see" the economic landscape best is seldom by direct observation but rather through confusing, ambiguous, and imperfect economic indicators.

In fact, the United States may already have passed its saddle point. Inertia may already be building to speed us down the incline. If this is the case, the problems that confront us are especially hard. We must not only change direction but overcome the momentum of past mistakes.

But this is perhaps too gloomy a scene for even a dismal scientist to want to describe. So let us assume, instead, that the United States is just now reaching the saddle point, the point of choice. What lies ahead if we continue on the present road? What if we turn? How can we change the course of such a large and unwieldy vehicle as a whole economy?

Doing the Right Thing

> Mankind, it seems, makes a poorer performance of government than of almost any other human activity. In this sphere, wisdom, which may be defined as the exercise of judgment acting on experience, common sense and available information, is less operative and more frustrated than it should be.
> Barbara Tuchman, *The March of Folly*

The saddle point presents difficult problems to an economy and its policymakers; and it is not really so surprising that at the critical moment, governments often make the wrong choices or even more often no choices at all.[1] That this folly is not unexpected (and has been repeated through history) does not make it less frustrating.

Sometimes the problem is that we do not recognize that there is a need for change. Today, for example, there are at least three groups of economists who argue that there is no need to be concerned with the problem of fiscal balance. They argue that deficits may be good, and if they are not good, at least they are not bad.

Robert Barro is one economist who argues that deficits do not matter either way, because of people's ability to adjust their lives to them.[2] In Barro's view, deficits are equivalent to postponed taxes and individuals can adjust their saving patterns to compensate for government practices. (This is called — incorrectly, I think — Ricardian equivalence, after a section in Ricardo's textbook about debt and taxes.)

In Barro's view, the private economy can offset imbalance in the public sector, leaving the overall economy always and everywhere in equilibrium. Barro sees the deficit as unimportant because he sees it overrated as a potentially destabilizing force. In this essay, however, I have focused on the deficit as a symptom of an unbalanced economy as much as the cause of disequilibrium; the budget deficit can only disappear in the long run if the economy reestablishes its balance within the world system. Thus, I reject Barro's view — deficits do matter.

In their recent book, *The Debt and the Deficit*, Robert Heilbroner and Peter Bernstein also propose that fiscal imbalance is a false demon.[3] They argue (correctly) that all deficits are not the same; there are good deficits and bad deficits. But their bottom line, I believe, is that they are concerned that wrong-headed deficit cutters will intentionally or unintentionally cut the wrong government programs in a mindless quest for a balanced budget. They see the deficit being used as an excuse to strip away fifty years of social progress, leaving the economy a hard, cruel place for the poor.

Perhaps Heilbroner and Bernstein are right to be worried about how fiscal balance will be restored. Indeed, I agree with many of their concerns; and in the next chapter I will argue for increased government activity, not cuts, in some areas that Heilbroner and Bernstein hold dear. But I think that they make a mistake when they argue too vehemently that the deficit is not a problem. The failure to achieve a fundamental balance in the economy — which would also lead to fiscal balance — would make impossible the kinds of programs that Heilbroner and Bernstein want to protect, by vastly increasing the magnitudes of the problems the programs address.

Finally, Robert Eisner has argued, on what must seem to most people to be very technical grounds that the national debt is not a problem.[4] Eisner points out that the debt and deficit as normally measured by government statistics really are not the same animals that appear in the sophisticated theories that economists use to understand macroeconomics. Eisner goes through elaborate arithmetic to show that properly adjusted, the debt has not changed very much and is not a really significant problem. Eisner misses the point, I think, by not seeing the relationship between fiscal balance and the greater economic balance on which the fiscal side depends. Searching for more sophisticated analytic techniques, he overlooks the need for fundamental economic change.

Even when the need for fundamental change is clear, there is still the question of what to change and how. In addition there is the problem that the benefits from changing course are often realized only in the long run while the costs are frequently immediate. This last problem can be particularly troublesome when economic and social policy is made by politicians facing election in the short run. Here political incentives can work decidedly against society's long-term interests.

Which Way Is Up?

One problem peculiar to economics at the saddle point is deciding what policy should aim for. What is the real problem and the real goal? If we aim to seek higher ground, which way is up?

The problem is that in economics, we are seldom able to measure anything directly. All the really important things in life are very hard to measure in the first place and then even more difficult to "aggregate" or add up, so that conclusions can be reached about the state of the national economy. Our best indicator of the health of the national economy is gross national product, for example, which measures the total dollar value of the things we produce. This total is an important indicator of how the economy is working, but equally important is what mixture of items is being produced, why, for whom, and how. We really need to know if the current batch of stuff is the right stuff, and GNP accounting simply cannot tell us that. Having the right stuff, after all, is at least as important as having lots of stuff.

In 1989, for example, a major oil spill in Alaska did tremendous harm to wildlife and the environment that may take generations fully to restore. The oil spill almost certainly made GNP go up for the year. More stuff was produced, but the wrong stuff. It is not a criticism of economists or GNP calculators that they use this kind of data, it is just a fact. Because our information about the economy is so limited and imperfect, we necessarily make wrong choices some of the time.

More important in the present context is the tendency in economic policy to confuse the indicators with what they indicate. The federal budget deficit and the nation's trade deficit, for example, are two indicators of fiscal crisis. They tell us the extent to which different parts of the economy have become unbalanced. The budget deficit measures the difference between government income and outlays directly. The trade deficit measures the difference between revenues from exports and the cost of imports directly. But they really tell us something else — they reflect the condition of our economic institutions.

The unbalanced condition of the economy causes these deficits. The true value of the trade and budget deficit economic indicators is not, therefore, their direct measurement, which is just dollars and cents, but rather what they can tell us about the bigger forces and problems that we cannot measure directly.

Sometimes the limits of economic statistics can totally dictate our perception of a problem. In Victorian Britain, for example, the only even vaguely reliable statistical indicator of the health of the national economy was the calculation of the trade balance. As a result, as Friedberg has shown, the British wrongly interpreted all their economic problems as fundamentally problems of international trade.[5] This compulsive concern with trade no doubt contributed to the lack of attention to other problems in other areas, which were probably more important in the long run.

An unbalanced economy is an abstract concept. In fact, the idea of a national economy, bigger and different from any piece of it that we can actually see with our own eyes, is pretty abstract in itself. The nature of cause and effect within this nebulous creature is even harder to understand or explain. It is small wonder, therefore, that the policymakers find it easier to attack the clear and simple indicators than to address the more complex and ambiguous problems that underlie them. Recent actions by the U.S. Congress show how important this distinction between the real and the measured economy is.

Since the late 1970s there has been growing concern about the U.S. bilateral trade deficit with Japan. Congress has considered many trade packages designed to reduce this deficit artificially through tariffs, quotas, or other trade sanctions. Of course, the real problem is one of fiscal balance. The United states has put itself in a situation where it must seek credit and investment from abroad. The United States benefits from investment inflows from Japan and, because of the nature of international finance, must balance this income with outlays for Japanese imports.

The problem (the need for foreign funds) is different from the measured problem (the fact of a trade deficit). But Congress persists, for the kinds of reasons already discussed, to attack the measured problem rather than what is very likely the real one. One interesting side effect of the threat of congressional trade sanctions against Japan has been the growth of Japanese-owned production facilities in the United States. United States citizens now purchase many more goods and services from Japanese firms than is measured by the trade figures. The measured problem improves somewhat, but it is not clear that the real underlying problem has changed in any significant way.

The difference between the real problem and the measured problem is even clearer when we examine the federal budget deficit. Congress adopted the Gramm-Rudman-Hollings bill as its "poison pill" defense against the rising national debt. Gramm-Rudman-Hollings is designed to force Congress to reduce the budget deficit in systematic steps by holding up as the painful alternative a highly distasteful package of mandatory outlay reductions.

Taking matters at face value, it appears that the Gramm-Rudman-Hollings law is working smoothly and well. With this fiscal sword of Damocles hanging over them, federal policymakers have had more success than in previous years in reaching agreement on policies to reduce the federal deficit. They have been successful in reducing the measured deficit, but they have arguably failed to solve (or even fully address) the underlying real problem of fiscal imbalance.

The progress that has been made under Gramm-Rudman-Hollings has come largely through the budget gimmicks, not the hard fiscal choices that will be necessary to transform the United States' fiscal institutions to accommodate the rapid pace of structural change. To keep the measured deficit within limits, federal policymakers have resorted to trick after trick.[6] Rosy scenario economic forecasts were used to generate phantom revenues. Perversely, Gramm-Rudman-Hollings requires only that a smaller deficit be forecast, not actually achieved—hence, the utility of falsely optimistic projections. Costly programs now tend to be funded under the table, either off-budget (through federally guaranteed credit programs for example) or even by back-dating, shifting expenditures to previous fiscal years that have already been certified Gramm-

Rudman-Hollings-compatible.[7] Finally, we have already seen how the accumulated surpluses of the social security retirement system are being employed to generate a false measurement of the federal government's annual budget balance.

Take away the accounting tricks and the federal fiscal imbalance has increased, not fallen, since Gramm-Rudman-Hollings was implemented. The real problem is now worse than before. But in enacting Gramm-Rudman-Hollings, Congress and the president were choosing to address one measurable indicator of fiscal imbalance. The relative ease with which they have been able to reduce the measured extent of the problem has allowed them to ignore the fact that the real problem has increased in size and scope.

Even when we overcome the confusion between the real economic problems and the indicators that inform us about those problems, the dilemma of the saddle point remains. If a change of direction is called for, what should change and how?

It has been argued in this essay that economic and social institutions need to be changed when, under the influence of rapid structural change, they can no longer balance successfully the competing forces in the economy. But institutions have tremendous momentum; the interests vested in the status quo are almost always the strongest interests around. It is hard to get people to give up a system that has worked for them in the past in favor of untried or previously unsuccessful institutional arrangements. It is not clear, therefore, that people (especially political groups) will do what needs to be done. This is particularly true because there are always two easier alternatives available that are less costly to adopt—in the short run.

Economic policy is a snap—if you set your standards low enough. An easy way out of the saddle point dilemma is to choose not to care about the future or to alter your standards (or how they are measured) so as to disguise the fact of decline. In the twentieth century, for example, both France and Britain have declined in their relative economic and political status in the world community (at least compared with their nineteenth-century expectations). One way that they have dealt with this situation is to replace the reality of power with the myth of influence. Myths can be almost as convincing as reality and are often cheaper to maintain. President Reagan certainly lived the myth of the budget balancer while the national debt grew.

Some might say that the United States has already bartered the reality of economic hegemony for its mythical equivalent. Lower real standards or fairy tales do not change the underlying problem of the saddle point.

A second and even more dangerous alternative is to pretend that the strong forces of structural change, which create fiscal crisis, can somehow be bottled up, walled out, or reversed so as to preserve the threatened institutional structure. It is a fact, however, that jinnis are seldom successfully stuffed back in their bottles. Those who try to insulate themselves from reality may gain relief in the short run but pay a correspondingly higher price in the long run.

Economic policy toward foreign competition often follows this road. In Europe, for example, the common market countries created a massive system of farm subsidies, the Common Agricultural Policy (CAP) so that they would not have to deal with the problems created by growing international competition in farm goods. At best they only postponed their day of reckoning. At worst, the European Community (EC) nearly blew apart in the 1980s over the high cost of the CAP program. Now the EC is forced to crack its farm nut, which has only become tougher in the meantime because other nations around the world felt forced to enact their own offsetting farm subsidies.

Trade barriers are a common medium for policies that try to insulate an industry or nation from larger forces. Less-developed countries sometimes pass domestic content legislation, for example, in an attempt to preserve and protect domestic production. At best, such protectionist policies take a nation out of the mainstream of change; they are simply left behind. At worst, the forces of change are diverted, corrupted, and distorted. Change still takes place, but not constructive change.

In thinking about the United States' choices at the saddle point it will be important to bear these issues in mind. We must not confuse economic indicators with the real forces at work on the economy. And we must try not to take the easy way out. We cannot, in the long run, live out myths; nor can we for long keep out the forces of change that are at large in the world economy.

Patterns of Past Experiences

The United States must soon make important choices about the direction it will take in the future. We have reached a crucial point in our economic history, we have come to the saddle point. But there is no sense of emergency or even immediacy abroad in the land. There is no common sense of the approaching choices that must be made and the consequences that must be faced. This is true even though many public leaders are well informed about our future prospects. Benjamin Friedman's excellent book, *Day of Reckoning*, provides a thorough analysis of past trends and their future consequences. The public seems little swayed, however, by even well written economic analysis on this point.

This lack of public interest or awareness, I think, is an essential element of the saddle point dilemma. The summit of a mountain pass is precisely the point where the climb eases and the imperative to ascend weakens.

Renaissance Florence and Victorian Britain were countries that had a lot in common with the postwar United States. They were the leading economies of their times. They were capitalist systems, dynamic, growing, and outward-looking. They were forced to deal with great and accelerating forces of structural change, which put their social institutions under tremendous stress and created large and persistent fiscal crises. Both nations reached the saddle point and failed to turn. They continued down the familiar road and fell into long-run decline relative to other nations of their time.

We should be able to learn something from past experiences with structural change and fiscal crisis. At the least, we should be able to learn the importance of policy choice at the saddle point. The British and Florentine experiences also provide us with good "stories" to help raise public consciousness regarding these issues. This is not an insignificant matter; all the equations, tables, charts, and graphs in the world are less persuasive than one well-told story. This being true, let me retell for emphasis the main points of the fiscal fables that history provides.

Renaissance Florence

The economy of Renaissance Florence was deeply rooted in the Middle Ages. The commercial revolution that built the city-states of the Middle Ages reached its peak in the Italian communes, particularly in Florence, where finance and commerce mixed thoroughly and served as strong catalysts for trade-driven economic growth. Florence was outward-looking and exploited its particular advantages, which were far more intellectual than natural or mechanical in nature. Renaissance Florence inherited the most successful economic system of the Middle Ages and, remarkably, kept it working through two centuries of more and more abrasive structural change.

The great economic success of Florence in the Middle Ages was its ability to adapt to the changes brought on by the commercial revolution. The great Florentine economic failure was its ultimate inability to transform itself to accommodate the changes of the Renaissance period.

The defining event of the Renaissance, from the perverse and dismal point of view of economics, was clearly the black death. The plague took so many lives that it altered for centuries the economic structure of the Western world — the pattern of production, division of labor, structure of markets, and distribution of income and wealth. Real wages increased, average wealth levels increased, and the quantity and quality of goods and services demanded shifted. A more dramatic and complete structural change is hardly imaginable, particularly when set against the stability and inertia that in so many ways characterized the preceding centuries.

In retrospect, what is most remarkable about the economic institutions of Renaissance Florence is how little they changed for two hundred years. The fundamental industries — cloth and finance — remained the same and were organized along similar lines. The particular goods and services produced did change with the times, evolving from the refinished wool of the Calimala Guild, to the finer wool of the Arte della Lana, to the costly silk brocades, and finally the decorative arts industry of the later years. But it is significant that these shifts were slow, modest, and really incomplete. Old products were never completely dropped and the new ones never wholly adopted. Florentine business played many variations on their familiar theme but never really learned the new tune or forgot the old one.

The social and economic institutions of Florentine government proved to be a remarkably accurate barometer of the extent of structural strain on the economy. Historians and political scientists have focused on the impact of changing economic structure on the political organization of the commune. The Ciompi Revolt, for example, derives from the growing relative importance of the lesser guilds, which, in turn, derives from the changing labor force and wealth structures.

The long series of wars that plagued Florence in the Renaissance and sapped its strength also have roots in the black death and the waves of change associated with it. Postplague government was more costly and was called on to perform more functions. Territorial expansion was necessary to supply the economic resources of the new governments and their new economic situations. As many city-states sought to expand at the same time, the result was mutually detrimental. Government costs increased for all of them, due mostly to the necessary employment of foreign mercenaries in this low-population era, while no long-term changes in territorial holdings was ever achieved. In the meantime, war distorted and disrupted economic structures and probably hardened tradition's already iron hold on the economy.

These war costs alone were enough to push the commune's budget out of long-run fiscal balance. The Monte Commune, the world's first funded public debt, was invented to be the first-order solution to this crisis. Government outlays increased further, however, as government became more involved in the economic life of the commune, adopting programs and policies that were designed to further local business interests.

The Florentine tax system was for decades still stuck in the patterns of the Middle Ages, when the population was larger and poorer and basic consumption goods, like salt and wine, were the broadest base on which to build a budget. Traditional tax sources were increasingly irrelevant as the consequences of the black death spread through the economy. Even very high tax rates ultimately could not extract the necessary resources from the populace using outdated tools.

The *catasto* tax reform of 1427 is tremendously significant in this context even though it did not generate sufficient new funds to save Florence from its growing fiscal crisis. The *catasto* was an important attempt to change direction. This reform moved the tax burden somewhat away from the traditional sources of medieval life — now much overtaxed — to put it on the incomes and occupations that had developed during the commercial revolution that peaked a century before. The *catasto* was also important as a political event; it symbolized the fact that in a labor-scarce world, taxes that fell almost exclusively on labor income could not support political balance.

Florence managed to survive in spite of the strong opposing economic currents of the period. This is a tribute to the fifth element that made Renaissance Florence a special time and place. But Florentine economic life had changed. From growth and prosperity, the focus shifted to maintenance, and finally to decline.

It is ironic that in a world plagued by war, *peace* accelerated the Florentine decline. The end of the Hundred Years' War in 1453 meant that the northern states, which had so long been preoccupied with their own conflict, could now turn their attention more toward peaceful pursuits and business transactions.

Suddenly, Florence faced a whole new world of competition, with the shifting patterns of trade, finance, and production that this entailed.

In a way the long years of war had limited the global impact of structural change. Each region had been put under some stress by the black death's legacy, but the total impact was in fact limited or contained by the persistence of military action. War moderated the extent to which greater economic and social adjustments were necessary across borders and between regions.

The end of the Hundred Years' War together with the Peace of Lodi, which caused a pause in the struggles among the Italian powers, had the total effect of accelerating structural changes that had been building up for a century. Markets shifted, centers of economic and political power shifted, and Florence declined dramatically in its relative political and economic influence.

As previous chapters have documented, the practical reactions to the Florentine fiscal crisis—the *catasto* and the Monte—did not help prepare the economy for the saddle point problem when it finally came in full-blown form in the second half of the fifteenth century. The Monte dug channels through which Florentine capital flowed. In the end, these mighty ruts were too strong to be overcome; they guided the wealth of Florence down the traditional routes that lead to eventual decline, away from the new opportunities that might have been pursued.

The tax reforms of 1427 also contributed to the Florentine failure in the end. The *catasto* was a good tax, but a flawed one. In static terms, it succeeded (better than earlier taxes) in placing the burden of government on those with the greatest wealth. In dynamic terms, however, it failed by providing an incentive for people and businesses to invest in conspicuous consumption, not productive capital. There was incentive enough, as it turns out, for Florentines to choose present consumption over investment in an uncertain future in a time of persistent decline. The *catasto* accelerated this undesirable trend.

The Florentines built palaces and produced decorative arts and crafts. Some of this work was very brilliant and we still celebrate its inspiration. Much of it, apparently, sold by the square foot, like cheap wallpaper, irrespective of inspirational content.

Perhaps there was nothing that Florence could have done to prevent its ultimate decline. The point is that *nothing* is precisely what they decided to do. The Florentines adopted policies aimed at preserving and protecting the status quo. They even adopted fiscal policies that deepened the patterns of the past to the point that they became awesome barriers to change.

The public debt—the Monte Commune—became the heart of the commune and in this way perhaps represents the choice that the Florentines made at the saddle point best. With decline plainly ahead and fiscal crisis all around, the Florentines chose myth over reality. They adopted policy after policy that preserved the myth of the funded public debt and therefore the myth of their own power and wealth. The price of the myth was an economic system that became locked in place. The myth of the Monte permitted the Florentines to extend for a while their high standard of living, but they paid the price in the long run.

What could the Florentines have done to change their fate? Were they doomed to decline? Perhaps, but not necessarily. Florentine fiscal policy — the *catasto* and the Monte — reduced the commune's flexibility and misallocated its resources. An unbiased tax system might not have saved the commune from relative decline, but it at least would not have persistently funneled business profits to conspicuous consumption. More realistic policies concerning the public debt would have had higher short-run costs. Nearly everyone in the commune would have been poorer and Florence might have fallen before the troops of Venice or Milan. But if Florence had survived, its public debt would not have so persistently diverted attention away from commerce towards finance, away from future growth toward present comfort. In short, the fiscal policies that accelerated the pattern of decline might, if reformed, have helped slow the decline instead.

Victorian Britain

Britain's economic experience in the Victorian era was decidedly different from the Florentine story but illustrates many of the same themes and morals. Britain successfully adapted to the structural changes that characterized the Industrial Revolution and, in so doing, broke out of the prevailing no-growth mold that had long formed the lives and expectations of people in the western world.

The driving force behind structural change in Victorian Britain was an unexpected increase in population. Perhaps the most significant triumph of the Industrial Revolution was Britain's ability to absorb this major increase in hands and mouths without the falling living standards that Thomas Malthus expected. This miracle was achieved through increased productivity on the farm and in the workshop, plus the unusual circumstances of the time that contributed to labor mobility, moving workers off the land and to the cities.

The Industrial Revolution was really a set of long, slow structural changes in the economic and social system, some of which were accelerated by the pressures of the Napoleonic Wars and others that were speeded up by Britain's growing role in the world economy. Britain's victory was its ability to adapt to these changes, especially in the years before 1850.

Certain political landmarks rise up to call out attention to the stresses and responses that structural change produced. The Factory Act, the Reform Bill, the income tax, and the Corn Laws all indicate the extent to which British economic and political institutions were strained and pulled by the winds of change. These laws also show us the remarkable degree of flexibility that normally rigid social institutions could exhibit under pressure.

Structural change led to fiscal crisis in Britain, as it did in Renaissance Florence. The burden of a large war-generated national debt was compounded in the 1830s and 1840s by continued deficits. These deficits slowly became the governing factor in fiscal policy. The need to control, reduce, or not increase the national debt often determined British actions and reactions in seemingly unrelated areas. As in Florence, the control of national debt became an end in itself, not a means to some greater goal.

Britain's eventual decline relative to competing nations, stemmed from its inability to adapt or respond to a second set of structural changes, those arising from the scientific revolution of the later years of the nineteenth century. Except in a few industries, notably shipbuilding, British firms failed to adopt and adapt the new technologies that appeared after the 1880s and ultimately played so large a role in the economic development of Germany and the United States.

British firms chose not to change when they reached their saddle point after 1850. They followed the direction set by earlier generations, paths as straight as a rail line, ruts as deep as a canal, and patterns as tightly woven as cotton cloth. Britain failed to make the crucial turn that could have led it to continued growth, perhaps at an accelerated pace. Other nations did turn, and they became the dominant economic systems of the twentieth century.

Government policies after 1850 perhaps best show how rigidity replaced flexibility. The fiscal institutions of government became increasingly set in stone. Gladstonian principles of finance kept a firm eye on the bottom line. No deficit could be tolerated and surpluses were always desired to reduce the accumulated debt. The compulsive need to achieve fiscal balance could accommodate only minor, incremental changes in fiscal policy.

As we have seen, there are many theories of the decline of Victorian Britain; these theories seek to explain why the institutional changes that were made elsewhere did not appear in Britain. This is a complicated problem, and it is no wonder that many factors played a part in the ossification of British industry. But the forces and rigid patterns laid down by the fiscal institutions of government no doubt played an important part in this story.

It is again ironic that the fiscal institutions that represented the most successful adaptations to structural change in the first half of the Victorian era, once they became rigid and inflexible, eventually played a significant role in the late-Victorian decline. The national debt and the tax system show clearly how institutions that are successful in one period can contribute to failure in changing times.

The efficient credit instruments created through Britain's public debt made possible the first industrial revolution. The national debt effectively channeled surplus resources to wartime needs without crowding out sources of industrial capital in the years before 1815. Britain could both grow at home and, at the same time, fight a long and costly war abroad. This really did make the national debt the "standing miracle" of the era.

The problem with financial flows is that they follow closely existing channels. The national debt, as the most important stream of highly organized financial activity, dug strong and deep channels that largely bypassed British industry. The city specialized in instruments that looked, smelled, and tasted like government bonds. Industrial finance was, for the most part, left to others; the financial channels that supplied British industry with working capital and investment funds were narrow and shallow, suffering from disrepair and disuse.

This unintentional effect of the deficit finance was exacerbated by the Baring indemnity. Once again, British finance was remarkably successful in meeting its short-run goals. In this case, the problem was to finance the post-Napoleonic indemnities without bringing international trade to a halt. The Baring indemnity provided a means for the British to lend funds to conquered countries, thus keeping the trade gates open, at least for a time. The crucial side effect of this action was that it established a strong, deep external channel that continued to divert British capital abroad for many decades. This made it even more difficult for British industry, cut off from the main channels of finance, to tap the most important sources of investment funds efficiently.

Britain used debt successfully as a flexible tool to adjust to the important structural problems of the early Victorian era. In doing so, however, the British established financial patterns that contributed to the later industrial decline.

It can also be argued that Peel's move to reinstitute the income tax in 1842 followed by the repeal of the Corn Laws represents the most significant fiscal reaction to the structural stresses imposed by the Industrial Revolution. Peel's Britain was faced with deficits that limited the scope of government, trade barriers that were detrimental to the industrial sector, and an excise tax system that fell heaviest the growing numbers of the working class. No small, incremental change could extract the budget from this box; only substantial structural change in the fiscal institutions of government would work, and that is what Peel accomplished.

With the income tax in place, Peel could repeal the Corn Laws and thereby open the door to the more prosperous years that followed, Victorian Britain's golden age. During these years the British were able to extract the maximum return from the structural changes that they bore earlier in the century. The tax reforms that Peel masterminded were like a magnifying glass that enlarged the gains of the first industrial revolution.

It is again ironic that these important reforms of the 1840s contained within them the dormant seeds of eventual economic decline. First, the repeal of the Corn Laws prized open the door to freer world trade. This had the short-term effect of increasing the market for British exports, but there were significant unintentional side effects. Most important was the effect of creating a much more "international" world economy, with a more international division of labor among the major trading nations. While other nations changed to find their place within the more open world economy, Britain clung fiercely to the niche that it had created earlier in the century. This meant that British exports moved further and further down the ladder in economic importance. Britain's export customers changed as production and consumption were reorganized. Soon Britain was in the second ranks, selling its cotton cloth to the poorer nations of the Third World.

The income tax also contributed directly to Britain's rigid industrial structure by overtaxing the capital investments in which the new technologies of the scientific revolution were embedded. Remember that Peel's income tax was a near-perfect copy of the tax that beat Napoleon and therefore embodied the economic theory and technological concepts of an earlier age.

The income tax that was in place during the critical decades of the 1880s and the 1890s was based on hundred-year-old economic theories and industrial technologies. The result was that the income tax correctly adjusted for the maintenance costs associated with the wear and tear to which a stable technology is subject. In a world of change, however, machines become obsolete due to technological progress long before they actually wear out. The old income tax could not account for this new problem. The result was that new investments of the kind that British industry needed were subject to yet one more obstacle—a higher tax rate than applied to investments in existing industries to make incremental repairs and upgrades to older equipment.

I do not want to make too much of the impact of this tax defect; I am sure it had an effect on economic development, but perhaps it was not a very large one. Certainly, there were many other forces also at work to prevent change. But the rigid tax system contributed to the problem, which is my point.

Together, the deep channels of debt finance and the barriers erected by the tax system must be considered to be significant factors in Britain's late-Victorian decline. They were certainly important barriers to the types of change that were critical at the saddle point.

It may be unfair to say so, but it seems that at the crucial moment, Britain rejected change. Britain did not lower her expectations but simply failed to raise them as others did. Remember that the Industrial Revolution was not a sudden spurt of rapid growth but instead a long, slow, gradual rise. Britain's problem was that it accepted this slow overall increase as a measure of success and therefore failed to transcend the norms of the past.

What could Britain have done at the saddle point to change its history? As with Renaissance Florence, this is a difficult question because so many factors conspired to keep Britain on the path that had caused it to grow but would soon lead to decline. Clearly, from the previous discussion, it appears that the British would have had a greater chance to break out of their rigid patterns if the fiscal institutions of government had been more flexible in the years after 1850. Ironically, this rigidity resulted from the British resolve not to repeat the errors of other nations (like Renaissance Florence) in dealing with fiscal crisis.

In Florence, as we have seen, the public debt grew and grew until it became fully integrated into the lifeblood of the economy. Real economic goals were sacrificed to preserve the appearance of a solvent public debt.

Britain erred on exactly the opposite side of this balance, illustrating the complex nature of what I call fiscal crisis. Under the principles of Gladstonian finance, the object was not just to keep the public debt from growing but to continually retire past debt, even if this required sacrifices in other areas. Government institutions in general, and the income tax in particular, were therefore frozen in time because of the fear that any small change would throw the budget completely out of balance and cause the fearsome monster of the national debt to rise up and strike out.

It is really interesting that the mountains of public debt in these two situations had so similar a result through such different mechanisms. In both cases debt became the overriding focus of government — to preserve the integrity of the rapidly compounding debt in Florence and to reduce the burden of the declining debt in Britain. But in each case, the need to cope with the national debt had the effect of freezing fiscal institutions, which meant that they could not change when the underlying economy changed — which means, ultimately, that fiscal institutions aided and even accelerated the ultimate decline of the economic system. The problem for the United States is to avoid the errors of the Florentines but not repeat the mistakes of the British.

Fairy Tales and Ghost Stories

One thing that can be learned from the study of Renaissance Florence and Victorian Britain is that structural change is a surprising slow process, which is why its causes can be confused and its effects so easily misunderstood. Ordinary people, living their lives one day at a time, wrapped up in their own lives, necessarily overlook the very gradual shifts and frictions that we have stressed here.

Perhaps the most interesting thing about the saddle point, therefore, is the way the landscape changes at this critical junction. Possible paths lead off in many directions: some rise higher; others, the easiest paths, descend. But the nature of change at the saddle point is subtle and slow. No sheer wall rises up to challenge the traveler. No sharp cliff provides a clear and sudden fall. There is a distinct lack of any sense of emergency to cause adrenaline to pump us up. In fact, the dominant sensation is likely to be one of relief that the hard climb has finally started to ease.

It would be convenient if the current fiscal crisis in the United States were to reach a head, generate an emergency, and require immediate action. Then the political and economic adrenal glands might kick into action and begin to make the policy changes that are necessary to achieve balance in the emerging world economy. Many people expect such a sharp blow and in its absence conclude that perhaps the concern about structural change and fiscal crisis is overstated, and they divert their attention to other seemingly more immediate concerns.

But fiscal crisis is likely to blow up with a wimper, not a bang. One recent study concludes that "if the United States is waiting for a crisis before taking action, the signal may never come. Rather the consequences . . . are likely to show up only slowly and imperceptibly as a steady erosion of the growth of U.S. living standards."[8]

If our policies remain unchanged, the United States is likely to travel a path of slow relative decline, like the ones followed by Florence and Britain. And it may be years, or even decades, before it is perfectly clear — even to politicians and self-interested businessmen — that the wrong path was chosen and the relative decline has become nearly inevitable.

What we need is a really good earthquake to shake us off the path we are following. But such a short, sharp shock is unlikely in the short run and the effects of such a future crisis are perhaps too dreadful, in human terms, rationally to desire. (Consider the riots, violence, death, and misery that some poor debtor nations have experienced when at last they have been forced to adopt the necessarily draconian policies needed to restore fiscal balance long after the saddle point has been crossed.)

We cannot count on a timely crisis to scare us into adopting appropriate new policies. In the meantime economists tell statistical horror stories of slower growth, declining living standards, and waning economic influence. But these numerical arguments are impotent; they penetrate the consciousness of the already-convinced but wither harmlessly before the practical people who believe only what they see with their own eyes.

What we need now, therefore, are fiscal fairy tales and ghost stories to teach us the lessons that we might otherwise be forced to live out. We need to be able to imagine and dream about alternative futures, so that we can pick roads to take and know the ones to avoid. Florence and Britain provide an outline on which to build a ghost story that might be meaningful today. A more difficult task is to construct a pleasant alternative—a fairy tale with a happy ending. What follows are two visions of alternative futures—on which an infinity of variations are possible—that may be reached from the ambiguous position of the saddle point.

Nightmare

Nightmares come in many forms, but some dark themes reoccur persistently. One of these is the nightmare where we are trapped by forces that seem beyond our control and are made to suffer as we are drawn inexorably toward some horrible punishment or doom. We are trapped on some giant spider's web, unable to escape. It is not always the pain at the end that is so frightful but the slow, pathetic, helpless anticipation of doom that makes the dreamer toss and turn, kick and groan. You want to break away, but you can't seem to move your arms or legs. You want to holler out for help, but you can't seem to speak. Down, down you travel toward unspeakable doom.

For the U.S. economy, the web is a complicated tangle of institutions, forces, and events. As we struggle with this net, we gain the sense that we are escaping it; but in fact we become more deeply ensnared.

Faced with the powerful forces of structural change that are abroad in the postwar world, economic institutions in the United States have made the mistake of standing firm, trying to preserve the appearance of prosperity, rather than accepting change for what it is and bending to accommodate change.

Debt has been the key tool in the struggle to maintain the appearance of economic hegemony. Individual families have used debt as a tool to increase their material level of welfare in the face of stagnant real incomes. Firms have found debt to be an artificial source of profits. Faced with relatively high tax rates and the need for costly, rapid, and repeated technological changes, many firms have chosen high debt (and low taxes) as the most reliable way to satisfy short-term bottom-line requirements.

The revolution in finance and the increasing internationalization of the world economy have provided firms and households in the United States with the liquidity they need to enmesh themselves more fully in the web of debt, which only seems to draw them tighter into its grasp. As real household incomes and corporate profits decline, debt as an escape becomes even more attractive while debt as the ultimate snare becomes even more effective.

Fiscal policy in the United States accelerated this trend. When the limits to private borrowing appeared, tax cuts allowed private consumption to surge forward, financed this time by increasing public debt. Public debt has overcome, temporarily at least, the limits to private debt as a means of preserving yesterday's expectations regarding living standards. Taken together, this combination of public and private responses to postwar structural change etched more deeply into the economy a pattern of debt and consumption, as opposed to saving and investment.

This story can end in at least three different ways. The first ending is the quickest — the crash and burn scenario. Stretched thin by debt, the U.S. economy is left tremendously susceptible to some unexpected shock, which tears the tight fabric of credit that now holds it together. Households, businesses, and perhaps even the government find that first some, then more of their debts cannot be repaid. The consumption boom ends and the United States is suddenly much poorer.

Crash and burn is an unlikely ending, however. As the great nonevent of the 1987 stock market crash demonstrated, the United States and the world economies are remarkably resilient and well protected from even major blows. If there is ever another Great Depression it will be a different and more subtle type of depression, not a sudden drop.

The second scenario is one that many people think most likely — high inflation. At some point, the economy encounters a major liquidity crunch, perhaps due to a force like that described above. The Federal Reserve System finds itself faced with the choice of either deep depression — perhaps on a worldwide scale — or a rapid increase in the money supply to keep the economy liquid. The inflation that would follow might reach banana republic levels, making the economy turn to barter and the complex real sectors essentially collapse (a variation on the first ending above). With prices so high, the economy is suddenly much poorer in real terms.

But Rudiger Dornbusch points out that even hyperinflation will not end debt problems in today's complex world.[9] Government debt today is held in the form of very short-term instruments. A quick dose of inflation will only serve to increase the future debt by driving up interest costs. This is a change from the past, when much government debt was held in very long term bonds and so could be handily inflated away before it needed to be refinanced.

In any case, hyperinflation is not really necessary to this scenario. It is unlikely that the Federal Reserve will be forced to engage in massive intervention that would trigger hyperinflation. Much more likely, all things considered, is the prospect that the Federal Reserve will find it necessary continually to bridge the gap between what the financial markets can support and the increasing liquidity needs of the economy. Inflation will thus be several points higher, on a yearly basis, than might otherwise be the case but still within the range that the postwar generations have come to expect and perversely come to regard as normal.

The effect of persistently higher (but not "abnormally" high) inflation will be to eat away purchasing power and living standards, a little at a time. Prolonged inflation, in this scenario, takes the place of deep depression as the mechanism by which people and firms in the economy adjust, reducing consumption down slowly toward the economy's ability to produce.

The best ending is also the worst and has been saved for last. This ending is closest to the nightmare of the spider's web. In this scenario, the patterns of debt and consumption become the driving force of the economy and lead slowly and steadily to its decline.

In the final ending, nothing happens to end the habit of debt-finance consumption. Households and businesses borrow to their limit to finance consumption, giving them the feeling of the high living standards to which they aspire. As limiting factors are reached, financial innovations are used to create artificial liquidity. When real incomes and other debt burdens cannot support new cars purchased with forty-eight-month loans, for example, sixty-month and seventy-two-month loans are created. Then leasing arrangements, which are already popular, come into play. More and more of each month's pay goes to meet the interest bills, but liquidity innovations constantly keep opening up to prolong the feeding frenzy.

U.S. citizens will have more and more, and at the same time they will have less and less that they really own and produce. Just as the funds to support this liquidity will come from abroad, so will many of the goods that are consumed.

It is not impossible to conceive this pattern continuing on and on for years, or even decades — until at last the baby boom generation grows old, and there is nothing there for them in retirement: no reserve of private resources, no reserve of public resources, no dynamic economy supported by earlier investments, no highly educated labor force. All has been sacrificed to debt and the appearance of high living standards.

This ending — the long, slow decline — was seen in different ways in both the Florentine and the Victorian experience. It remains the most likely ending today. At some future date a nervous International Monetary Fund official dictates the conditions for international assistance to the debt-heavy United States. Austerity arrives.

What are the implications of this conclusion to the "American century" and the "American crisis"? In simple economic terms, this is a nightmare of lowered expectations and relatively lower living standards. In social terms, the consequences are probably more significant. Social tensions in the United States have been calmest in periods of rapid economic growth, when greater measures of opportunity, generosity, and material rewards have been available.

In the prosperous 1960s, for example, the nation could confidently think of assisting the minority groups, the elderly, and the young. This sacrifice was made easier by the tide of prosperity that lifted all groups. But access to debt is always uneven and always favors the haves over the have-nots. Debt-driven consumption is therefore inherently unequal and unavoidably divisive.

In a stagnant economy, however, sacrifice comes harder and self-interest is more rigidly held. Tensions grow between the old and the young, the creditors and the debtors, rich and poor. The future, in this scenario, is therefore likely to contain more than simple but unexpected economic hardship. Life itself may become less pleasant, even for the individuals who have beat the odds and secured for themselves the resources for a comfortable life. Consumption, which insulates us from the cold reality of economic decline, will necessarily be sacrificed to purchase the walls and fences that try unsuccessfully to protect us from the colder reality of the social problems of the age of decay.

Fairy Tale

Is a fairy-tale ending possible, given the patterns of the past? Or is the fate of the United States sealed, our path locked into one of the nightmare scenarios just described? Is change possible without some miracle or a lucky coincidence? I think that there is reason to hope that we have not gone too far past the saddle point to effect the changes necessary to secure a less-dismal economic future. The task now is to imagine a scenario of success, to dream of a world where the United States turns at the saddle point and continues to climb to high ground.

There is a *New Yorker* cartoon that shows two scientists contemplating a blackboard covered with complex equations and calculations, in the middle of which are the words *Then a miracle happens*. One scientist says to the other, "I think you need to be more specific here." It is time to be specific regarding the types of changes needed to turn the U.S. economy from the path followed by Florence and Britain.

It is foolish to think that the tremendous forces of structural change in the world economy are temporary or that we can in some meaningful way insulate ourselves from their consequences. The future of the happy ending requires short-term change so that the people and institutions of the economy may begin to move in the same direction as the waves of structural change, so that change can carry us along.

That said, it is important to be clear about the forces that are driving the world economy and to inventory our strengths and weaknesses realistically. In this way we can best navigate the untraveled path ahead.

The fundamental dynamic of this age is the global reorganization of economic activity—production, distribution, and consumption. This reorganization has been made possible by the demographic, technological, financial, and communications revolutions of the postwar period. These revolutions have also made the global economy necessary.

These revolutionary structural transformations have created tremendous stresses, which individual economies cannot easily bear. These stresses have burst the effective national borders that separated economic systems in the nineteenth century. This has relieved the stress in the short term, because international payments and transactions could compensate for domestic imbalances, making adjustment to each successive wave of change less traumatic. The emerging global economy has therefore been a safety valve for the stresses caused by structural change. This was perhaps most apparent in the 1970s, then the international system experienced a series of severe shocks, which were made less severe overall because of the increased flexibility of the global financial system.

In the long run, however, the global economy has generated even greater stresses, which are compounded, not absorbed, by international economic relations. The speed at which the international division of labor is taking place has accelerated as the nature of technology has changed, making older products and processes obsolete; the nature of finance has changed, making possible more rapid and dramatic capital movements; and the nature of communications has changed, enlarging the scale and scope of the firm and market.

The United States must find its place within this changing world economy. In an international system based on specialization and exchange, where does the United States fit in? In the nightmare scenario of the last section, we looked at the consequences if the United States continues to specialize in consumption while others change and produce. The myth of affluence can be sustained in this scheme for quite a long period because of our accumulated wealth and the increasing ability to leverage assets. But the future does eventually come.

The other, better, choice is to choose to enter fully the world economy with the new roles of specialization and exchange that this requires.[10] As the world economy grows, it will shift more and more from the primary sector (natural resources and agriculture) to the secondary sector (manufacturing), and from the secondary to the tertiary sector (services broadly defined) in terms of both consumption and production. This long-standing trend is unlikely to be reversed. While the U.S. economy, by its nature, will always include elements of all three sectors, it is in fact a policy question as to which of these sectors will play the leading role in our economic future.

The future of the United States within the world economy seems not to lie in simple mass production manufacturing. One lesson of the 1970s and 1980s is that other nations are now better positioned for this field. The growth of the primary sector in the United States will always be constrained by the limits imposed by nature and by market demand. We are left therefore with services, the tertiary sector.

The rise of the "service economy" is precisely what many people fear. They see "deindustrialization" and assume that high wages and high incomes will disappear with industrial jobs. This is clearly wrong however, at least according to the theory of structural change outlined in the first chapter of this essay. As an economy (and therefore the world economy) grows, it necessarily shifts more and more toward consumption (and therefore production) of services. The choice to resist the growth of the tertiary sector is, it seems, the choice to resist growth, period. This is especially true in the world economy, where missed opportunities for growth by one nation are quickly snapped up by others.

It is ironic that the movement toward a service economy is resisted at all, given the population boom of the postwar period. It would be difficult to absorb the huge work force of the baby boom generation into capital-intensive industry without pushing wage rates to very low levels. The growth of the necessarily labor-intensive service sector of the economy comes at precisely the right time to match the growth in population.

But all services are not the same. Labor that embodies low levels of education or training (or is used in conjunction with poor physical capital) is incapable of supporting a high and rising standard of living. The appropriate strategy for the United States, then, is to specialize within the world economy in the production of high-quality services and of goods that intensively use these services, directly or indirectly.

In this scenario, the United States would specialize to a greater degree in the production of high-productivity services, which often embody substantial amounts of education and training, and in the production of goods that depend critically on the contribution of high-quality services. This may seem like an unrealistic proposal, but in fact the most successful sectors of the U.S. economy have long relied on precisely this strategy for success in the international economy. The least successful sectors — those built on mindless mass production — assume implicitly the existence of a work force, income pattern, and world economy that ceased to exist in the 1970s and is unlikely to reappear.

In agriculture, for example, the high U.S. productivity is critically dependent on the skill of highly trained U.S. farmers, the agricultural agents who advise them, and on the scientific and technological services that are embedded in the seeds, machines, and chemicals that they use. Where the contribution of these high-quality services has become unimportant, the U.S. advantage in agriculture has disappeared.

This story is repeated in manufacturing. The most dynamic U.S. manufacturing sectors, such as the aerospace industry, are precisely those that directly and indirectly employ high-quality science, design, and engineering services and then marry these services to a skilled manufacturing system.[11]

In a competitive world, high-quality services must be produced but they must also be continually updated. With the rapid pace of technological change in the world economy, all capital now becomes more quickly outdated, and this applies to human capital as well as any other. It is not enough, therefore, to create this service economy but we must constantly recreate it if it is to prosper.

Government policies have accelerated the movement toward the high-consumption economy of today. How can government policies change to put the U.S. economy firmly on the path toward a growing high-quality service sector? Fortunately, there are policies available to government that could further this end.

First, the key to high-quality services is high-quality education and training. In the United States, most general education and training is provided by government, with state and local governments bearing a large share of the responsibility for providing these services. The quality, standards, and funding of education must be raised throughout the U.S. educational system. This will require a substantial increase in resources devoted to education directly and in training the educators. In addition, the scope must be broadened to provide education and training more completely through the life cycle.

Second, government actions must be taken to increase the advance of science and the growth of technology. This is appropriately a responsibility of the federal government. The federal government should focus on research, where private risks tend to exceed social risks. A greater government role in nondefense research would allow private firms to specialize more completely on the more profitable development function. Clearly, however, the task of increasing research and development will also have a substantial resource cost.

Finally, the government should attempt to alter, where possible, the undesirable private sector incentives that currently divert resources away from education, research, development, and productive investment and toward debt-financed consumption.

Policies that promote or achieve these goals would not necessarily guarantee the United States a better future in the world economy, but they would clearly point the economy in the right direction, the path towards higher living standards and greater competitiveness.

10

Changing Directions

It is one thing to identify the problem of the saddle point and point out the need for policies to move the economy in a new direction. It is another thing actually to conceive of policies that might realistically alter the economy's course. Finally, it is a very hard thing to overcome the forces of institutional momentum and actually implement these policies.

The policy problem at the saddle point is that any institutional changes that are adopted will need to do so much at once. First, they should move the government and the economy back toward fiscal balance. The lack of fiscal balance is, as we have seen, more of a symptom of economic stress than a cause of it; but it is also true that the vast, almost unparalleled imbalances of the U.S. economy in recent years have acted to accelerate structural change and so have magnified the stresses and strains to which the economy would anyway be subject. A greater measure of balance between income and outlays needs to be achieved for government, consumers, business, and for the U.S. economy relative to the world economy. The mountains of debt must stop their rapid growth.

Second, the saddle point policy must take positive public action to integrate the United States successfully into the global economy. We must find our place within the emerging international pattern of specialization and exchange. Given the resources of the United States, its history, and the expectations of its people, it seems logical to conclude that the U.S. should increasingly specialize in the production and export of high-quality services and the products and processes that most directly embody high-quality services. The cost of the education and training that is necessary to secure the nation's place at the top of world's service-manufactures-resources pyramid will be very high. A way must be found to generate the public funds necessary for a major thrust toward improved education, training, and research without creating an even greater fiscal imbalance.

Finally, it is clear that public sector actions alone will never achieve the change that is now needed. The most important task is to change the pattern of the private sector. Some call for public "industrial development policy" to guide or coerce businesses to make better choices, but this is not a realistic solution. It is better to examine the extent to which current government policies send incorrect messages to businesses and provide inefficient incentives. The third goal of policy, then, is to remove the visible hand of government from business decisions (where transparent market forces are more effective) and to create an "incentive revolution" in other areas (where government policies can provide a positive stimulus to structural change in the private sector).

Perhaps no set of economic policies can achieve these goals. Perhaps there are many different ways to get from here to there; certainly there is no lack of advice for U.S. firms and politicians to follow.[1] I offer one plan with some hope of shifting the economy's momentum without thoroughly distorting private sector incentives or resorting to a heavy-handed and ultimately unsuccessful layer of coercive government controls.

The Saddle Point Plan

The Saddle Point Plan has three main parts: income tax reform, deficit reduction, and a major new program of federal grants to state and local governments for education and training programs.

Income Tax Reform

The federal income tax was thoroughly reformed in 1986, but it is now clear that the many changes that were adopted at that time have had unintended and undesirable side effects. Shifting the tax burden from individuals to businesses has encouraged the consumption binge by U.S. households and, at the same time, penalized the U.S. private sector and pushed it more deeply into the broadest and deepest remaining tax expenditure, corporate debt. The 1986 tax reforms have therefore contributed to the growth of the consumption-debt society at the expense of needed saving and investment.

There is nothing simple about income taxes, so it is really foolish to suggest that simple changes should be made in the tax system. But relatively simple corrections could help undo some of the damage that the income tax now does. First, the burden of the tax must be redivided between individuals and corporations. The best way to do this is to raise tax rates for individuals, without changing the tax rates facing corporations. This would generate additional revenue to reduce the federal deficit while at the same time applying a brake to the current consumption binge. Even relatively small increases in tax rates, of one, two, or three percentage points in each tax bracket, would generate a substantial increase in tax revenues without, it seems to me, having any alarming effect on work incentives.

Currently, the income tax provides very strong incentives for the accumulation of debt by individuals and corporations; this must be changed because the rapid growth of public and private debt is simultaneously accelerating the world's structural change while acting as a barrier to successful U.S. participation in that world economy.

The tax system must put saving and consumption on a more equal footing. To this end some favor (for both economic and political reasons) implementing additional tax incentives for saving. But this is costly and the track record of this type of tax expenditure is not excellent. It is politically more difficult but economically critical that we instead remove the existing tax expenditures for debt, which will be defended vigorously by the special interests that have grown up around them.

Removing debt incentives on the corporate side of the income is relatively easy (and would simplify the incomprehensible and nearly unenforceable corporate tax at the same time). Many economists have suggested that the current corporate income tax be replaced by a corporate "cash flow" tax.[2] There are many variations on a cash flow corporate income tax, but the differences are less important here than the similarities. A cash flow income tax would treat all corporate outlays equally. Payments of dividends to corporate shareholders would bear the same tax treatment as interest payments to bondholders. Research and development costs, the expense of purchasing new capital equipment, and all other business costs would be "expensed"—deducted fully from corporate taxable income in the year in which they are made. No one type of investment would be favored over others and, more important, there would be no tax advantage associated with debt finance and the use of financial leverage generally.

The cash flow income tax would remove many of the inefficient incentives that currently exist, which have promoted unprofitable investment and exacerbated the economy's problem of fiscal imbalance.

It will be necessary, however, to add one additional "loophole" to the tax system. A perfectly "neutral" tax, which treats all types of corporate investment equally, tends to generate an inefficiently low level of basic research and employee education and training. This is because the firm is often unable to capture all the benefits of basic research (which tends to generate knowledge and ideas that go beyond the bounds of patent protection) or all the benefits of training employees (who are free to move on to other jobs, taking their costly human capital with them). An otherwise neutral tax system encourages firms to undertake proprietary product development and physical capital investment (where they stand a better chance of capturing all available profits) over basic research and human capital investment (where others, including competing firms, stand to gain as well).

To solve this incentive problem, I propose partial tax credits for basic research and employee education and training expenses, over and above the "expensing" granted these business outlays. Society gains "externalities" from these types of expenditures along with the firms that undertake them, and the tax system is a relatively effective mechanism to subsidize these otherwise underprovided investments. Research will be needed to determine the optimal rate of tax credit to efficiently subsidize these activities.

It is more difficult, from the practical standpoint, to reverse the debt incentives built into the individual income tax. The Tax Reform Act of 1986 was a major assault on the tax system's implicit subsidy of consumer debt. The congressional tax writers were able to close the deduction loophole for consumer interest expenditures, a category that includes interest on car loans, credit cards, installment purchases, and so on. But the parallel attempt to eliminate or significantly reduce the deduction for home mortgage interest failed. Worse, perhaps, the new law allows a good deal of debt reswitching. In many cases, consumers can keep the deduction for auto interest, for example, by financing the purchase through second mortgages on their homes.[3] Perversely, this bit of the tax code makes the major debt of a home mortgage even more valuable because of its potential ability to shelter from taxes additional tax-deductible consumer debt.

This result was perhaps inevitable, and the basic tax treatment of the owner-occupied home might be impossible to change in any significant way. Such is the power of the coalition of interests—representing realtors, home builders, mortgage banks, and others—associated with the home mortgage deduction. But this might still be a battle worth fighting, even if it is ultimately lost. The home mortgage deduction of the U.S. income tax encourages, both directly and indirectly, the social emphasis on consumption and debt that lies at the heart of the economy's inability to adjust to the global pattern of structural change.[4]

This tax reform proposal would not create any enormous redistribution of tax burdens among income groups or among generations or occupations groups. By increasing federal revenues, it would make possible significant deficit reduction. With spending discipline, a truly balanced budget (a balance of outlays and revenues without resort to accounting tricks regarding the social security surplus) is possible. At the same time, it would create a modest "incentive revolution" in favor of research and education and away from debt and consumption.

Deficit Reduction and Fiscal Balance

The second thrust of the saddle point plan is deficit reduction. To a large extent, reducing the deficit requires the tax reforms—especially the personal income tax rate increases—just discussed. But there is more to do to bring down the deficit.

First some of the real damage of the Gramm-Rudman-Hollings years must be undone. This will involve more than repeal of the Gramm-Rudman-Hollings Act itself.

The spectre of draconian automatic spending cuts proved a powerful incentive for Congress and the president to bury important government programs "off budget" where they are hard to find and hard to fix but safe from cuts. A variety of accounting tricks and traps have also been introduced to hide the true size and composition of federal expenditures.

The federal budget must be cleanly reconstructed to make the true picture of the fiscal balance problem visible. When the smoke is cleared away and social security surplus and off-budget adjustments made, it will be plain that the federal deficit is even larger than now appears and in no danger of finding its own balance in this century. Then and only then can tax increases — and probably additional spending cuts — be effectively implemented, as they must be.

Reducing and eliminating the federal deficit will accomplish several important goals at once. First, obviously, it will provide governmental fiscal balance. More important, however, it will also make a giant contribution toward international fiscal imbalance. The largest source of the nation's current account deficit in the 1980s has been the large credit needs of the federal government. Reducing the federal deficit will automatically and necessarily also reduce our payments imbalance with other nations.

The process by which reductions in the budget deficit generate a lower current account deficit will be advantageous to the economy. As government borrowing declines, the investors in Japan and Europe will demand fewer dollars to use to buy Treasury obligations. The dollar should decline as a result. The falling dollar will increase the price of BMW cars, stereo VCR systems, and the many other imported consumer goods that U.S. citizens have learned to love. This might further encourage saving by raising the cost of conspicuous consumption. At the same time, however, the dollar's lower cost abroad should encourage exports of U.S. goods. This is important; the rise in the foreign demand for U.S. goods and services will be needed to offset the fall in domestic demand resulting from income tax increases.

The dollar's fall will not only help us achieve balance between imports and exports, it will also act to create more jobs, specifically in the U.S. export sector. This is exactly the part of the economy that will grow the most in the future, as the nation becomes more fully integrated into global patterns of specialization and exchange. Short-term employment shifts toward the sectors that rely on high-quality services will send the right message throughout the economy.

As you can see, deficit reduction is not an end in itself. Rather, balancing the federal budget is part of the solution to the broader problem of structural change and fiscal balance. True reduction of the federal deficit does not guarantee that balance will be achieved completely elsewhere. But it is difficult to imagine that overall balance is possible with federal outlays and revenues so very far from balance as they are now.

Upgrading the Nation's Education System

The best thing that can be said about the U.S. system of public education is that it is not as bad as it might be. This is a sad comment, but it is still something of a positive achievement. Given the problems that U.S. education faces, resources it has available, and the process by which those resources are used, it is indeed possible for education to be much worse than it is.

Just about every objective measure available shows U.S. education in decline, both in absolute terms and relative to other countries with whom we compete. There are exceptions, of course; a fraction of our students receive an excellent education by any standard. But the average or typical level is too low; and there is no clear hope, under the present system, for the dramatic improvement that the U.S. will need if it is to avoid relative decline in the global economy.

The U.S. education system has failed, and it is really no wonder. Education is a national concern, but it is also a decidedly family concern. Families have an obvious interest and an important stake in what their children learn and how well they learn it. The U.S. system of public education is weighted to reflect the local stake in schooling decisions heavily. It is ironic, therefore, that the result has been to give children less education of lower quality than their parents probably desire and than the nation surely needs.

This irony results from the fact that education decision making and education finance have, by design or by tradition, been closely linked in the United States. In no part of U.S. government are the decision to spend and the decision to tax more directly tied than in public school finance. There are too few resources allocated to education precisely because of how it is financed.

While individual parents want the best education for their own children, these same people, as voters, do not want to impose high taxes on themselves to pay to have other people's children schooled. In large measure this is due to the fact that public education in most parts of the United States is financed through local property taxation systems, which are the least responsive to short-run changes in individual and community economic circumstances. People vote against what they see as bad taxes, but at the same time they also necessarily vote for bad schools. This might be formulated as Gresham's Law of Local School Finance: *Bad taxes drive out good schools.* The result has been a low and uneven pattern of school finance, with the consequent low and uneven pattern of educational quality.

It is time to recognize that public education is a national concern, which should be financed at least in part at the national level. This does not mean, however, that local control and influence (and the existing system of local school districts and state administrative agencies) must be replaced by a federal educational leviathan. Federal finance and local control can be effectively combined through a system of intergovernmental grants designed to provide high-quality education to all U.S. children.

There are three problems to address in the design of the federal education program. First, there is the matter of deciding how to distribute the federal funds among the thousands of school districts in a way that accounts for annual school enrollment totals and composition, capital needs, local cost differentials, and other factors. There is no perfect formula to use in slicing this pie; but there are plenty of imperfect ones that would provide a higher level of funding, more stable funding, and more equal funding than now exists.

The second problem is that throwing money at the education problem alone is no solution. More resources must be provided to educators; then they must be used wisely and effectively. Teacher salaries should rise, if only to begin to attract more of our brightest people to the teaching profession. But higher teacher salaries are not enough. On-going teacher training programs, curricular improvements, and new equipment are all necessary. Emphasis on mathematics and science is important; but reading, writing, and language skills also need work. The problem is made even harder by the fact of the poor educational background of today's young adults. The problem of continuing and remedial education for adults cannot be ignored if this generation is to avoid a permanent place in the bottom of the income distribution.

There is so much to do and it is all so expensive. A mountain of money is needed. Some of it will be wasted or inefficiently spent, this is clear. But the payoff on the successes is likely to be so great as to make the certainty of some waste tolerable. (And the high cost of failure to improve education is so high as to make it difficult not to attempt such a massive plan.)

The final problem is finance. Where can the federal government get the billions of dollars it will need to provide supplemental finance for state and local education programs without adding to the mountain of debt and without reversing the progress made in the first two components of this plan?

One answer to the education finance problem is a national value-added tax (VAT), which would be conceptually similar to the type of tax system already in wide use in Europe. The value-added tax is like a national sales tax except that it is collected directly from businesses (not added on at the cash register like a state sales tax) and it is possible to impose different tax rates on different classes of goods and services.

I propose a VAT for education because it can raise revenue and at the same time help achieve the other goals of the Saddle Point Plan. Even at a relatively low rate of tax, the VAT would be able to collect remarkably large sums. In fact, many conservatives have long opposed a national VAT precisely because of its ability to command resources for government use. The time has come, however, to use this powerful tool to educate our children and so secure their future and our own.[5]

A national VAT would have two distinct advantages in addition to its ability to mobilize an army of social resources in service to education and therefore the economy. First, movement toward a VAT would make the U.S. tax system more closely aligned to the fiscal systems of Europe and Japan, which are currently the largest potential markets for the high-quality service products we hope to produce. Equivalent tax systems tend to ease business relations, making U.S. firms more competitive in foreign markets.

The second advantage is that the VAT taxes consumption, but implicitly defers taxes on saving. Thus, the VAT would be one more positive incentive to move U.S. consumers away from the unsuccessful consumption-debt pattern of the past and toward the saving-investment pattern that is needed for future growth.

Taken together, the three components of the Saddle Point Plan—tax reform, deficit reduction, and educational reform—have the potential to correct many of the problems that currently plague our economic system and create positive incentives toward creation of the economy of the future. This is not a perfect plan, nor is it likely to find complete political acceptance — which is why it is painted in broad strokes only, with precise rates and detailed programs left for later. But it is a step in the right direction.

Leverage

There is reason to believe that fiscal reform is still possible. There remains an opportunity — a chance — to help change the economy's course through prompt federal action. There is hope that Congress and the president might adopt the Saddle Point Plan just presented or some other plan, different in minor detail or in overall outline, that points toward the same goals of saving, investment, and education.

The above paragraph will be read as pure fiction or hopeless optimism by many people who have followed the course of fiscal politics in the United States. One need not be a cynic to doubt the ability or the will of Congress and the president to act boldly to solve the nation's problems, especially given this essay's contention that no short-term crisis to galvanize support for reform is likely.

Pure momentum is the most important characteristic of institutions. The momentum of current fiscal policy is constantly reinforced by the activities of special interests and the cost-benefit calculus of elected politicians and the inherent rigidity of government bureaucracy. This momentum has carried us to the saddle point and will carry us past it, past the summit and down the steep decline, if no pressure is brought to bear quickly to alter the economy's direction.

The key to fiscal reform at the saddle point is leverage. The forces that can be mobilized to enact fiscal reform are small compared to the vast institutional momentum of the status quo. But even a weak force can be powerfully felt if equipped with the right lever to magnify its thrust.

Social security is the lever that makes fiscal reform possible in the United States. The social security system, the largest government program in the world, is also the fiscal program most important to the U.S. public and their elected officials. It is the only government program for which U.S. citizens have consistently been willing to make personal sacrifices. It is the only government program for which Congress and the president have consistently been willing to make hard choices and take political heat. Willingness to preserve the stability and solvency of the social security system is the ultimate political shibboleth in the United States.

The social security system provides the political leverage to achieve structural fiscal reform because, under present policies, the social security system is essentially bankrupt. If the present patterns of public and private consumption and debt continue, it seems decidedly unlikely that our economy will be able to meet the obligations it has made to the baby boom generation that retires in the years after 2020. Social security surpluses over the next thirty years, given current trends, will be absorbed by government and private consumption. The technology, physical capital, and human capital that are the necessary prerequisites of a growing nation in the global economy will not exist. In short, if current trends continue as they are likely to without fiscal reform, the economic foundations of the social insurance system will crumble, leaving the baby-boomers and their children much worse off.

Structural fiscal reform along the lines of this essay's Saddle Point Plan offers a way to preserve and protect the social security system while, at the same time, helping to change the economy's course. It is no accident that one set of policies has the potential to solve two problems. The 1983 social security reform was essentially a bet on the future of the economy — on the ability of the U.S. economic system to outgrow its retirement obligations, given the helping hand of the saving and investment that the social security surpluses was designed to stimulate.

This bet on the future can be won only if the economy can restore fiscal balance and make the critical turn at the saddle point. The reforms outlined here would help achieve the goals of fiscal balance and structural change and would thereby also restore balance and solvency to the social security program.

The Saddle Point Plan promotes the long-run solvency of the social security program in three main ways. First, income tax reform removes the tax incentives that have, increasingly in recent years, resulted in inefficient patterns of consumption, debt, and investment. Individuals and businesses would be far more likely to make short-term choices that would be in the long-term interests of the economy, particularly with respect to research and development, investment in equipment and technology, and worker training. All these forces would tend to improve the quality of the goods and services produced in the United States, increase the rate of economic growth in the long run, and shift the economy toward the specialization in high-quality services that seems to hold the key to the future in the global economic system of tomorrow.

Deficit reduction is the second component of the Saddle Point Plan; it would contribute to restoration of the social security system in several ways. The most important contribution would be to free up the surpluses in the social insurance trust funds for their intended purpose: private sector investment. Currently, as we have already noted, all of the trust fund surpluses are absorbed by the federal government in its deficit. It is true that this does indirectly increase private saving and investment, but only because without the social security surpluses government borrowing would cut even more deeply into the resources available for the private sector. This is not what the 1983 reforms had in mind when the surpluses were first conceived, and the current combination of fiscal imbalances will not assure the long-run health of either the economy or the social insurance programs that depend on the health of the economy.

In addition, as discussed in the last section, deficit reduction would also have international effects, transmitted through the exchange rate, that would tend to encourage economic growth and structural change in the short run. These short-term changes would help create a new momentum that could carry the economy in the right direction in the long run.

The third piece of the Saddle Point Plan involves implementation of the value-added tax to finance a large-scale program of intergovernmental grants to stimulate education and training. These policies also promote the long-run stability of the social security system in several ways. The VAT would further encourage saving and investment over debt and consumption while also removing some institutional barriers to the more thorough integration of the United States into the world economy. The improved programs of education and training that VAT revenues would make possible are clearly needed if the United States is to develop its comparative advantage in high-quality services.

Without these saddle point programs, or alternative policies like them, the United States will be left to find its niche at a lower level in the integrated structure of the world economy. Lower living standards in the short run and social security crisis in the long run are the unavoidable consequences of inaction.

Social security provides the lever to use in implementing fiscal reforms, but someone must pick up this lever and put it to use. It is not an accident that there are no lines now forming to grasp this tool. Each piece of the Saddle Point Plan, on its own, is potential political dynamite. And any one piece, enacted separately, cannot guarantee success in the short run or the long run. No individual legislator or single political party is likely to take the risks built into the Saddle Point Plan.

Fortunately, the ill-fated social security reforms of 1983 provide us with a model for gaining the leverage that we need. Congress can muster the political will to make hard choices, history tells us, if (1) the tough and unpopular choices are seen as necessary to save the social security system, and (2) responsibility for the needed policies is taken by a bipartisan "blue-ribbon" panel, like the distinguished group that generated the 1983 reform plan.

Finally, the reforms must be presented as a unified plan, delicately balanced. It must be known that any single substantive amendment will cause hundreds of others to follow; and reform will die, with fingers pointed, and blame assigned, to the individuals responsible. In such a condition, voting for the entire package is the only politically safe strategy. Credit for saving social security can be claimed, while blame for unpopular details can be shifted to the vast majority of other legislators who voted the same way. Once even a single substantive amendment is introduced, however, politicians are forced to go on the record for potentially damaging details and must choose the consequences of votes on single issues versus the credit they may gain from passage of the entire package.

Fortunately, Congress and the president have learned well how to play this complex game of electoral "chicken," so there is reason to believe that they might, in this gamelike situation, be prepared to summon the will and maintain the momentum necessary to pass a complex package of reforms. The economic consequences of failure are great, and the potential gains from success are too important for them to fail.

This book therefore ends on a hopeful note. Renaissance Florence and Victorian Britain suffered the stresses and strains of structural change and fiscal crisis. Both economic systems proved unable to change at the critical point when they were required to adapt to a new global environment. The United States economy faces the same saddle point landscape. Our problems are made more severe, however, by the fact that the changes have been larger, in some respects, than those of the past and have taken place over a shorter time period; and the challenge of global integration is greater.

A pessimist looks at this scene and sees the United States falling inexorably into the declining patterns of the past. But there is reason for optimism. Policies like those outlined in the Saddle Point Plan stand a reasonable chance of turning the economy from its current self-destructive path. The leverage to bring this change about exists in the form of the social security system. And a structure of political choice has evolved in the United States that could enact such large-scale fiscal reforms in the near future.

The optimist therefore hopes to see a rebirth of the Florentine "fifth element" in the United States. In choosing a future that exploits our comparative advantage in products and processes that make use intensively of the high-quality services we are capable of producing, the United States would be choosing to rekindle the special spark that lit Florence so many years ago.

Notes

1 STRUCTURAL CHANGE AND FISCAL CRISIS

1. Ricardo, *Principles*, chap. 7.
2. A good discussion of Engel's Law and structural change is found in Kindleberger, *Economic Development*, pp. 168–70.
3. Fisher's theory is explained in more detail in Kindleberger, *Economic Development*, pp. 171–81.
4. See Clark, *Conditions* for the statistical analysis mentioned here.
5. Or, in economic jargon, it is a problem of Harberger triangles, not Okun gaps.
6. This study is cited in Kindleberger, *Economic Development*, p. 175.
7. See Olson, *Rise and Decline*.

2 RENAISSANCE FLORENCE: DEATH, BIRTH, AND THE FIFTH ELEMENT

1. This remark is widely quoted. My source is Schevill, *History*, p. 291.
2. This quote is from Marshall, *Principles*, p. 116. The comment was not intended to describe Florence, but the shoe does fit her.
3. Jacob Burckhardt (*Civilization*) popularized the notion that Florence's most important characteristic was "individualism." This may or may not be true in general; but the force of individual self-interest was important, I think, in the political and economic spheres of Florentine life.
4. Two centuries later the Florentines had their own popes, but by then the flame of the fifth element was burning far less brightly.
5. Ehrenberg, *Capital and Finance*, p. 193.
6. Bagehot, *Economic Studies*, p. 69.
7. Olson, *Rise and Decline*, pp. 147–50. Olson generally looks at the guild system as an example of how structural rigidities can slow economic growth. This was not true of the Florentine guilds in the fourteenth century, but Olson's analysis fits the fifteenth-century experience much better. The Medici oligarchy government introduced rigidities into the economy that might well have slowed the growth of the commune. For example, Lopez describes the guilds of the late fifteenth century as "rigid hierarchies," ("Hard Times," p. 37).
8. de Roover, "Labour Conditions" provides an excellent description and analysis of the role of the cloth guilds within the main Florentine industries.
9. Burke, "Republics," p. 220.
10. Ibid., p. 221.
11. The decline of the Italian city-states is discussed by Cipolla, e.g., *Before the Industrial Revolution*, pp. 253–63.
12. The best general reference (in English, at any rate) to the economy of Renaissance Florence is probably Brucker, *Renaissance Florence*, pp. 51–88.

13. See de Roover, "Commercial Revolution" for a detailed discussion.

14. Listed in de Roover, "Commercial Revolution," pp. 24–25.

15. Cloth was also an appropriate industry for the years after the Black Death because, according to Lopez ("Hard Times") it was not a particularly labor-intensive product and thus suited the labor-scarce economic environment of the fourteenth and fifteenth centuries well.

16. The Calimala Guild's operations are discussed by Luzzatto, *Economic History*, p. 97.

17. Brucker, *Renaissance Florence*, pp. 60–61.

18. There is an exception to every rule, and the capital requirements and use in silk throwing in Genoa is one.

19. The silk industry is discussed in Brown, *In the Shadow*, esp. chap. 3.

20. This point is made in de Roover, "Labour Conditions," pp. 298–99.

21. See Swetz, *Capitalism and Arithmetic* for both an excellent discussion of the use of arithmetic in northern Italy and also a translation of an early manual.

22. Although landlocked, Florence eventually built and operated its own publicly owned fleet in the fifteenth century and required that Florentine commerce use these vessels exclusively. This, of course, helped to increase their interest in maritime insurance. The Florentine insurance industry is examined in Laven, *Renaissance Italy*, pp. 94–96 and also in Lopez, "Hard Times."

23. Bergier's studies indicate that many important ideas about risk, return, and accounting were not absorbed by merchants and financiers in other countries even after the decline of the Italian economies in the sixteenth century. There is no obvious reason for this knowledge to be lost except perhaps that Germans and others, already set in their own ways of transacting business, just did not want to try new processes. See Bergier, "From the Fifteenth Century."

24. Discussed in Brown, *In the Shadow*, pp. 163–65.

25. Lane, "Investment and Usury," pp. 51–52.

26. This is discussed in Goldthwaite, *Building*, pp. 78–79 and also in Laven, *Renaissance Italy*, pp. 91–92.

27. Goldthwaite, *Building*, p. 79.

28. Goldsmith, *Premodern Financial Systems*, p. 158.

29. The critical role of gold coins is stressed by Lopez, "Dawn," pp. 18–21.

30. Cited by Cipolla, *Monetary Policy*, p. 5.

31. Cipolla (ibid., pp. 1–29) presents an excellent analysis of this period. I have summarized and simplified Cipolla's analysis here.

32. Cipolla, *Monetary Policy* is again the best reference to the monetary phenomena discussed here.

33. Ibid., p. 48.

34. This is cited by Cipolla (ibid., pp. 54–55).

35. The best discussion of the Monte Commune is Becker, *Florence*, pp. 151–200. Much of the information given here concerning the Monte derives from this reference.

36. de la Roncière, "Indirect Taxes" is the principal source for information concerning the gabelles.

37. Quoted in Brucker, *Society*, p. 180.

38. Cipolla (*Monetary Policy*) supplies this information. Cipolla makes a strong case for the proposition that these monetary changes are the root of the discontent that caused the Ciompi Revolt. He sees the proposed reforms as an attempt to reestablish the desirable (for the *arti minori*) economic conditions of the "fat cattle" years.

39. My discussion here of the Ciompi uprising is intentionally superficial in all but the economic aspects. The political and social sides of these events are done justice in Brucker, "Ciompi Revolution," which I find to be the best overall treatment of the Ciompi. My discussion leans heavily on this work, as well as Cipolla, *Monetary Policy*.

40. Martines, *Power and Imagination*, pp. 135–36. Martines puts the revolt in Florence in the perspective of similar tensions in other Tuscan city-states.

41. See Braudel, *Wheels*, pp. 232–48 for a useful discussion of the history and development of the term and concept of *capitalism*.

42. Brucker, "Ciompi Revolution," p. 354.

43. Ibid., p. 355. Brucker holds that the leaders of the Ciompi Revolt were quite conservative and in their actions very respectful of tradition and ancient institutions — an attitude that would not be consistent with the leaders of a class struggle.

44. Quoted in Brucker, *Renaissance Florence*, p. 81.

45. Holmes, "How the Medici," p. 358. Holmes provides a thorough account of the relationship between the Medici and the Roman church.

46. Becker, "Florentine Territorial State," p. 125. Becker's study of the Monte has convinced him that it was the key element in the birth of civic humanism in Florence.

47. See Kirshner and Mohlo, "Dowry Fund," for an excellent analysis of its records.

48. Ibid., p. 408.

49. This is noted in Mohlo, *Florentine Public Finance*, pp. 128–29. The growth of the silk industry also attracted other trades to Florence. The *battiloro* (gold beaters) craft, for example, grew due to the demand for the fine gold threads that were a distinctive feature of Florentine silk brocades.

3 MOUNTAINS OF DEBT AND THE HEART OF FLORENCE

1. This is, of course, Paul Kennedy's thesis in *The Rise and Fall of the Great Powers*.

2. Machiavelli, *Prince*, p. 74.

3. Mohlo, *Florentine Public Finance* is the most complete source on this topic.

4. Smith, *Wealth of Nations*, vol 2, p. 402.

5. Quoted in Herlihy and Klapusch-Zuber, *Tuscans*, p. 5.

6. Machiavelli, *History*, p. 172.

7. Ibid., pp. 172–173.

8. Ibid., p. 174.

9. Indeed, this data is available in machine-readable form.

10. Unless otherwise noted, this statistical portrait of Florence in 1427 is based on the analysis of the *catasto* records found in Herlihy and Klapisch-Zuber, *Tuscans*.

11. Herlihy and Klapisch-Zuber (*Tuscans*) focus their study on the social aspects of Florentine life revealed by the *catasto*. Goldsmith (*Premodern Financial Systems*) uses these data to examine the financial lives of the people more closely.

12. These conclusions and the data that follow are found in Goldsmith, *Premodern Financial Systems*, pp. 151–55. Goldsmith's study is based on earlier work by Herlihy.

13. Goldsmith, *Premodern Financial Systems*, pp. 148–49.

14. Goldsmith makes alternative estimates of income using other data sources, which tend to confirm the general magnitudes given here. It would be an error, however, to understate the potential for error in any estimates of this nature.

15. Data based on author's calculations, using Goldsmith, *Premodern Financial Systems* as a source of income estimates; Mohlo, *Florentine Public Finances* as a source for communal budget data; and Brown, *In the Shadow* for per capita tax figures.

16. Goldsmith, *Premodern Financial Systems*, p. 154.

17. Herlihy and Klapisch-Zuber, *Tuscans*, p. 26. But these authors prove that the *catasto* was a great success in other ways. Their volume provides us with a priceless detailed picture of Florentine social and economic life based on *catasto* returns, which would not otherwise be possible to reconstruct.

18. Years later, in *The Prince*, Machiavelli specifically warned his Medici patron against repeating the error of imposing new taxes on conquered territory. Of course, many future "princes" would also ignore this advice, some with success.

19. Schevill, *History*, pp. 361–62.

20. de Roover, *Rise and Decline*, p. 74.

21. Lopez, "Hard Times," pp. 45–47. Arpad Kadarkay warns that it is an error to push the intellectual link between Savonarola and Lorenzo beyond the strict definition of *pessimism* used here.

22. Lopez, "Hard Times," p. 45.

23. Quoted in Brucker, *Renaissance Florence*, p. 262.

24. Quoted in Brucker, *Society*, p. 27.

25. Goldthwaite's "optimistic" thesis is introduced in his *Private Wealth* and more completely developed in his *Building of Renaissance Florence*.

26. See Brown, *In the Shadow*, p. 173.

27. Both of Goldthwaite's books discuss this idea. Note, however, that this data, even if it is the most reliable available, is still based on the records of just four families.

28. See Lopez, "Hard Times," for his theory of art as an investment.

29. Lopez, *Three Ages*, p. 14.

30. Goldthwaite, *Building*, pp. 182–85.

31. Ibid., p. 418.

32. Ibid., pp. 422–23.

33. Baron, "New Attitude" p. 176.

34. Herlihy and Klapisch-Zuber, *Tuscans*, p. 17.

35. Lopez, "Hard Times," p. 51.

36. This is cited in Marks, "Financial Oligarchy," p. 127.

37. This is also cited in Marks, "Financial Oligarchy," pp. 133–34.

38. See Laven, *Renaissance Italy*, pp. 101–3 for a discussion of Monte finances and Florentine tax policy in this period.

39. Stephens, *Fall*, pp. 182–90, discusses the various means used, including the sale of Florentine citizenship and the levy of forced loans on the guilds themselves (in addition to collections from individual members). Every cord was used to tug revenues from Florentine pockets, it seems.

40. The dowry fund terms became more and more generous in the last years of the fifteenth century and the first decades of the sixteenth century in an attempt to attract new investors whose funds could repay old obligations. It was like an ever-more-generous Ponzi scheme. See Stephens, *Fall*, pp. 188–90.

41. Marks, "Financial Oligarchy" p. 132.

42. Ibid., p. 144.

43. Kirshner and Mohlo ("Dowry Fund") have studied the records of the dowry fund. The continuing importance of the fund is discussed in Butters, *Governors and Government*, pp. 37–38.

44. See Lopez and Miskimin, "Economic Depression" for evidence of this depression.

45. Laven, *Renaissance Italy*, p. 36.

46. Cipolla is the accepted authority on the uneven decline of the city-states in Italy. For a brief discussion, see *Before the Industrial Revolution*, chap. 10.

47. See Bergier, pp. 105–15, for an analysis of the decline of Italian banking and the rise of the Germans in this field.

48. Bergier, p. 114.

49. Cochrane, *Florence*, p. 55.

50. Cochrane (*Florence*) calls these the "forgotten" years of Florentine history, a reflection of Florence's place in the world during this period.

51. Butters (*Governors and Government*, pp. 1–4) discusses the rise of a class system in Florence and the growing gap between rich and poor.

52. Cochrane, *Florence*, pp. 114–15.

53. Ibid., p. 110.

54. Ibid., p. 202.

55. Marks, "Financial Oligarchy" p. 144.

56. These are the conclusions reached by Cipolla, "Economic Decline."

4 SIMPLE PATTERNS: BRITAIN AND THE INDUSTRIAL REVOLUTION

1. *Crystal Palace*, pp. xxi–xxii.

2. This is quoted by Thomson, *England*, p. 909.

3. From the *Illustrated London News* of June 28, 1851 as quoted in Gash, *Age of Peel*, p. 181.

4. *Crystal Palace*, p. vi.

5. Visiting the Centennial Exhibition of 1876, the U.S. intellectual William Dean Howells wrote that "all that Great Britain and Germany have sent is insignificant in amount when compared with our own contributions; the superior elegance, aptness, and ingenuity of our own machinery is observable at a glance" (cited in Weymouth, *America*, p. 27).

6. This is the type of "failure" that Paul Kennedy is concerned with in his best-selling book, *The Rise and Fall of the Great Powers*. Kennedy's decline is relative, unlike the absolute decline that McCloskey considers and rejects in the case of Victorian Britain.

7. It is more accurate to say that Toynbee *popularized* the phrase, which had first appeared in some French discussion in the 1830s.

8. Toynbee's lectures presented a more complex view, of course; but now no one reads his lectures and everyone uses his language. Revisionist economic historians led by Crafts and others are challenging Toynbee's terminology in an attempt to correct the general perception of this period.

9. Quoted in Deane, *First Industrial Revolution*, p. 3. Rostow suggests that the British Industrial Revolution and its leading sector takeoff set the pattern that all economies necessarily follow as they become modern industrial systems. Deane's critique of Rostow's theory is devastating.

10. Cannadine has written an excellent historiography of the Industrial Revolution ("The Present and the Past"). One of his main points is that each generation of historians has produced a distinctly different theory or interpretation of the industrial period in Britain. These various interpretations seem to be deeply colored by that generation's economic events and theories. Following Cannadine's arguments, it is not surprising that writers in today's slow-growth world end up focusing on the slow-growth aspects of the Industrial Revolution.

11. Bagehot, *Economic Studies*, pp. 71–72.

12. In fact, most of these impressions are derived from a casual reading of James Burke's popular book, *The Day the Universe Changed* (pp. 163–93), which was written to accompany his even more popular television series of the same name.

13. McCloskey, "Industrial Revolution," p. 103. He also notes that "the British economy from 1780 to 1860 was unpredictable because it was novel, not to say bizarre."

14. Cited in Braudel, *Perspective*, p. 539. Braudel follows this with the comment that "it is not fair to expect great men of an age . . . to be skilled at the art of prophecy." Since prophecy is the one task people generally expect modern economists to perform regularly, it is clear that either we are not "great men" or they expect prophesy of us unfairly.

15. Crafts's neat little book (*British Economic Growth*) is the best source for a thorough but concise summary of the British growth experience as informed by the most recent data analysis available.

16. Marshall, *Principles*, p. 603.

17. Kindleberger, *Economic Growth*, p. 62.

18. Chapman, *Cotton Industry*, p. 31–32.

19. Cited by Sabine, *History*, p. 47.

20. Quoted in Seligman, *Income Tax*, p. 130.

21. Quoted by Sabine, *History*, p. 61.

22. McCloskey ("Did Victorian Britain Fail?") seems to be one of the few dissenters, although even his strong views might be tempered by recent empirical work. In any case, McCloskey argues only that Britain did not fail in the absolute sense, whereas my discussion here views failure as a relative phenomenon.

23. See Crouzet, *Victorian Economy*, pp. 380–81. The service sector was very important to Britain's industrial development, as detailed by Hartwell, *Industrial Revolution*, pp. 201–25.

24. Like every other general statement about the economy of Victorian Britain, this assertion is challenged by some scholars, at least in regard to specific industries.

25. See Crafts, *British Economic Growth*, p. 162, for an analysis of the revealed comparative advantages of different nations.

26. Sayers, (*History*, pp. 60–77) discusses Britain's response to the new industries.

27. Crafts ("British Industrialization") argues that comparative advantage was a very powerful organizing force in Britain and so had a very large impact on the economy.

28. Hobsbawn, *Industry and Empire*, pp. 161–62.

29. But the best attempt to analyze all the different theories is found in Levine, *Industrial Retardation* esp. chap. 6. My particular favorite, not developed here, is Sayer's (*History*), who concludes that decline might have been due to simple "hard luck."

30. I have listed this as a "general theory" of change, but it is hard to believe that Schumpeter's ideas (*History*) were not informed and probably influenced by his detailed knowledge of British economic history.

31. Olson (*Rise and Decline*) does not specifically apply his model to Victorian Britain, so he might argue with the examples I use here; but they are clearly in the spirit of Olson's analysis.

32. This is not meant as a criticism of Olson's work. Indeed the strength of his written work is his critical self-analysis and thorough use of supporting examples.

33. The overcommitment thesis is both well presented and effectively criticized in Crafts, *British Economic Growth*, pp. 157–65.

34. Crouzet, *Victorian Economy*, p. 420.

35. Good sources for a deeper analysis of this special theory are Hobsbawn, *Industry and Empire*, pp. 152–161 and Mathias, *First Industrial Nation*, p. 419.

36. This view is certainly not shared by all. For a distinctly opposing statement, see Levine, *Industrial Retardation*, pp. 145–47. Chapman (*Cotton Industry*, p. 26) seems to take my point of view, however.

37. See Payne, *Industrial Entrepreneurship*, for a thorough analysis of the entrepreneurship hypothesis of decline.

5   THE ODIOUS TAX AND THE STANDING MIRACLE

1. Sabine, *History*, p. 20.

2. Seligman (*Income Tax*, p. 58) notes that the colonial excises of the Stamp Act became necessary when Parliament refused to increase land taxation.

3. Ibid., p. 60.

4. Ibid., p. 62.

5. This is cited in Seligman, *Income Tax*, p. 63.

6. This data and the information in the next paragraph are found in Seligman, *Income Tax*, p. 65.

7. Ibid., p. 68.

8. This is the title of Sabine's chapter on the wartime income tax (*History*).

9. Quoted by Sabine, *History*, p. 29.

10. Seligman, *Income Tax*, p. 74–75.

11. Seligman (*Income Tax*, pp. 92–97) and Sabine (*History*, pp. 35–39) provide details on the tax schedules and their various provisions.

12. This is especially true when the revisions adopted in 1806 are considered.

13. Seligman, *Income Tax*, p. 99.

14. Ibid., p. 100.

15. Ibid., pp. 116–17.

16. Sabine, *History*, p. 53.

17. Seligman, *Income Tax*, p. 49.

18. This is Richard Whitlock, quoted in Seligman, *Income Tax*, p. 134.

19. Ibid., p. 138.

20. Hicks, *British Public Finances*, pp. 93–94.

21. Cited by Seligman, *Income Tax*, p. 140.

22. Ricardo, *Principles*, p. 95.

23. Groves (*Tax Philosophers*, pp. 34–35) discusses Mills's views on differentiation.

24. The tax continues to the present day in pretty much the same form; this study, however, halts at the beginning of the Great War.

25. Hicks, *British Public Finances*, p. 77.

26. Schumpeter, *History*, p. 404.

27. This periodization is arbitrary but serviceable. I am not saying that the tax changed in any important way in 1873. Rather, the tax stayed much the same, but the economy changed; and the combination of the old tax and the new world economy produced a different reaction than before.

28. This is the general concept; modern economists would adjust this description in a variety of ways to account for changing price levels, technologies, and other factors. These adjustments are important to efficient taxation, but we need not become this technical here just to capture the basic idea. The interest rate is also an important

determinant of the level of investment spending, but the peculiar pattern of British finance, which is discussed later in this chapter, reduces its impact during the Victorian era. Even low interest rates do not necessarily produce higher investment spending if there is no financial channel to accommodate this flow.

29. Seligman, *Income Tax*, pp. 189–90.

30. See Sayers, *History*, pp. 93–99 on the British shipping industry. Britain's dominance in this area eroded unevenly after the turn of the century.

31. Sayers, *History*, 162–63.

32. Smith, *Wealth of Nations*, vol. 2, pp. 410–11; Ricardo, *Principles*, p. 163; Jonathan Swift quoted in Dickson, *Financial Revolution*, p. 26.

33. Hume, *Writings*, pp. 94–96.

34. Braudel, *Wheels*, p. 528.

35. Ibid., p. 528.

36. Kindleberger, *Financial History*, p. 75.

37. These brief descriptions are too oversimplified except to suggest the basic nature of these instruments. Dickson, *Financial Revolution*, and Fisk *English Public Finance* provide more detail.

38. The debate on this point is found in Williamson, "Why Was British Growth" and Heim and Mirowski, "Interest Rates."

39. See Chapman, *Cotton Industry*, chap. 5. The necessary small coins were silver, and Britain was at this time a net exporter of silver coin (and importer of gold) due to exchange rate imbalances. Thus, this problem is not wholly the result of weak local banks but does serve to illustrate this weakness.

40. Crouzet, *Victorian Economy*, p. 335.

41. This was not a problem in Germany, where banks were stronger from the start and established close early links with their industrial customers.

42. Halberstam (*Reckoning*, p. 332) discusses the modern version of the "missing middle." Schumpeter, of course, would argue that the largest firms can only hope to stay dominant by adopting the latest technology. This is clearly true of some large firms but not all of them, and not even most of them in Britain during this period. See also Best and Humphries, "City" regarding imperfections in city markets.

43. Kindleberger, *International Capital Movements*, p. 29.

44. Kindleberger, *Financial History*, p. 219.

45. Capital was widely exported, not narrowly channeled to Britain's colonial allies, as one might have expected.

46. Data found in Kindleberger, *Financial History*, pp. 219–25.

47. Ibid., p. 220.

48. Bagehot, *Economic Studies*, p. 74.

49. Weiner (*English Culture*) discusses the "gentrification" of British entrepreneurs.

50. As in the epigraph from Marshall, *Principles*, p. 269.

51. Webber and Wildavsky, *History*, p. 325.

52. Hicks, *British Public Finances*, p. 143.

53. Webber and Wildavsky, *History*, pp. 325–26.

54. Ibid., p. 342.

6   THE AMERICAN CENTURY AND THE AMERICAN CRISIS

1. Epigraph quoted in Halberstam, *Reckoning*, p. 63.

2. Ibid., pp. 45–46.

3. Ibid., p. 45.

4. I use the term *revolution* here not so much because it is the best or most accurate word but because it is the word that has been applied in previous sections to sets of events and forces associated with structural change.

5. This table and the others presented in this section show data for a few selected, evenly spaced years, not the entire period. The data in the intervening years varies somewhat due to changing macroeconomic conditions. But the figures cited in these tables do not distort in any important way the patterns they are meant to describe. It should also be noted that conventions used in measuring some of these variables also necessarily distort their interpretation somewhat.

6. It is worth noting here that throughout this period the United States has been a "service economy," with over 60 percent of total output flowing from the service sector. Observers who see this as a new event or a sudden threat lack an accurate understanding of economic history.

7. Note that these figures do not include nonpayroll jobs, but they still provide a representative indication of the changing pattern of civilian employment in the United States.

8. Kennedy, *Rise and Fall*. Kennedy's thesis is that economic power is the source of strength and weakness in international affairs.

9. Maddison, *Phases*, pp. 30–31, marks 1890 as the year of transition between British economic hegemony and the dominance of the United States.

10. These figures and the others cited in this section are taken from tables in the appendix to Easterlin, "American Population." The actual calculations, as cited by Easterlin, are largely based upon the work of Kuznets.

11. See Fuchs, *How We Live* for a thorough analysis of the needs and choices at each stage in life.

12. This is not an exhaustive list of the types of government and nongovernment institutions that address social problems at different stages of life.

13. In each case it is necessary to oversimplify the problems and ignore much data and theory; but the goal here is to provide a general understanding of these events, not a detailed analysis.

14. Electronic devices are different from electrical ones in my taxonomy, at least in the sense that electrical tools use electromagnetic force to operate machines whereas electronic devices rely on the properties of the charged particles themselves for operation. Compare an electric clock (which uses electromagnetism to drive the motor that turns the clock hands) with an electronic timer, which uses electron charges to keep and display the time directly.

15. *Economic Report of the President* 1989, p. 227.

16. While this is perhaps the best available measure of innovation, it is clearly imperfect for at least two reasons. First, some innovations are held as trade secrets and not protected by patent for strategic reasons. Second, differences in international patent laws distort the numbers. In Japan, for example, any small change in a product or process must be patented individually to be protected, whereas under U.S. law a patent can provide much broader protection. This difference partly accounts for the very large number of Japanese patents relative to those of U.S. firms.

17. These points are explained in greater detail in Levich, "Financial Innovations" and Friedman, "Postwar Changes."

18. Friedman, "Postwar Changes," p. 16.

19. Friedman, *Day of Reckoning*, p. 116.

20. Halberstam, *Reckoning*, pp. 247–48.

21. Ibid., p. 691.

22. Levy, "Incomes, Families," pp. 109, 146.

23. The other side of this coin is that high labor wages was much of the explanation for the high and rising U.S. standard of living.

24. The shift to investment and production abroad is complex. It cannot be explained only in terms of relative wage rates. And high U.S. wage rates cannot be explained only in terms of population trends. This analysis should make clear that these structural changes involve a combination of factors, some of which are also discussed in chap. 8.

25. This is a gross oversimplification, of course, but the purpose of this section is to sum up.

7 THE CHANGING STRUCTURE OF AMERICAN GOVERNMENT

1. The epigraph is from Shultz, "Comparative Advantage," p. 656.

2. This discussion will henceforth use the terms *government* and *federal government* pretty much interchangeably, although a more detailed analysis of postwar government changes would necessarily need to look at the entire federal-state-local government system and take account of the substantial diversity within that system. I focus on the federal government here.

3. A good analysis of the changing structure of government is found in Break, "Role of Government," Shultz, "Comparative Advantage," and Samuelson, "Public Role."

4. But less heavily than in the future.

5. See Boskin, *Too Many Promises* for an excellent analysis of social security and its development.

6. Kennedy, *Rise and Fall*, p. xxii.

7. Ibid., p. 534.

8. These are the broad trends for the long period under consideration here. The tax reforms of 1986 modify these general trends somewhat. They will be discussed in chap. 8.

9. See Witte, *Politics and Development*, chap. 6.

10. Ibid., p. 144.

11. This is the conclusion of Auerbach and Poterba, "Why Have Corporate Tax Revenues."

12. Figures on corporate profitability are taken from Auerbach and Poterba, "Why Have Corporate Tax Revenues," p. 6, table 2.

13. I believe that Stanley Surrey coined this phrase. His books (*Pathways* and, with Paul McDaniel, *Tax Expenditures*) on this subject are the best reference.

14. Figures from Surrey and McDaniel, *Tax Expenditures*, p. 35, table 2.

15. See Auerbach and Poterba, "Why Have Corporate Tax Revenues."

16. Friedman, *Day of Reckoning*, p. 116.

17. Ibid., p. 4.

18. The change in the tax burden overall was much less than ERTA's implied promise; social insurance taxes necessarily increased as benefit costs rose, offsetting some of the effects of lower income tax rates.

8 THE NEW MOUNTAINS OF DEBT

1. This is the average change relative to a basket of currencies of our trading partner countries. Changes with respect to individual currencies will vary from this average.

2. This technology gap is far from equal in all industries, as the case studies contained in Dertouzos et al., *Made in America* make clear.

3. There are those who take a different view, namely, that the Reagan administration intended to run up huge deficits in order to handcuff future administrations and prevent them from undoing Reagan's "legacy" of a downsized federal government. This view is difficult to accept. It is refuted by both critical outsiders (Benjamin Friedman, for example) and by sympathetic insiders such as William Niskanen. Although this theory cannot be completely dismissed, it cannot be accepted, either, and will receive no further treatment here.

4. Although not completely, as anyone who files a tax return can attest.

5. Under a negative tax rate, such an investment would generate a positive offset for the investor against other types of income. In effect, the investor receives a net payment from the government over and above forgiveness of tax on the particular investment.

6. The most controversial aspect of the 1983 reforms, in fact, seems to have been the treatment of the "notch babies," a small cohort whose benefits unexpectedly changed as they approached retirement age.

7. Data are from Aaron, Bosworth, and Burtless, *Can America*. Precise dates and amounts cited here are highly sensitive to the actuarial assumptions and macroeconomic conditions in the future.

8. See Boskin, *Too Many Promises* for a detailed analysis of social security's many problems and Boskin's innovative proposal to solve some of them.

9. Wisely so, perhaps. The Medicare problem is so difficult that including it in the 1983 agenda might have prevented any reforms from being produced at all, so difficult would the economic and political trade-offs have been.

10. There are other reasons why investment may not take place. Martin Feldstein, for example, has analyzed the effect of promised social security benefits on private saving and has found a substantial impact. An additional dollar of social security "saving" may reduce private saving by as much as fifty cents to a dollar. For a discussion of Feldstein's views on this and other subjects, see Boskin, *Too Many Promises*, chap. 4.

11. See Litan, Lawrence, and Schultze, *American Living Standards*.

9 SADDLE POINTS

1. The epigraph is from Tuchman, *March of Folly*, p. 4.

2. Barro's views are summed up in his "Ricardian Approach."

3. See Heilbroner and Bernstein, *Debt and the Deficit*, for a fuller summary of their views.

4. Eisner, "Budget Deficits" captures the essence of his approach.

5. Friedberg, *Weary Titan*, p. 70.

6. See William G. Gale's description of these accounting tricks and traps ("Budget Gimmick") and Herb Stein's *Wall Street Journal* analysis of them ("Congress's Amazing Budget Tricks").

7. At least this back-dating was being seriously considered in the multibillion dollar thrift industry assistance package in 1989.

8. Litan, Lawrence and Schultze, *American Living Standards*, p. 4.

9. See Dornbusch, *Dollars, Debts*, pp. 188–89.

10. Robert Reich ("As the World Turns") believes that the United States must specialize in "symbolic-analytic" services, based on his analysis of the global economy. The MIT Commission on Productivity (Dertouzos et al., *Made in America*) holds out greater hope for U.S. manufacturing. These studies (and others) are not so far apart as

they appear at first glance because they tend to talk about the same goal (similar to mine stated here) in different terms.

11. The industry-specific studies contained in Dertouzos et al., *Made in America*, (the report of the MIT Commission on Productivity) are enormously interesting and useful to people who are interested in the future of manufacturing in the United States.

10 CHANGING DIRECTIONS

1. Dertouzos et al., *Made in America*, the MIT Commission on Productivity's report, not only provides its own set of recommendations but also usefully summarizes the findings of some of the other studies. While the MIT commission focused on the micro aspects of productivity and competition, Cuomo Commission on Trade and Competitiveness, *Cuomo Commission Report*, provides a good analysis of the macro issues.

2. An excellent analysis of a cash flow income tax plan is found in Rivlin, *Economic Choices*, pp. 87–117. This particular plan, which differs only in detail from other proposals of the same nature, is due mostly to Henry Aaron and Harvey Galper. The idea of a cash flow tax is taken seriously by tax policy analysts, if not by legislators.

3. There are limits and restrictions on these activities, of course; but individuals are relatively skilled at navigating the loopholes, which I think have been, on balance, far less restrictive than was initially intended.

4. In a presentation before the National Tax Association, I said that one lesson fiscal history teaches us is not to mess around with the tax treatment of owner-occupied housing. I now suggest this politically "imprudent" step.

5. Liberals, on the other hand, have opposed the VAT because of its apparent regressivity. This problem may be overstated; but in any case it may be overcome, on average, through the use of offsetting credits or lower tax rates on food, housing, and other necessities.

Bibliography

Aaron, Henry J. "Politics and the Professors Revisited." *American Economic Review* 79(May 1989): 1–15.

Aaron, Henry J., Barry P. Bosworth, and Gary Burtless. *Can America Afford To Grow Old?* Washington: Brookings Institution, 1989.

Aaron, Henry J. et al. *Economic Choices 1987.* Washington: Brookings Institution, 1986.

Aaron, Henry J., Harvey Galper, and Joseph A. Pechman, eds. *Uneasy Compromise.* Washington: Brookings Institution, 1988.

Alt, James E. "The Evolution of Tax Structures." *Public Choice* 41(1983): 181–222.

The Crystal Palace Exhibition Illustrated Catalogue. 1851. Reprint. New York: Dover, 1970.

"America's Wasting Disease." *Economist.* March 25, 1989.

Ashton, T. S. *The Industrial Revolution.* London: Oxford University Press, 1948.

Ashworth, William. *An Economic History of England 1870–1939.* London: Methuen, 1960.

Auerbach, Alan. "Corporate Taxation in the United States." *Brookings Papers on Economic Activity* 1983: 451–506.

_____. "Taxation, Corporate Financial Policy, and the Cost of Capital." *Journal of Economic Literature* 21(1983): 905–40.

Auerbach, Alan, and James M. Poterba. "Why Have Corporate Tax Revenues Declined?" In *Tax Policy and the Economy,* vol. 1, ed. Lawrence W. Summers. Cambridge: National Bureau of Economic Research and MIT Press, 1987.

Bagehot, Walter. *Economic Studies.* Ed. Richard Holt Hutton. Stanford: Academic Reprints, 1953.

_____. *Lombard Street.* Homewood, IL: Richard D. Irwin, 1962.

Baily, Martin Neil. "The Productivity Slowdown by Industry." *Brookings Papers on Economic Activity* 1982: 423–60.

Baily, Martin Neil, and Alok K. Chakrabarti. "Innovation and Productivity in U.S. Industry." *Brookings Papers on Economic Activity* 1985: 609–39.

Baron, Hans. "A New Attitude toward Wealth." In *Social and Economic Foundations of the Italian Renaissance,* ed. Anthony Molho. New York: John Wiley & Sons, 1969.

Barro, Robert J. "The Ricardian Approach to Budget Deficits." *Journal of Economic Perspectives* 3,2(1989): 37–54.

Becker, Marvin B. *Florence in Transition.* Vol. 2. Baltimore: Johns Hopkins University Press, 1968.

_____. "The Florentine Territorial State and Civic Humanism in the Early Renaissance." In *Florentine Studies,* ed. Nicolai Rubinstein. London: Faber & Faber, 1968.

Bergier, Jean-François. "From the Fifteenth Century in Italy to the Sixteenth Century in Germany: A New Banking Concept?" In *The Dawn of Modern Banking,* ed. Robert S. Lopez. New Haven: Yale University Press, 1979.

Bernanke, Ben S., and John Y. Campbell. "Is There a Corporate Debt Crisis?" *Brookings Papers on Economic Activity* 1988: 83–126.

Bernheim, B. Douglas. "Budget Deficits and the Balance of Trade." In *Tax Policy and the Economy*, vol. 2, ed. Lawrence H. Summers. Cambridge: MIT Press, 1988.

Best, Michael H., and Jane Humphries. "The City and Industrial Decline." In *The Decline of the British Economy*, ed. Bernard Elbaum and William Lazonick. Oxford: Clarendon, 1986.

Birnbaum, Jeffrey H., and Alan S. Murray. *Showdown at Gucci Gulch*. New York: Random House, 1987.

Boskin, Michael J. *Reagan and the Economy*. San Francisco: Institute for Contemporary Studies Press, 1987.

_____. *Too Many Promises*. Homewood, IL: Dow Jones–Irwin, 1986.

Boskin, Michael J., and Douglas J. Puffert. "Social Security and the American Family." In *Tax Policy and the Economy*, vol. 1, ed. Lawrence H. Summers. Cambridge: MIT Press, 1987.

Boskin, Michael J., and Aaron Wildavsky, eds. *The Federal Budget: Economics and Politics*. San Francisco: Institute for Contemporary Studies, 1982.

Bosworth, Barry P. "Capital Formation and Economic Growth." *Brookings Papers on Economic Activity* 1982: 273–318.

_____. "Taxes and the Investment Recovery." *Brookings Papers on Economic Activity* 1985: 1–39.

_____. *Tax Incentives and Economic Growth*. Washington: Brookings Institution, 1984.

Bowsky, William M. *The Finance of the Commune of Sienna, 1287–1355*. Oxford: Clarendon, 1970.

_____. "The Impact of the Black Death." In *Social and Economic Foundations of the Italian Renaissance*, ed. Anthony Molho. New York: John Wiley & Sons, 1969.

Bradford, David F. *Untangling the Income Tax*. Cambridge: Harvard University Press, 1986.

Bradford, David F. and the U.S. Treasury Tax Policy Staff. *Blueprints for Basic Tax Reform*. 2d ed. Arlington: Tax Analysts, 1984.

Branson, William H. "Trends in United States International Trade and Investment since World War II." In *The American Economy in Transition*, ed. Martin Feldstein. Chicago: University of Chicago Press, 1980.

Braudel, Fernand. *The Perspective of the World*. Trans. Sian Reynolds. Vol. 3 of *Civilization and Capitalism, 15th–18th Century*. New York: Harper & Row, 1984.

_____. *The Wheels of Commerce*. Trans. Sian Reynolds. Vol. 2 of *Civilization and Capitalism, 15th–18th Century*. New York: Harper & Row, 1984.

Break, George F. "The Role of Government: Taxes, Transfers, and Spending." In *The American Economy in Transition*, ed. Martin Feldstein. Chicago: University of Chicago Press, 1980.

Brown, Judith C. *In the Shadow of Florence*. New York: Oxford University Press, 1982.

Brown, Kenneth M. "Changes in Industrial Structure and Foreign Competition—The Policy Arguments." In *Contemporary Economic Problems: Deficits, Taxes, and Economic Adjustments*, ed. Phillip Cagan. Washington: American Enterprise Institute, 1987.

Brucker, Gene A. "The Ciompi Revolution." In *Florentine Studies*, ed. Nicolai Rubinstein. London: Faber & Faber, 1968.

_____. *Renaissance Florence*. Rev. ed. Berkeley: University of California Press, 1983.

_____., ed. *The Society of Renaissance Florence*. New York: Harper & Row, 1971.

Burckhardt, Jacob. *The Civilization of the Renaissance in Italy*. New York: Phaidon, 1950.

Burke, James. *The Day the Universe Changed*. Boston: Little, Brown, 1985.

Burke, Peter. "Republics of Merchants in Early Modern Europe." In *Europe and the Rise of Capitalism*, ed. Jean Baechler, J. A. Hall, and M. Mann. London: Basil Blackwell, 1988.

Butters, H. C. *Governors and Government in Early Sixteenth-Century Florence*. Oxford: Clarendon, 1985.

Cameron, Rondo. *A Concise Economic History of the World*. New York: Oxford University Press, 1989.

Cannadine, David. "The Present and the Past in the English Industrial Revolution 1880–1980." *Past and Present* 103(1984): 131–72.

Chamberlin, E. R. *Everyday Life in Renaissance Times*. New York: Capricorn, 1965.

Chambers, Jonathan D. *The Workshop of the World*. London: Oxford University Press, 1961.

Chapman, Stanley D. *The Cotton Industry in the Industrial Revolution*. 2d ed. London: Macmillan Education, 1987.

Cipolla, Carlo M. *Before the Industrial Revolution: European Society and Economy, 1000–1700*. 2d ed. New York: W. W. Norton, 1980.

_____. "The Economic Decline of Italy." In *The Economic Decline of Empires*, ed. Carlo M. Cipolla. London: Methuen, 1970.

_____. *The Monetary Policy of Fourteenth-Century Florence*. Berkeley: University of California Press, 1982.

Clark, Colin. *The Conditions of Economic Progress*. 2d ed. New York: St. Martin's Press, 1951.

Clark, Peter K. "Issues in the Analysis of Capital Formation and Productivity Growth." *Brookings Papers on Economic Activity* 1979: 423–46.

_____. "Productivity and Profits in the 1980s: Are They Really Improving?" *Brookings Papers on Economic Activity* 1984: 133–68.

Cochrane, Eric. *Florence in the Forgotten Centuries*. Chicago: University of Chicago Press, 1973.

"The Cost of Growing Old." *Economist*. June 3, 1989.

Cuomo Commission on Trade and Competitiveness. *The Cuomo Commission Report*. New York: Simon & Schuster, 1988.

Crafts, Nicholas F. *British Economic Growth during the Industrial Revolution*. New York: Oxford University Press, 1985.

_____. "British Industrialization in an International Context." *Journal of Interdisciplinary History* 19(1989): 415–28.

Crouzet, Francois. *The Victorian Economy*. Trans. A. S. Forster. New York: Columbia University Press, 1982.

Deane, Phyllis. *The First Industrial Revolution*. New York: Cambridge University Press, 1965.

_____. *The State and the Economic System*. New York: Oxford University Press, 1989.

Deane, Phyllis, and W. A. Cole. *British Economic Growth, 1688–1959*. London: Cambridge University Press, 1962.

"Debt Wish II." *Economist*. April 1, 1989.

de la Roncière, Charles M. "Indirect Taxes or 'Gabelles' at Florence in the Fourteenth Century." In *Florentine Studies*, ed. Nicolai Rubinstein. London: Faber & Faber, 1968.

de Roover, Raymond. "The Commercial Revolution of the 13th Century." In *Social and Economic Foundations of the Italian Renaissance*, ed. Anthony Molho. New York: John Wiley & Sons, 1969.

_____. "Labour Conditions in Florence around 1400: Theory, Policy, and Reality." In *Florentine Studies*, ed. Nicolai Rubinstein. London: Faber & Faber, 1968.

_____. *The Rise and Decline of the Medici Bank*. Cambridge: Harvard University Press, 1963.

Dertouzos, Michael L. et al. *Made in America*. Cambridge: MIT Press, 1989.

Dickson, P. G. M. *The Financial Revolution in England*. New York: St. Martin's Press, 1967.

Dornbusch, Rudiger. *Dollars, Debts, and Deficits*. Cambridge: MIT Press, 1986.

_____. "Trade, the Dollar, and the Decline of America." *Harvard International Review* 10(1989): 95–99.

Drucker, Peter F. "Demographics and American Economic Policy." In *Toward a New U.S. Industrial Policy*, ed. Michael and Susan Wachter. Philadelphia: University of Pennsylvania Press, 1983.

Easterlin, Richard A. "American Population since 1940." In *The American Economy in Transition*, ed. Martin Feldstein. Chicago: University of Chicago Press, 1980.

Eckstein, Otto, and Robert Tannenwald. "Productivity and Capital Formation." In *Toward a New U.S. Industrial Policy*, ed. Michael and Susan Wachter. Philadelphia: University of Pennsylvania Press, 1983.

Ehrenberg, Richard. *Capital and Finance in the Age of the Renaissance*. Trans. H. M. Lucas. London: Jonathan Cape, 1928.

Eisner, Robert. "Budget Deficits: Rhetoric and Reality." The *Journal of Economic Perspectives*. 3,2(1989): 73–93.

Feldstein, Martin. "The Budget Deficit and the Dollar," *National Bureau of Economic Research Macroeconomics Annual* 1986: 355–92.

_____., ed. *The American Economy in Transition*. Chicago: University of Chicago Press, 1980.

_____., ed. *The United States in the World Economy*. Chicago: University of Chicago Press, 1988.

Feldstein, Martin, and Lawrence Summers. "Inflation, Tax Rules, and the Long Term Interest Rate." *Brookings Papers on Economic Activity* 1978: 61–100.

Fisk, Harvey E. *English Public Finance*. New York: Bankers Trust, 1920.

"The Folly of Raiding the Piggy-Bank." *Economist*. April 8, 1989.

Frankel, Jeffrey A. "International Capital Flows and Domestic Economic Policies." In *The United States in the World Economy*, ed. Martin Feldstein. Chicago: University of Chicago Press, 1988.

Friedberg, Aaron L. *The Weary Titan: Britain and the Experience of Relative Decline, 1895–1905*. Princeton: Princeton University Press, 1988.

Friedman, Benjamin M. "Crowding Out or Crowding In? Economic Consequences of Financing Government Deficits." *Brookings Papers on Economic Activity* 1978: 593–642.

_____. *Day of Reckoning*. New York: Random House, 1988.

_____. "Financing Capital Formation in the 1980s: Issues for Public Policy." In *Toward a New U.S. Industrial Policy*, ed. Michael and Susan Wachter. Philadelphia: University of Pennsylvania Press, 1983.

_____. "Postwar Changes in the American Financial Markets." In *The American Economy in Transition*, ed. Martin Feldstein. Chicago: University of Chicago Press, 1980.

Fuchs, Victor R. *How We Live*. Cambridge: Harvard University Press, 1983.

Galbraith, James K. *Balancing Acts*. New York: Basic Books, 1989.

Gale, William G. "The Budget Gimmick of the 1990s?" *Wall Street Journal*. May 3, 1989.

Gash, Norman, ed. *The Age of Peel*. London: Edward Arnold, 1968.

Goldsmith, Raymond W. *Premodern Financial Systems*. Cambridge: Cambridge University Press, 1987.

Goldthwaite, Richard A. *The Building of Renaissance Florence*. Baltimore: Johns Hopkins University Press, 1980.

_____. *Private Wealth in Renaissance Florence*. Princeton: Princeton University Press, 1968.

Groves, Harold M. *Tax Philosophers*. Ed. Donald J. Curran. Madison: University of Wisconsin Press, 1974.

Halberstam, David. *The Reckoning*. New York: William Morrow, 1986.

Hale, John R., ed. *A Concise Encyclopedia of the Italian Renaissance*. New York: Oxford University Press, 1981.

Hartwell, R. M. *The Industrial Revolution and Economic Growth*. London: Methuen, 1971.

Heilbroner, Robert, and Peter Bernstein. *The Debt and the Deficit*. New York: W. W. Norton, 1989.

Heim, Carol E., and Philip Mirowski. "Interest Rates and Crowding-Out during Britain's Industrial Revolution." *Journal of Economic History* 47(1987): 117–39.

Herlihy, David, and Christiane Klapisch-Zuber. *Tuscans and Their Families*. New Haven: Yale University Press, 1985.

Hicks, John. *A Theory of Economic History*. Oxford: Clarendon, 1969.

Hicks, Ursula K. *British Public Finances*. London: Oxford University Press, 1954.

Hinrichs, Harley H. *A General Theory of Tax Structure Change during Economic Development*. Cambridge: Harvard University Law School, 1966.

Hirst, F. W., and J. E. Allen. *British War Budgets*. London: Oxford University Press, 1926.

Hobsbawn, E. J. *The Age of Empire, 1875-1914*. New York: Pantheon, 1987.

_____. *Industry and Empire*. London: Weidenfeld & Nicholson, 1968.

Hollander, Samuel. "Ricardo and the Corn Laws: A Revision." *History of Political Economy* 9: 1–47.

Holmes, George. "How the Medici Became the Pope's Bankers." In *Florentine Studies*, ed. Nicolai Rubinstein. London: Faber & Faber, 1968.

Hume, David. *Writings on Economics*. Ed. Eugene Rotwein. Madison: University of Wisconsin Press, 1970.

Jacob, E. F., ed. *Italian Renaissance Studies*. London: Faber & Faber, 1960.

Kennedy, Paul. *The Rise and Fall of the Great Powers*. New York: Random House, 1987.

Kennedy, W. P. "Foreign Investment, Trade, and Growth in the United Kingdom, 1870-1913." *Explorations in Economic History* 11(1973-1974): 415–43.

Kindleberger, Charles P. *Economic Development*. New York: McGraw Hill, 1965.

_____. *Economic Growth in France and Britain 1851-1950*. Cambridge: Harvard University Press, 1964.

_____. *A Financial History of Western Europe*. London: George Allen & Unwin, 1984.

_____. *International Capital Movements*. Cambridge: Cambridge University Press, 1987.

Kirshner, Julius, and Anthony Molho. "The Dowry Fund and the Marriage Market in Early Quattrocento Florence." *Journal of Modern History* 50(1978): 403–438.

Koenigsberger, H. S. *Medieval Europe, 400-1500*. New York: Longman, 1987.

Landau, Ralph. "U.S. Economic Growth." *Scientific American*. June 1988.

Lane, F. C. "Investment and Usury." In *Social and Economic Foundations of the Italian Renaissance*, ed. Anthony Mohlo. New York: John Wiley & Sons, 1969.

Laven, Peter. *Renaissance Italy, 1464-1534*. New York: Capricorn, 1966.

Lee, C. H. *The British Economy since 1700*. Cambridge: Cambridge University Press, 1986.

Lee, Susan, and Mary Beth Grover. "Social Security Faces a $60 Billion Question." *New York Times*, July 23, 1989.

Levich, Richard M. "Financial Innovations in International Financial Markets." In *The United States in the World Economy*, ed. Martin Feldstein. Chicago: University of Chicago Press, 1988.

Levine, A. L. *Industrial Retardation in Britain 1880-1914*. New York: Basic Books, 1967.

Levy, Frank. "Incomes, Families, and Living Standards." In *American Living Standards*, ed. Robert E. Litan, Robert Z. Lawrence, and Charles L. Schultze. Washington: Brookings Institution, 1988.

Lipsey, Robert E. "Changing Patterns of International Investment in and by the United States." In *The United States in the World Economy*, ed. Martin Feldstein. Chicago: University of Chicago Press, 1986.

Litan, Robert E., Robert Z. Lawrence, and Charles L. Schultze, eds. *American Living Standards: Threats and Challenges*. Washington: Brookings Institution, 1988.

Lopez, Robert S. "The Dawn of Medieval Banking." In *The Dawn of Modern Banking*, ed. Robert S. Lopez. New Haven: Yale University Press, 1979.

_____. "Hard Times and Investment in Culture." In Wallace K. Ferguson, et al., *The Renaissance*. New York: Harper & Row, 1962.

_____. *The Three Ages of the Italian Renaissance*. Charlottesville: University Press of Virginia, 1970.

Lopez, Robert S., and H. A. Miskimin. "The Economic Depression of the Renaissance." *Economic History Review* 14(1961-62): 408-26.

Luzzatto, Gino. *An Economic History of Italy*. Trans. Phillip Jones. London: Routledge & Kegan Paul, 1961.

McCloskey, D. N. "Did Victorian Britain Fail?" *Economic History Review* 23(1970): 446-59.

_____. "The Industrial Revolution, 1780-1860: A Survey." In *The Economic History of Britain since 1700*, Vol. 1, ed. Roderick Floyd and Donald McCloskey. New York: Cambridge University Press, 1981.

Machiavelli, Niccolo. *History of Florence and the Affairs of Italy*. Washington: M. Walter Dunne, 1901.

_____. *The Prince*. Trans. George Bull. New York: Penguin, 1981.

Maddison, Angus. "Growth and Slowdowns in Advanced Capitalist Economies." *Journal of Economic Literature* 25(1987): 649-98.

_____. *Phases of Capitalist Development*. New York: Oxford University Press, 1982.

Mansfield, Edwin. "Technology and Productivity in the United States." In *The American Economy in Transition*, ed. Martin Feldstein. Chicago: University of Chicago Press, 1980.

Marks, L. F. "The Financial Oligarchy in Florence under Lorenzo." In *Italian Renaissance Studies*, ed. E. F. Jacob. London: Faber & Faber, 1960.

Marshall, Alfred. *Principles of Economics*. 8th ed. London: Macmillan, 1920.

Martines, Lauro. *Power and Imagination: City-States in Renaissance Italy*. New York: Vintage, 1979.

Mathews, R. C. O., C. H. Feinstein, and J. C. Odling-Smee. *British Economic Growth, 1856–1973*. Stanford: Stanford University Press, 1982.

Mathias, Peter. *The First Industrial Nation*. New York: Charles Scribner's Sons, 1969.

———. *The Transformation of England*. New York: Columbia University Press, 1979.

Melis, Federigo. *Tracce di una storia economica di Firenze e della Toscana in generale dal 1252 al 1550*. 2d ed. Florence: Universita degli studi di Firenze, 1966–67.

Mill, John Stuart. *Principles of Political Economy*. 7th ed. London: Longman, Green, 1929.

Miskimin, Harry A. *The Economy of Early Renaissance Europe, 1300–1460*. New York: Cambridge University Press, 1975.

Molho, Anthony. *Florentine Public Finances in the Early Renaissance, 1400–1433*. Cambridge: Harvard University Press, 1971.

———., ed. *Social and Economic Foundations of the Italian Renaissance*. New York: John Wiley & Sons, 1969.

Niskanen, William A. *Reaganomics*. New York: Oxford University Press, 1988.

Norsworthy, J. R., Michael J. Harper, and Kent Kunze. "The Slowdown in Productivity Growth: Analysis of Some Contributing Factors." *Brookings Papers on Economic Activity* 1979: 387–433.

North, Douglass C., and Robert Paul Thomas. *The Rise of the Western World: A New Economic History*. New York: Cambridge University Press, 1973.

Olson, Mancur. *The Logic of Collective Action*. Cambridge: Harvard University Press, 1971.

———. *The Rise and Decline of Nations*. New Haven: Yale University Press, 1982.

Organization for Economic Co-operation and Development. *Structural Adjustment and Economic Performance*. Paris: OECD, 1987.

Osborne, John W. *The Silent Revolution*. New York: Charles Scribner's Sons, 1970.

Payne, Peter L. "Industrial Entrepreneurship and Management in Great Britain." In *The Cambridge Economic History of Europe*, vol. 7, ed. Peter Mathias and M. M. Postan. Cambridge: Cambridge University Press, 1978.

Pechman, Joseph A. *Federal Tax Policy*. 5th ed. Washington: Brookings Institution, 1987.

———., ed. *Comparative Tax Systems: Europe, Canada, and Japan*. Arlington, VA: Tax Analysts, 1987.

Poterba, James M. "Tax Policy and Corporate Saving." *Brookings Papers on Economic Activity* 1987: 455–504.

President's Council of Economic Advisors. *Economic Report of the President*. Washington: GPO, various years.

Rauch, Jonathan. "Is the Deficit Really So Bad?" *Atlantic Monthly*. February 1989.

Reich, Robert B. "As the World Turns." *New Republic*. May 1, 1989.

———. "Whither Protectionism?" *Harvard International Review* 10(1989): 100–102.

Ricardo, David. *The Principles of Political Economy and Taxation*. 1821. Reprint. London: J. M. Dent & Sons, 1973.

Rivlin, Alice M., ed. *Economic Choices, 1984*. Washington: Brookings Institution, 1984.

Rohatyn, Felix. "America's Economic Dependence." *Foreign Affairs* 68(1989): 53–65.

Rosenberg, Nathan, and L. E. Birdzell, Jr. *How the West Grew Rich*. New York: Basic, 1986.

Rostow, Walt Whitman. *British Economy of the Nineteenth Century*. London: Oxford University Press, 1948.

———. *The Stages of Economic Growth*. Cambridge: Cambridge University Press, 1960.

Rowthorn, R. E., and J. R. Wells. *De-industrialization and Foreign Trade*. Cambridge: Cambridge University Press, 1987.

Rubinstein, Nicolai, ed. *Florentine Studies*. London: Faber & Faber, 1968.

Rudder, Catherine E. "Tax Policy: Structure and Choice." In *Making Economic Policy in Congress*, ed. Allen Schick. Washington: American Enterprise Institute, 1983.

Sabine, B. E. V. *A History of Income Tax*. London: George Allen & Unwin, 1966.

Samuelson, Paul A. "The Public Role in the Modern American Economy." In *The American Economy in Transition*, ed. Martin Feldstein. Chicago: University of Chicago Press, 1980.

Sayers, R. W. *A History of Economic Change in England, 1880–1939*. London: Oxford University Press, 1967.

Schevill, Ferdinand. *History of Florence*. New York: Harcourt, Brace, 1936.

Schumpeter, Joseph A. *History of Economic Analysis*. New York: Oxford University Press, 1954.

Seligman, Edwin R. A. *The Income Tax*. 2d ed. New York: Macmillan, 1914.

Shultz, George P. "The Comparative Advantage of Government." In *The American Economy in Transition*, ed. Martin Feldstein. Chicago: University of Chicago Press, 1980.

Smith, Adam. *The Wealth of Nations*. 2 vol. London: J. M. Dent, 1964.

Southgate, George W. *English Economic History*. Rev. ed. London: J. M. Dent and Sons, 1948.

Stein, Herbert. "Congress's Amazing Budget Tricks." *Wall Street Journal*. June 27, 1989.

Stephens, J. N. *The Fall of the Florentine Republic*. Oxford: Clarendon, 1983.

Steuerle, C. Eugene. *Taxes, Loans, and Inflation*. Washington: Brookings Institution, 1985.

Summers, Lawrence, and Chris Carroll. "Why Is U.S. National Saving So Low?" *Brookings Papers on Economic Activity* 1987: 607–42.

Surrey, Stanley S. *Pathways to Tax Reform*. Cambridge: Harvard University Press, 1973.

Surrey, Stanley S., and Paul R. McDaniel. *Tax Expenditures*. Cambridge: Harvard University Press, 1985.

Swetz, Frank J. *Capitalism and Arithmetic*. La Salle, IL: Open Court, 1987.

Thomson, David. *England in the Nineteenth Century*. New York: Penguin, 1950.

Tuchman, Barbara W. *A Distant Mirror*. New York: Ballantine, 1978.

_____. *The March of Folly*. New York: Ballantine, 1984.

Veseth, Michael. *Public Finance*. New York: Reston, 1984.

_____. "Reaganomics vs. Medici-conomics: Public Finance in Renaissance Florence." *Proceedings of the National Tax Association Conference on Taxation* 1987: 271–78.

Wachter, Michael L., and Susan M. Wachter, eds. *Toward a New U.S. Industrial Policy?* Philadelphia: University of Pennsylvania Press, 1983.

Webber, Carolyn, and Aaron Wildavsky. *A History of Taxation and Expenditure in the Western World*. New York: Simon & Schuster, 1986.

Weiner, Martin J. *English Culture and the Decline of the Industrial Spirit, 1850–1980*. Cambridge: Cambridge University Press, 1981.

Weymouth, Lally. *America in 1876*. New York: Vintage, 1976.

Wildavsky, Aaron. "Budgets As Compromises among Social Orders." In *The Federal Budget: Economics and Politics*, ed. Michael J. Boskin and Aaron Wildavsky. San Francisco: Institute for Contemporary Studies, 1982.

Williamson, Jeffrey O. "Why Was British Growth So Slow during the Industrial Revolution?" *Journal of Economic History* 44(1984): 687–712.

Witte, John F. *The Politics and Development of the Federal Income Tax.* Madison: University of Wisconsin Press, 1985.

Index

WIDENER UNIVERSITY
WOLFGRAM LIBRARY
CHESTER, PA.